The Wife of the First Consul

Josephine Bonaparte

THE

WIFE OF THE FIRST CONSUL

BY

IMBERT DE SAINT-AMAND

TRANSLATED BY

THOMAS SERGEANT PERRY

ILLUSTRATED

WILDSIDE PRESS

THE CAXTON PRESS, NEW YORK

CONTENTS.

—◆◆◆—

v

PART II.

THE CONSULATE FOR LIFE.

THE WIFE OF THE FIRST CONSUL

THE WIFE OF THE FIRST CONSUL.

INTRODUCTION.

IN the modest church of Rueil, on each side of the altar, there stand, face to face, two funeral monuments which call forth a host of memories. The one to the right represents a woman kneeling at a prayer-desk, in full dress, but with no royal insignia, and the simple inscription runs thus: "To Josephine. Eugene and Hortense, 1825." The statue, which is of Carrara marble, is the work of the sculptor Cartellier. In the foundation of the pedestal rests the body of the woman who was Empress of the French and Queen of Italy. Opposite, a group in white marble, the work of the sculptor Barre, represents a woman and an angel. The woman, who is kneeling, wears a regal diadem, and she is wrapped in the folds of a long veil. Her attitude is that of prayer, with her hands lowered towards the earth, and her eyes raised towards heaven. Before her one may see a crown, a few laurels, and a lyre, but her melancholy face expresses a feeling of contempt for these toys which are so trivial on earth, and so much more trivial in face of eternity. It is indeed the sad woman, rid of all illusions, who in 1807 said to Napoleon: "My reputation is tainted, my health broken, I expect no further happiness in this life; expel me from your heart, if you wish it, bury me in a convent, I desire neither throne nor wealth. Give my mother peace, grant to Eugene the glory which he deserves, but let me live quiet and alone." Above the statue floats an angel who, with a gesture at once protecting and consoling, shows to the unhappy queen the eternal spheres. On the pedestal is cut this inscription: "To Queen Hortense, her son Napoleon III."

The remains of the Queen do not lie in the foundation of this monument; they rest beneath it in a crypt shut off by a gate of wrought iron, to which leads a staircase in the corner of the church. The arches of the vault are upheld by clusters of short and massive columns. A funeral lamp and two bronze candelabra cast a dim glow over this vault, into which the light of day never falls. At the back of the crypt, beneath an arcade, may be descried the huge tomb, which seems to be covered with a royal mantle, carved in stone, and surmounted by a golden palm, with the arms of the French Empire and those of Holland. On the tomb is this inscription: "Hortense Eugénie de Beauharnais, Duchess of Saint-Leu, Queen of Holland, born in Paris, April 10, 1783; daughter by her first marriage of Marie Rose Josephine Tascher de la Pagerie, Empress of the French,

and of Viscount Alexandre de Beauharnais; daugh-
ter-in-law and sister-in-law of Napoleon I., Emperor
of the French; married in Paris, January 3, 1802, to
Louis Napoleon, King of Holland; died at her castle
of Arenenberg, October 5, 1837." The two women,
the mother and the daughter, are united in death, as
they were in life. It is impossible to look without
emotion at this last resting-place of such vanished
splendor, of such fallen greatness, and Bossuet's
thoughts on the nothingness of human things occur
to one in this village church with its two eloquent
graves.

These two graves are appropriately placed under
the vaults of the modest church, the bells of which,
according to Bourrienne, made a deep impression
upon Bonaparte. Near by is the estate of Malmaison,
which was for Josephine what the Little Trianon was
for Marie Antoinette, a poetic and fateful spot, which,
after having been the abode of enchantments, success,
and boundless hopes, became that of despair, humilia-
tion, of cruel struggles, of agony, of death, and which
finally deserved its name of evil omen, Malmaison,
mala mansio.

I am approaching the region of legend, and recall
Isabey's celebrated drawing; I seem to see the First
Consul walking alone, in uniform, before the building.
I summon memories of the beautiful days and starlit
nights, of Malmaison in the year VIII., of the dinners
in the open air, the games upon the grass, of the balls
in which all the women are dressed in white. I see

Hortense de Beauharnais, a bright and merry girl, running, swift as Atalanta, in the garden; or in the theatre at the end of the gallery, playing Rosina in the "Barber of Seville" like a consummate actress. I am back in the consular court, which is still republican, full of charm, of vivacity, rich in youth, glory, and hope, with but little dread of the catastrophes hid in the dark future.

Nine years pass, and what a change! Poor Josephine, broken with grief, enters once more the house where not long before she had arrived in joy. Her dark presentiments have been realized. The woman to whom the conqueror of Italy used to write burning love-letters is now disgraced, disowned, and driven forever from the Tuileries. She has just drunk to the dregs the chalice of the bitterness of divorce which she had prayed to be spared. It is a cold, wet December night; the withered leaves lie about like dead illusions; the wind wails, and nature moans. The abode of happiness is become a Calvary. What a night the wretched woman passes in the room which she used to occupy with Napoleon! And when she wakes in the morning, what a sad eye she turns towards the trees which once shaded so much happiness! In the course of the day Napoleon comes to pay an icy visit to his divorced wife; he walks for a few moments with her in the park and leaves her without a kiss.

I picture to myself the melancholy scenes of May 29, 1814, Whitsunday. Josephine is lying at the point of death in that chamber of Malmaison, surrounded by her children, visitors, and friends, "as gentle in the face of death as she always had been to every one." When the Emperor left for the island of Elba, she said, "Napoleon is in distress, and I can't be with him." The impossibility of devoting herself to him was a terrible blow to her. "I have been a witness," said Mademoiselle Avrillon, "of the sleeplessness of the Empress Josephine, and her terrible dreams. I have known her to pass whole days buried in gloomy thoughts. I know what I have seen and heard, and I am sure that it was grief that killed her." In her last moments she awoke from her stupor only at intervals, and in a sort of quiet delirium these few words escaped her, betraying all the anguish of her heart: "Bonaparte, Elba, Marie-Louise!"

A year later, during the Hundred Days, Napoleon went to Malmaison before the ceremony of the Champ de Mai. He was received by Queen Hortense, and at his entrance into the vestibule he betrayed profound emotion. This he controlled, however, with his wonted energy, and he desired to visit everything, the house and the park. He wandered about, deep in thought; one would have said that from one path to another he was pursuing a shadow. Then he took his place at the table, where he saw the place that Josephine had left empty. The breakfast was short and silent. On rising from the table, the Emperor passed into the gallery, and looked at every one of the pictures, which were fixed in his memory. Then he went upstairs, and came to the door of the room where his wife, whom he had loved so warmly, had died. Hortense wished to follow him. "No, my daughter," he said; "I wish to go in alone." Abandoned by the ungrateful Marie-Louise, Napoleon fell into meditation before the death-bed of the grateful Josephine. Doubtless he craved forgiveness for the divorce; and he said to himself, at the bottom of his heart, "It's because I deserted this woman that fortune has deserted me." The whole drama of his life unrolled itself before his eyes. A world of memories rose before him like a tide. Oh, if one could but seize some part of the past! If hope could take the place of memory! If faded flowers would but bloom again! But, alas! everything had slipped through his fingers. Napoleon left Josephine's room with tears in his eyes.

Possibly he had thought that at Malmaison he would, as it were, dip into a healthful spring, and that there, in this home of his glorious youth, he should find again his self-confidence, his faith in his star; but it was a vain hope. The wife who had brought him good fortune was no more. Once again he was to return to Malmaison, but after Waterloo; and it was there that he stayed after his second abdication for five days, from the 25th to the 29th of June, 1815. It was again Queen Hortense who received him, a respectful and faithful friend in his misfortune. The sky was clear, the sun brilliant, but the heart of the

man who was about to become a prisoner was as dark
as the tomb. Long before he had said: "One sees
everything through a gilded veil which makes it
bright and clear. Gradually, as one goes on, this
veil thickens, until at last it becomes almost black."
This moment had come; a long crape veil stretched
over the shadows over the horizon. The beaten soldier of Waterloo walked until he was worn out in
the park of Malmaison, where he passed his last
hours as a free man, talking continually to Hortense
about Josephine, whose portrait he wished to have.
But what did he hear? The roar of the cannon in
the plain of Saint Denis. What did he see? Officers and old soldiers arriving in ragged uniforms,
stained with dust, who told him of the progress of
the enemy. Blücher had unwisely separated himself
from Wellington; the Allies were advancing in two
columns of about sixty thousand men each, leaving
so much space between them that either could be
crushed before the other could come to its rescue.
The man of battle felt all his genius aroused. In
the night between the 28th and the 29th of June he
made his plans; if he could be given the command,
he promised to beat in detail the Prussians and the
English with the ruins of his Waterloo army. In
the morning of the 29th he commissioned General
Beker to carry the following message to Fouché and
the other members of the Provisional Government,
sitting at the Tuileries. "I offer," he said, "to place
myself at the head of the army, which at the sight of

me will recover all its spirit, to fall upon the enemy
with desperate energy, and to punish him for his
rashness. I give my word as a general, a soldier, and
a citizen, not to retain the command for one hour
after the certain and crushing victory which I promise to gain, not for myself, but for France."

Napoleon, in full uniform, waited with his aides
for the answer of the Provisional Government; if it
were favorable, he meant to mount his horse at once.
General Beker returned, bringing a refusal, and the
man of Austerlitz submitted. If Napoleon sinned by
pride, how severely he was punished! He, who a
short time ago made the world tremble, was compelled to consult a regicide, a former accomplice of
the cruelties of the comedian Collot d'Herbois. He,
the hero of battles, consecrated by the Pope, the man
of destiny, the modern Cæsar, the new Charlemagne,
obliged to submit to the refusal and the contempt
of Fouché !

It is easy to imagine the wrath of the young aides-
de-camp, impatient to follow him, certain of victory,
when they were obliged to sheathe their swords
again, to unsaddle their impatient steeds, and to see
the last dream of patriotism and glory disappear.
Who can describe the torture of such an hour for a
character like Napoleon's? The plaudits of the multitude, the enthusiastic shouts of the soldiers, the
intoxicating joys of the triumph, the solemn entry
within the walls of conquered capitals, the bulletins
of famous victories, ovations, hosannas, — they were
all cruelly avenged!

All was over. He had to bow before an implacable fate; he had to leave before the end of the day.
The preparations for departure were completed. The
Prussians were advancing on the left bank of the
Seine, between Argenteuil and Chaton; if he had
remained a few hours longer, he would have been
their prisoner. He had just taken off his uniform
and put on citizen's dress. His mother, his brothers,
and a few soldiers, a few courtiers of misfortune, had
assembled to bid him an eternal farewell. Since he
had not thought of providing himself with money,
Queen Hortense begged him to accept a diamond
necklace. At first he refused; but when she insisted
with tears, he let her hide the necklace in his coat.
After having urged unity and courage upon them all,
he embraced his faithful friends for the last time.
The last one of whom he took leave was his mother.
Their separation recalls the grand scenes of antiquity, which were sublime in their simplicity.
"Farewell, my son," said Madame Letitia. The
Emperor answered, "Mother, farewell." He got
into his carriage, and left Malmaison forever.

To the right of the castle is to be seen a stone pedestal, on which there stood, until 1870, a bronze eagle
with this touching inscription: "The last step of
Napoleon, when leaving for Rochefort, June 29, 1815,
at four o'clock in the afternoon." Why was the
eagle torn from the pedestal with the inscription?
It could not excite anger. It was no longer the
royal bird, floating in the clouds, gazing at the sun;

it was the wounded eagle, fluttering along the
ground, like the swallow before a storm. Oh, the
melancholy of greatness! Vicissitudes of fate! how
eloquent is your language in these times of revolution, when fortune seems to make sport of kings and
emperors! How insignificant is man, and how hard
it is to find any trace of his footsteps!

In the month of August, 1831, a woman was weeping before the iron gate of Malmaison; with her was
a young man of twenty-three, who shared her grief.
This young man was her son. She insisted on being
admitted, but entrance was obstinately refused. This
woman was Queen Hortense; the young man was
the future emperor ´Napoleon III. The mother and
the son had just been kneeling before the tomb of
Josephine in the church of Rueil, and it is thus that
the former queen describes the emotion that she felt
then : " What a drear feeling came over me when I
knelt before that cherished image and sadly thought
that of all whom she had loved I alone remained
with my son, isolated, and compelled to flee the spot
where she reposed. The great number of flowers
covering this monument, which my brother and I
had such difficulty in getting permission to build,
proved to me that at any rate she was lying among
friends who held her memory dear. Her daughter
only was forgotten."

It was after this pious visit to the church of Rueil,
where she herself was one day to be buried, that
Queen Hortense and her son wished to revisit Mal-

maison. She said : "I stopped at the gate of the castle, and insisted upon entering. It is from there that the Emperor started to leave France forever. . . . It was impossible to secure any remission of the orders of the new proprietor, who had forbidden entrance to the castle without a card. My nephew had sold Malmaison to a banker, who kept a part of the gardens and the castle, and had sold the rest. It was difficult to recognize the place, and I could not believe myself at the same spot which I had left so beautiful, where I had always been so gladly received, when admission to it was so cruelly denied me."

How painful it must have been to see strangers thus occupying a dwelling which she had inhabited with those she loved! It is a bit of the irony of fate, which seems to take a pleasure in persecuting wretched humanity with refined cruelty. The Malmaison of Napoleon and of Josephine, the home of his glory as consul, the last refuge of the defeated soldier of Waterloo before his departure for the rock of Saint Helena, all this belonging to strangers, while the woman who had so shone there had not the right to enter the house to go and pray in the room where she had seen her mother draw her last breath! No one recognized her. She had hoped to find there what her heart had left, to catch in the song of the birds some trace of departed joys, or of her old griefs in the murmur of the wind. But nature is insensible to our sorrows, and nothing remains of our dreams and illusions.

In 1842 another unhappy sovereign, Queen Christina of Spain, in one of her excursions in the neighborhood of Paris, visited the estate of Malmaison, attracted by the painful memories which clung about the place. She bought the castle and lived in it until 1861. On one side she built a chapel, now empty; but the arms of the Spanish Bourbons yet remain above the place where the Queen used to pray. In 1861 she consented to sell Malmaison to the Emperor, who paid eleven hundred thousand francs and presented it to the state as a sort of national jewel. The castle was restored and decorated, and assumed its former aspect under the days of the Consulate and the Empire. One day Napoleon III. shut himself for several hours in the gallery, and with his own hands hung up the principal pictures in the places where he remembered having seen them when he was a child.

In 1867, at the time of the Exposition, the Empress Eugénie conceived the excellent idea of collecting at Malmaison and the Little Trianon the various objects, pictures and furniture, which could be proved to have belonged to the illustrious occupants of these two historic mansions. The French, and even more noticeably foreigners, crowded thither and gazed with a sort of awe at the two valuable museums; for foreigners take perhaps a deeper interest in the glories of France than do the French themselves. At Malmaison they saw the council-table of the ministers, Josephine's tapestry-frame and harp, the Emperor's field-desk, the clock that stood in his room at Saint Helena, the little iron bed with green silk curtains in which he died. Malmaison had never been so crowded with visitors ; but this climax of its fame was not far removed from a probably final decay.

The janitress, who was in the service of Queen Christina, and has been in the castle ever since, describes the last incidents that have come under notice, with a sort of vigorous and popular eloquence. She says that in 1867 she noticed in the park some Germans in civil dress, who were examining everything about them with the greatest care, and that in the war she saw the same Germans again, this time in uniform, take possession of the castle ; and that a few days before the war broke out, the young Prince Imperial came to visit Malmaison, and that she was struck by his melancholy expression. She adds, that just as he was leaving, a thunder-storm broke forth, and a tree which had been planted by Napoleon and Josephine was half shattered by the lightning. "An evil omen," she said. Then she goes on to tell how they managed to bind up the old tree-trunk ; but that when they began to divide the place into house-lots, in 1879, the tree was cut down and uprooted. At the same time Josephine's descendant, the heir of the Napoleons, was dying in Zululand.

After the fall of the Second Empire, the state sold Malmaison to a private person. The park was cut up into lots and sold to different buyers, who are building houses. The façade of the castle is intact, but the interior is in a melancholy state of dilapidation, shorn of ornaments, furniture, and hangings.

Malmaison, which at the beginning of the century was, as it were, a symbol of France under the Consulate; Malmaison, still full of the gigantic plans and the proud dreams of the ambitious hero of Marengo; Malmaison, sacked in 1815 by Blücher's soldiers, — became in the last war a Prussian barrack. The troops of the victor at Sedan installed themselves in triumph where the First Consul, in his military court, had worn his most martial air.   Silent and deserted, Malmaison seems like a tomb.   Its bare walls are gloomier than ruins.   Yet there is a certain majesty in their bareness.   The stones of the castle speak that mysterious language which may be heard in the silence.   No man with feeling for poetry or history can enter this house without being filled with respect.   One lowers one's voice and steps softly, as if dreading to disturb the sleep of illustrious hosts. The deserted halls seem to be tenanted by phantoms of the past.   In the twilight one would say that it is a haunted spot, and haunted by what ghosts!

How many cataclysms there have been in France during the last century!   The scythe wielded by war and revolution commits more grievous ravages than those of time.   Of all the buildings which were the scene of the last agonies of Louis XVI. and Marie Antoinette, what is now left?   The Tuileries are burned.   There is not one stone left of the Manége where Louis XVI. was tried, of the Temple tower

which served as prison for the unhappy monarch and
his family. The little dungeon of the Queen in the
Conciergerie alone remains, and the crowds who daily
pass through the place of her execution do not know
even where the martyr's scaffold stood. And what
is left of what one may call the scenery of the consular epoch? The house in the rue de la Victoire,
whence issued the 18th Brumaire, is destroyed, its
very site is not to be determined; Saint Cloud and the
Tuileries [1] are mere stone skeletons. Shells and petroleum have destroyed everything. Great stretches
of the sky appear through the empty arches, and one
would say that these fresh ruins are as old as Pom-
peii or Herculaneum. The superb appearance of the
two palaces which they were in their splendor is so
deeply printed on the memory, that at certain moments one, gazing at the ruins, would think himself
the victim of a nightmare, and would expect on
waking to find the two monuments as they were
before the fire. If Josephine could come back to life,
how surprised she would be at this destruction!
What would be her reflections before the ruins of the
Tuileries and of Saint Cloud! What an impression
would be produced by Malmaison dilapidated and
deserted!

Well, if revolutions destroy, let history yet try to
build up what they have pitilessly overthrown! History is a reconstruction, which will permit us to see

---

[1] The ruins of the Tuileries have been removed since the above
was written. — Tr.

again with the eyes of our soul what we can no longer
see with our real eyes, to build up ruins, to people
empty halls, to hear amid the silence the echo of conversation, of the trumpets, of the orchestras of former
days.   There may reach our ear the distant sound of
Josephine's gentle voice which the First Consul used
to prefer to the applause of his people and his army.
Let us summon forth the image of this woman under
the ancient trees which have survived so many disasters.   While we think of her, we shall gaze at the
views which so often charmed her, at the prospect
which was for her a consoling friend, at the river
which flowed beneath her feet.   Let us consult her
friends : here are her husband's secretaries, Bourrienne and Méneval ; here is the lady in waiting,
Madame de Rémusat ; there is the Duchess of Abrantès, Miot de Mélito, Rœderer, General de Ségur,
Thibaudeau, Marmont, Lavalette.   After long study
of their memoirs, one seems to know the authors, to
be near them, in the same room, exchanging ideas
with them, listening to their reminiscences, hearing
their anecdotes and their talk about the persons and
events of bygone days.   Let us ask them, in this
sketch, to make us understand the character of the
wife of the First Consul, and the part she played,
to describe to us this period of four years and a half
which was so brilliant and busy, to show us society
forming itself anew, with drawing-rooms opening
again, the foreign aristocracy resuming its journeys
to Paris, the reopening of the opera balls, as luxury,

elegance, and fashion reassert themselves, while at the same time the populace easily exchanges liberty for glory, and sets a man above every institution.

Fox said in 1802 that in the person of the First Consul there were three Bonapartes equally worthy of study; the one of Malmaison, of Saint Cloud, and of the Tuileries. As for Josephine, she was always and everywhere the same : affable, gracious, obliging, always seeking peace, sharing none of the severities, the anger, or the petulance of her husband, dissuading him from thoughts of vengeance, anxious to see him kind, generous, and inclined to pity. This modest, disinterested woman, who was essentially tender and good, is one of the most amiable and sympathetic figures of history. If her statue has been removed from the avenue leading from the Arch of Triumph which bore her name, her memory at any rate cannot perish. The charm which she exercised upon her contemporaries has survived, and even when one thinks, whether rightly or wrongly, that he has discovered flaws in her private life, one feels an attraction towards her. Whether alive or dead, good women deserve our love. That greatest quality, a woman's real ornament, kindness, would make us pardon many faults. Josephine wished to call forth no tears but those of joy and gratitude. Her ambition was to be Bonaparte's good angel. She often gave him wise advice, and the time of his most earnest devotion to her was that of his greatest success.

In our opinion the Consulate is Napoleon's high-water mark; his fall began with the murder of the Duke of Enghien, the inauguration of the imperial period. From that moment a cloud hangs over his star: this cloud is at first but a black point, but it grew from year to year, and at last produced the dense gloom of the final catastrophe. It was in vain that Napoleon accumulated crown upon crown for himself and his family; the glory of the Emperor could not outshine the glory of the citizen. Josephine had a presentiment of this, and the throne filled her with a secret dread. She knew that as her greatness increased, her happiness would diminish, and yearned to descend as much as her husband aspired to rise.

PART I.

THE TEMPORARY CONSULATE.

I.

O N the 21st Brumaire, year VIII., there appeared in the *Moniteur* the following short paragraph: "Paris, 20th Brumaire. The three Consuls have taken their seats in the Luxembourg. In the evening the public buildings and many private houses were illuminated." From the moment of his installation at the Luxembourg the future Cæsar regarded himself as the absolute head of the state. "He is a pike who will swallow the two other fish," said Madame de Permont to his mother, Madame Bonaparte. "O Panoria!" replied Madame Letitia, with reproachful accent, for at this moment she still believed in the genuine republicanism of her son. "The surprising thing," said Edgar Quinet, "is the way in which all combined to blind themselves. In fact, every one was new to servitude. Even those who ran towards it most eagerly imagined that they were acquiring a new form of liberty. . . . Not a day passed without an approach to absolute power, but no one seemed to perceive it." Bonaparte, a sovereign in fact, was not yet one in appearance; he regarded

21

republican susceptibility, but gradually, by crafty and astute steps, he began to accustom men to his rule. The old customs begin to reappear one by one. Josephine ceases to be called Citoyenne Bonaparte, and the woman who is soon to be Empress of the French and Queen of Italy is designated as Madame Bonaparte. For a little while there are preserved the names of things which no longer exist, such as liberty and the Republic, and the future Emperor is still called the citizen First Consul.

Bonaparte occupied in the little Luxembourg the apartment on the ground floor, to the right as one enters from the rue de Vaugirard. His office was near a hidden staircase leading to the first floor, where Josephine lived. After breakfast, which was served at ten o'clock, Bonaparte used to talk for a few minutes with his aides-de-camp, and then he betook himself to his work.

" On leaving the council," says his secretary, Bourrienne, "he would go to his office singing, and Heaven knows how out of tune he used to sing. He would sign a few letters, stretch himself in his easy-chair, and read a few letters of the evening before and the occasional publications of the day. When there was no council, he would stay in his office and talk with me, always singing and cutting the arm of his chair, sometimes looking like a big boy. Then he would start up, and sketch the plan of some monument which was to be built, or dictate the vast things which were to astonish or appal the world. . . . Din-

ner was at five o'clock. After dinner the First Consul used to go up to Josephine's apartment, where he
was accustomed to receive the ministers; he always
took pleasure in seeing the minister of foreign affairs,
especially after that portfolio was in the hands of M.
de Talleyrand. At midnight, and often earlier, he
used to give the signal for breaking up, by saying
suddenly, ' Let us go to bed ! ' "

Josephine began to receive at the Luxembourg
people of the old régime. The title of *Madame*
pained more than one Republican who longed for the
simpler *Citoyenne.* "They consoled themselves afterwards at the Tuileries," says Bourrienne, "by using
Your Highness, on occasions of great ceremony, and
merely Monseigneur in private." The First Consul
took the most careful precautions to combine certain
revolutionary memories with the symptoms of reaction. He abolished the holiday of January 21, the
anniversary of the execution of Louis XVI., but
he preserved as national holidays the 14th of July
and the 1st of Vendémiaire, in memory of the taking of the Bastille and the establishment of the Republic. He let his wife surround herself with people
of the old court, but he married his third sister to a
soldier of fortune, the son of an innkeeper of Cahors.

It was at the Luxembourg that was celebrated,
January 20, 1800, the civil marriage of Caroline
Bonaparte with Murat, a general in command of a
division. Not till two years later was the nuptial
benediction given to the couple, on the occasion of

the marriage of Hortense de Beauharnais with Louis
Bonaparte. Murat, who was born at Cahors, March
25, 1771, was not yet twenty-nine years old when he
was married. Caroline, who was born at Ajaccio,
March 25, 1782, was under eighteen. According to
the author of the Recollections of Madame Récamier (Madame Récamier was very intimate with
Madame Murat), "of all the sisters of Napoleon
Caroline was the one who most resembled him. She
was not so regularly beautiful as his sister Pauline
(Madame Leclerc), but she belonged distinctly to
the Napoleonic type; she was of a marvellously rich
coloring; her intelligence was quick, her will imperious, and the contrast of the girlish grace of her face
with the decision of her character made her a very
attractive person. She continued to come, as she
had done when a young girl, to all the entertainments at Madame Récamier's, in the rue du Mont
Blanc." This is the portrait which the Duchess of
Abrantès drew of her: "Caroline Bonaparte was a
very pretty girl, as fresh as a rose, but in no way
comparable, in regularity of feature, to Madame
Leclerc. Still, she was very attractive on account
of her expression and the astounding brilliancy of
her complexion. Her skin was like white satin tinted
with pink; her feet, hands, and arms were even perfect models, her teeth were charming, like those of
all the Bonapartes." Prince Metternich, who was a
great admirer of her, said of her : "Caroline combined
with an agreeable face a rare mind. She had care-

fully studied her brother's character, and had no
illusion about any of his faults; she also knew the
weak points in her husband's character, and would
have guided him if he had submitted to guidance."

Young, handsome, full of military enthusiasm,
Murat shone in the first rank among these knights-
errant of democracy; he was one of those illustrious plebeians who have no need of ancestors, because
they are themselves ancestors. In the whole French
army there was not such a proud cavalier. His pro-
verbial bravery, his dashing steeds, his rich uniforms,
the fire and gayety of his southern nature made him
a popular figure. He could not make his appearance
on the battle-field or at a review without attracting
every eye. Yet, in fact, the First Consul had no
sympathy for this brilliant officer. The Duchess
of Abrantès thus explains his coolness: " The true
cause of Napoleon's moderate friendship for Murat
(for in spite of their relationship, he never loved
him) was nothing but Murat's rash conduct when
he came to Paris to bring the first flags won by the
army of Italy. Those who know Napoleon's character will easily understand how Murat injured himself
by quietly boasting of his influence in the Directory,
at the Ministry of War, through Madame Bonaparte
and Madame Tallien."

In his Memoirs, Bourrienne refers to the same
incident. He says that Madame Bonaparte and
Madame Tallien had Murat appointed brigadier-gen-
eral; that on his return to Italy he had incurred the

disapproval of the commander-in-chief; that by the influence of these ladies he obtained a place in the army of Egypt, but that on the voyage thither, on board of the *Orient*, Bonaparte did not once speak to him. Bourrienne, indeed, goes so far as to insinuate that at Messoudiah, Murat's was one of the two names mentioned by Junot to excite Bonaparte's jealousy and his distrust of Josephine. But the bold officer performed such prodigies of valor, and was notably so conspicuous on the field of Aboukir, that the commander-in-chief could not refuse him the expression of his satisfaction.

Murat's conduct at Saint Cloud on the 19th Brumaire brought about a perfect reconciliation with Bonaparte, who appointed him commander of the Consular Guard. Nevertheless, when he came to the Luxembourg to ask for the hand of Caroline, Bonaparte at first did not favor his suit. He hesitated to give to a plebeian his sister, who had already been sought by a great Italian nobleman, the Prince of Santa Croce. He thought, too, that there were in the army abler and more famous generals than Murat; as, for example, Moreau and Augereau. But Caroline and Murat had been in love since the Italian campaign, and their marriage was warmly favored by Josephine.

When Murat made his demand, Bonaparte received him with unbending gravity, and gave no positive answer. In the evening this proposal was the subject of conversation in the drawing-room of the

Luxembourg. Josephine, Hortense, and Bourrienne warmly pleaded Murat's cause. To their earnest arguments the First Consul replied: "Murat is the son of an innkeeper. In the lofty rank in which fortune and glory have placed me, I cannot mingle his blood with mine. Besides, there is no hurry; I will see about it later." Murat's two supporters were not discouraged; they spoke earnestly of his love for Caroline, of his devotion to the First Consul, of his excellent conduct in Egypt. "Yes, I acknowledge," said Bonaparte, "that Murat was superb at Aboukir." Josephine and Hortense redoubled their solicitations, and before the end of the evening the First Consul had given his consent. Before he went to bed he said to Bourrienne, "Well, you ought to be satisfied; and I am, too. On the whole, Murat suits my sister, and then people won't say that I am proud, and seeking grand marriages. If I had given my sister to a nobleman, all your Jacobins would have been shrieking out, Counter-revolution."

According to General de Ségur, two considerations had decided the First Consul: "one, which the study of the innermost secrets of the human heart, everywhere the same, can alone explain, was the secret satisfaction that he felt at Madame Bonaparte's intercession in favor of the marriage; the other, which was entirely political, proved the truth of what Napoleon said about himself; namely, that his ambitious advance was gradual and the result of events; that his ambition grew always according to

the circumstances, and that finally the lofty height
to which it attained was in no way premeditated at
the beginning." If, in 1800, he married his sister to
the son of an innkeeper, it was because he was not at
all sure of becoming one day Emperor, and because
he wanted to please the army, reassure the Republicans, and give a pledge to the democracy. As General de Ségur points out, the man who accepted Murat for his brother-in-law was probably not thinking
of ever putting on his head the crown of Charlemagne or of allying himself with the house of
Austria.

Bonaparte's regard for the Republican opinions
could not last long. It would have had a longer life
if public sentiment had shown itself firmer, and there
would have been no Emperor if the citizens had not
transformed themselves into subjects.

" What a pleasure for a master," says Edgar Quinet,
" to feel beneath his feet the proud spirit of a people
which but just now was defying heaven and earth!
That a general, drunk with victory, should impose
himself upon a nation which adores him, is in the
order of events. That armies which had sworn to
live free or die should carry their leader on a shield,
is a thing to be read in every history. But that a nation should not feel the yoke that is heavy on its neck;
that, far from suffering from it, it should accept it as
a benefit and a deliverance; that the men of liberty,
Daunou, Cabanis, Grégoire, and Carnot, even La
Fayette, should be the first to glorify their own over-

throw; that they should run to their suicide with no presentiment to warn them; that evidence should not affect them; that the bare sword should not warn them, — all this is a new fact such as the world had not yet seen." Reaction appeared everywhere. Carnot accepted the Ministry of War. The destroyer of the Bastille, Palloy, "the lifelong patriot," celebrated the accession of the First Consul with a handsome engraved medallion. The "Almanack of the Nineteenth Century" contained the following dialogue between Diogenes and a man of the Revolution: —

What did you do to be a man?

I made the 10th of August, the 31st of May, the 18th Fructidor, the 30th Prairial.

You are a mere destroyer; you are not a man.

I have worked at three constitutions with which people have become disgusted.

You are a mere fool.

I have made more than a hundred speeches from the tribune.

You are a mere babbler.

I have understood how to please all parties.

You are a mere weather-cock.

I have proposed more than two hundred toasts to equality and fraternity.

You are a mere sot.

I cursed Robespierre the eve of his death, and spoke against Barras the 29th Brumaire.

You are a mere slave.

I invented some fine phrases about liberty.

You are a mere rhetorician.

I wrote a good book on morality.

You are a mere hypocrite.

I have had my enemies shot, who were accused of being hostile to the state.

You are a mere monster.

I followed orders.

You are a hangman.

The demagogic fury had died out, and to call a man a Jacobin was the deepest insult. The phrases which previously had aroused and inspired the masses now seemed like old-fashioned empty formulas. The following chapter of the " Brief Revolutionary Catechism " was on every one's lips: —

Question. What is the aim of a revolution?

Answer. To destroy in order to change, and to change in order to destroy.

Q. How many elements are there in a revolution?

A. Four: deficit, poverty, audacity, and fear.

Q. How many virtues?

A. Two: robbery and assassination.

Q. Who profit by revolutions?

A. The rascals and the ambitious.

Q. What becomes of the people in a revolution?

A. They cut a sorry figure.

Q. Why so?

A. Because whether they take part in it or not, they are always the victims.

Q. In what way?

A. In this way: all means are good for crime in attack, but not for virtue in defence.

Q. How does a revolution end?

A. By an excess of evil, in the blindness of the leaders, and in the awakening of the people.

Aided by such a state of public opinion, Napoleon himself must have been astonished at the ease and rapidity with which his plans were accomplished. Nevertheless, he deemed it wise to take many precautions in the form, at least, if not in the substance. He preserved some appearance of respect for the ideas and the institutions which he had so often sworn to defend. He saw that if he changed too suddenly, he would be exposed to the bitter reproaches of his old fellow-soldiers, before whom he had so often protested his faith in the Republic. He had seen too clearly the grand and terrible side of the Revolution to trifle with it. Since the hour for throwing off his mask had not yet struck, he assumed the appearance of a sort of citizen-king, who, while really the master of France, continued to call himself simply General. He decided to install himself at the Tuileries; but the Convention and the Committee of Public Safety had sat there, and the famous palace recalled both royal and revolutionary memories. Besides, it was called the Government Palace; and since the First Consul was averse to living there alone, he determined to bring the Third Consul there too, but to establish him in the Pavilion of Flora, and take for himself the royal apartments, which had been occupied by Louis XIV., Louis XV., and Louis XVI.

While the First Consul was thus aspiring to the palaces of kings, Josephine gave no evidence of any desire to leave the Luxembourg, which would have been perfectly satisfactory as a winter residence; as a summer residence, she could ask for nothing better than Malmaison, and she did not care for Saint Cloud or Compiègne or Fontainebleau.

She was passionately fond of jewels, but she did not care to wear them fastened in a royal crown. She did not deem it necessary to change into ladies-in-waiting those women of the old régime whose society she enjoyed. Singularly enough, she would have been a monarchist, but on the condition that the monarch should not be her husband, and one of her greatest fears was that of seeing Bonaparte become emperor or king. The Tuileries, which were yet full of memories of the 20th of June, the 10th of August, and of the Convention, seemed to her a fatal residence, and she felt that if she were to live there, she should be assuming a position that did not belong to her, that she would be like a servant taking possession of the master's drawing-room. She said to herself that those who climb too high are exposed to giddiness, and she feared lofty mountain-tops because of the precipices beneath them. She had presentiments and scruples which made her regret leaving first her little house in the rue de la Victoire, and then the Luxembourg. But Bonaparte did not trouble himself about Josephine's uneasiness; he was driven by a secret impulse, by a mysterious and irresistible force, to pursue his onward course swiftly and victoriously. Whatever height of fortune he reached, it never occurred to him to say, This is enough. The Tuileries will not satisfy him. One day he will want Potsdam, the next the Escurial; one day Schoenbrunn, and another the Kremlin.

II.

ON the 30th Pluviose, year VIII. (February 19, 1800), Bonaparte, when he woke up in the Luxembourg, said to his secretary, " Well, Bourrienne, here's the day when we are going to sleep at the Tuileries. You are very lucky, for you haven't got to make a show of yourself; you will go your own way. As for me, I have got to go in a procession. It's a great bore; but we must make a show and impress the people. The Directory was too simple, and so was not respected. Simplicity is all very well in the army; but in a large city, in a palace, the head of the government must attract all eyes in every possible way."

The Tuileries of Catherine of Medicis, of Louis XIV., of Louis XV., of Louis XVI., of the Convention, is now about to become the Tuileries of the First Consul. His removal to this palace was to show himself as master; for there is a certain relation between men and public buildings. Bonaparte knew from his instinct of power what an influence a name has on the imagination of the masses. Does not the

33

man who installs himself in the abode of kings substitute himself for them? From the moment when the First Consul occupies a palace, he will necessarily have a court and courtiers. Etiquette will grow up of itself. The friends of childhood and his college comrades will not dare to be too intimate with the head of the state. Republican familiarity will disappear before the monarchical spirit. The people who are accustomed to live on the favors of princes will feel themselves attracted to the Tuileries, as if Bonaparte were a Bourbon. The manners, the ideas, the language of royalty, will gradually reappear.

At one o'clock in the afternoon all Paris was astir; every one wanted to see the procession starting from the Luxembourg for the Tuileries. Madame Bonaparte had already gone there; since she possessed no claims to royal honors, she had come modestly with her daughter Hortense and with her sister-in-law, Madame Murat, and the three stationed themselves, not on the balcony of the Pavilion of the Clock, which would have been too formal, but at the windows of the apartment of Consul Lebrun, in the Pavilion of Flora. Then the procession arrived with the regiments commanded by Lannes, Murat, and Bessières. The three Consuls were in a carriage drawn by six white horses presented to General Bonaparte by the Emperor of Germany after the peace of Campo Formio. The First Consul was on the back seat, with Cambacérès at his left and Lebrun opposite. Then followed the Council of State and the senators, most of them in cabs with the numbers hidden by pieces of paper. The impressive thing in the procession was the fineness of the troops, — three thousand picked soldiers, all veterans. The whole Carrousel was filled by a dense crowd who shouted wildly, " Long live the First Consul ; long live Bonaparte ! " Everywhere on the way people were saying, " How young he is ! What a fine head ! What a fine face ! The Emperor of Germany gave him those white horses, and he gave him his sabre too. Do you see Josephine ? She has brought him good luck."

Patriotic joy shone on every face. The people, the workmen, the poorer classes, were contented. All the social classes, indeed, were united in one common thought. Windows were bought at high prices from which to view this grand spectacle, this review which would become a matter of history. What pretty women ! what rich dresses ! Napoleon was not sincere when he told Bourrienne in the morning that he did not care for this pomp and show. His entrance into the Tuileries would be one of the finest days of his life, full as it was of triumphs. There was a keen joy in hearing the shouts of the populace mingling with those of the troops, and real intoxication in all this military display, in the blare of the trumpets, and the roar of the drums. Starting from nothing, to be everything, what a dream ! and to get to the topmost pinnacle at thirty years of age, what a wonder it is !

The Consular Guard formed a line on both sides from
the entrance into the Carrousel to the door of the Tuileries. There was a certain contrast between this imitation of royalty and the inscription which still stood
there, on the guard-house to the right of the middle
grating: "August 10, 1792, Royalty was abolished
in France, never to reappear." As they looked at
this inscription, many of the soldiers broke out into
denunciation of royalty, with no notion that at this
moment they were bringing it back. When they
had got into the Tuileries, the troops drew up in
order of battle. The Consuls' carriage passed the
gateway and stopped. Bonaparte got out quickly and
vaulted on the horse which was brought up for him,
while Cambacérès and Lebrun made their way slowly
to the reception rooms.

He was now in his element, and had become really
himself in the presence of the troops, of the men to
whom he owed everything. For if he had entered
the Tuileries, it was the soldiers who had led him
there; and he acknowledged himself their debtor,
for it was through them that he had become all-
powerful. Hence he was glad to find himself among
his companions in arms, those brave men whose sun-
burnt faces recalled many victories. He was happy
to see the old bullet-riddled flags, black with powder,
and in rags, which were real treasures, holy talis-
mans. Was there one of the three thousand soldiers
there who would not have given his life to defend
these glorious insignia? The marching past began,

and Bonaparte took his place before the Pavilion of the Clock, with Murat at his right and Lannes at his left. The 43d half-brigade advanced, and the color-bearer saluted the First Consul with the flag which was a mere staff with a few shreds of bunting full of bullet-holes. Bonaparte regarded it with respect and emotion, taking off his hat and returning the salute. The flags of the 30th and 96th were in the same state. When they passed, Bonaparte saluted them too, and his emotion appeared to increase. All this time his mother was weeping with joy.

When the review was over, the First Consul descended from his horse, entered the Pavilion of the Clock, and ascended briskly the staircase of the king's palace. The next day there was to be read in the *Moniteur:* "30 Pluviose, Year VIII. The Government installed itself in its Palace to-day; the Councillors and Secretaries of State, the Secretary General, the Ministers and the Consuls, all in full dress, drove to the Tuileries, preceded by a band, and accompanied by the staff of the 17th Division. The First Consul, alighting from his carriage, mounted his horse, and passed by the lines of the different bodies of troops drawn up in the courtyard. Later, in one of the halls of the Palace, the Minister of the Interior presented to the Consuls the members of the governing boards of Paris. This ceremony was accomplished with perfect order. The public testified its satisfaction by warm applause: hope and joy shone on every face."

Bonaparte then installed himself in the chamber of
Louis XIV., the Sunlike King; Josephine had the
room of Marie Antoinette. Who, a few years earlier, could have foreseen so strange a thing? When
the future conqueror of Arcola, obscure in, lost in
the crowd, looked in anger at the invading rabble
of the 20th of June and the 10th of August, could
he have thought that he would so soon take the place
at the Tuileries of the sovereign whose humiliations
so moved him?

The next morning, on entering Bonaparte's room,
Bourrienne said to him: "Well, general, here you
are at last, without difficulty, with the applause of
the people. Do you remember what you said to me
two years ago in the rue Sainte Anne? 'I could
make myself king, but it's not yet time.'" "Yes,
that is true; but do you know we have done a good
many things since then? On the whole, I am perfectly satisfied; yesterday went off very well. Do
you think that all those people who came to toady
me are sincere? Of course not; but the joy of the
people was genuine. The people are right. And
then, you can consult the real thermometer of public
opinion. Look at the stocks. So I can let the Jacobins grumble; but they mustn't grumble too loud."

Then the First Consul dressed and went to stroll
in the Gallery of Diana. He looked at the busts
which had been placed there by his orders, — Demosthenes, Alexander, Hannibal, Scipio, Brutus, Cicero,
Cato, Cæsar, Gustavus Adolphus, Turenne, Condé,

Duguay-Trouin, Marlborough, Prince Eugene, Marshal Saxe, Washington, Frederick the Great, Mirabeau, and four generals of the Republic who had been
killed in battle, Dugommier, Dampierre, Marceau,
and Joubert. Then he passed through the halls,
which were full of memories of the youth of Louis
XIV., of the childhood of Louis XV., of the agonies
of the martyred king and queen, of the bloody rule
of Robespierre. In the Pavilion of Flora is the
room where the terrible Committee of Public Safety
used to sit. At the other end of the Gallery of
Diana is the Council Hall of the Ministry, where
were held all the important meetings during the
minority of Louis XV., and in the last hours of the
monarchy. There is the bed-chamber, a showy room,
where the Sunlike King used to appear in such
majesty, and where the Imperial throne was soon
to be raised. It was in the next room that, on
the 20th of June, the rioters put the red cap on the
head of Louis XVI. After that is the large room,
which under the king used to be called the Hall of
the Hundred Swiss, where, at the time of the Convention, Robespierre appeared in triumph at the festival of the Supreme Being. In the future this is
to be the Hall of the Marshals. As he passed these
rooms, Bonaparte, who was deeply impressed, said to
Bourrienne: "Getting into the Tuileries isn't everything: the thing is to stay here. Who is there who
hasn't lived in the palace? Thieves, and members
of the National Convention. Do you see? There's

your brother's house. It's from there that I saw them besiege the Tuileries, and carry the good Louis XVI. away. But don't be uneasy. Let them try it."

The same day Bonaparte had the Liberty Trees, which had been planted in the courtyard of the Tuileries, cut down. Liberty was itself disappearing, and nothing really takes its place, not even glory.

III.

THE First Consul installed himself at the Tuileries, on the first floor in that part which, in the time of Louis XIV., had been called His Majesty's winter apartment. The windows looked upon the garden. The working-room was of moderate size and lit by but one window. This room, by the side of which there was a closet full of maps, opened into a large bedroom, containing a gorgeous bed, which was not that of Louis XVI. "I must not forget to say," Bourrienne tells us, "that the First Consul slept there very seldom; for he troubled himself very little about his quarters, and concerned himself about external luxury only out of calculation, regarding it as a means of impressing people. To speak plainly, Bonaparte, at the Luxembourg, at Malmaison, and during the first part of his stay at the Tuileries, occupied the same room with his wife." Every evening he went down a little staircase to Josephine's apartment below, on the ground floor. She had taken the apartment of Marie Antoinette, and had fitted

41

it up very simply. By the side of her dressing-room were the rooms of her daughter Hortense, consisting of a bed-chamber and a little sitting-room.

As yet there was no thought of appointing chamberlains, equerries, and ladies-in-waiting. Public opinion was not prepared for them, and nothing more was demanded than could be performed by State-counsellor Bénezech, who was a sort of master of ceremonies in charge of the domestic administration of the palace, and in fact really managed the court. On the occasion of the First Consul's solemn entry into the Tuileries, Josephine had modestly stationed herself at a window of the Pavilion of Flora, but a few days later, the 2d Ventose, when her husband was receiving the ambassadors of Spain and Rome, the ministers of Prussia, Denmark, Sweden, Baden, and Hesse-Cassel, and the ambassadors of the Cisal-pine, Batavian, Swiss, and Ligurian Republics, she had all the diplomats presented to her, and held a levee very much like a queen. It was Bénezech who made the presentations.

This return to the old ways did not fail to displease those who still nourished republican sentiments. Thibaudeau, the author of "Memoirs on the Consulate," says about this: "So high was the respect for the civil magistracies, and so strong the hostility to court etiquette, that the Counsellors of State were scandalized at seeing a former Minister of the Interior, one of their colleagues, with an usher's rod in his hand, playing the part of master

of ceremonies, and even of head butler of the First
Consul. There were as yet no titled servants, called
chamberlains; the aides-de-camp took charge of what
would have been their duties, but that had too much
the air of the camp. It was clear that the Tuileries
required a regular court and fixed etiquette, just as
a temple requires priests and service. A court in
process of formation was a new sight for most of the
spectators as well as for the courtiers themselves."

At first it was not very easy to make up the society
of the Tuileries. The "Memorial of Saint Helena"
describes the First Consul's difficulties. Since he
had spent the last few years in the army, he knew
very few people, and he was continually obliged to
consult Consul Lebrun about men and things. The
Republicans, and especially the generals, would have
been horrified if he had received people who belonged
to the old régime, royalists, émigrés. All these did
not begin at once to mount the grand staircase of
the Tuileries, familiar as they grew with it later.
Under the pretence of discriminating between the
wife and the husband, they began by appearing only
on the ground floor, in Josephine's apartments, visiting her in the morning. The bankers and business
men who set the tone under the Directory, were
anxious to gather about Bonaparte; but the First
Consul, who disliked doubtful characters, repelled
their advances with some severity. Their wives were
pretty, amiable, and charming, but could not fasci-
nate him, and he told Josephine not to admit them

to the Tuileries. It was he who said in regard to
the contractors and speculators who were very influ-
ential at the Luxembourg in the time of Barras:
" One of the ways in which I most furthered the
reaction of society towards the condition and habits
of the past was by driving all this false brilliancy
back into the crowd; I never wanted to raise one
of these men to honor, for of all forms of aristocracy
that seemed to me the worst."

Since the nobility and the bankers were thus ex·
cluded, the First Consul could at first have no other
society than that of officials, civil and military, and
their wives. " At first," he says in his "Memorial
of Saint Helena," " everything for a while was like
a magic-lantern, very mixed and forever changing.
The combination soon acquired a color, a tone of its
own, and was by no means without its good side. At
Moscow, the Viceroy (Prince Eugene) found some
letters of the Princess Dolgorouki, who had been
in Paris at that time. She spoke very well of the
Tuileries; she said it was not exactly a court, but
that on the other hand it was not a camp; that the
etiquette and the ways were quite new; that the First
Consul did not carry his hat under his arm, or wear
a rapier, to be sure, but that he was not a rough
soldier." The ladies who attended these receptions
were, for the most part, young, timid, and without
experience of the world; but Madame Bonaparte set
them at their ease by her amiable grace and kindness, and the young women who at first were intimi·

dated by the growing etiquette of a palace, and especially by the rank and glory of the First Consul, gradually acquired familiarity with the customs of good society, and were wise enough to take Josephine for a model. At that time Madame Bonaparte used to give breakfasts from which men were rigorously excluded.

" In my opinion," said the Duchess of Abrantès, " it was a delightful custom, that of inviting to such entertainments women who were still too timid to be agreeable in a drawing-room in the presence of men so much their superiors as to alarm them. By talking at these informal breakfasts about the fashions, the new plays, the little commonplaces of society, the young women acquired courage, and ceased to be mere wallflowers in the drawing-room of the First Consul, when he sought distraction there. Madame Bonaparte did the honors of the breakfast with charming grace. Generally there were about half-a-dozen of us, and all, with the exception of our hostess, of about the same age."

Let us once more consult the Duchess of Abrantès, whose graceful, womanly Memoirs, and " History of the Paris Drawing-rooms," with its curious and amusing details, give a most vivid and attractive picture of this period. In the chapter called " Madame Bonaparte's Drawing-room," she describes all the women who were intimately allied with Josephine in 1800 and 1801. There was Madame de La Rochefoucauld, " a little hunchback, a very kind

woman, although witty," who was related to the
family of Beauharnais; then Madame de La Valette,
"sweet, good, always pretty, in spite of the small-
pox, and of the many who found her too handsome
notwithstanding her misfortune." And Madame de
Lameth, " round as a ball and bearded, — two unattractive things in a woman, but good and witty, — two
very attractive qualities"; then Madame de Lauriston,
" kind to every one and generally popular "; Madame
de Rémusat, "a superior woman and very charming
to those who understood her "; Madame de Talhonet,
" who remembered too well that she had been pretty,
and forgot that she was so no longer "; and Madame
d'Harville, " systematically impolite, and only polite
by accident."

The intimate friends of Madame Bonaparte used
to meet in the drawing-room on the ground floor,
and the official visitors used to appear on the first
flight, in the grand reception rooms. But there
were many different types, curious combinations, and
striking contrasts even in the society downstairs.
All opinions met there. An émigré just a few days
returned would sit by the side of a former member
of the Convention, who a few years earlier had condemned him to death; a Republican general would
elbow a member of the Vendean army; but, by her
exquisite tact, Josephine was able to enforce, if not
peace, at least a truce between men whose antece-
dents seemed to make them irreconcilable enemies,
and from the beginning of the Consulate she worked

more energetically than any one to bring about the reconciliation and fusion which her husband desired.

The great receptions of the first floor were called mobs by those who had admission to the ground floor. Every decade, or week of ten days, there was served, in the Gallery of Diana, a dinner of two hundred plates. The senators and the generals were received on the second day of the decade; the members of the Legislature, on the fourth day; the Tribunes and the members of the Court of Appeal, on the sixth day.

The question of a consulate for life, or of making the position hereditary, had not yet arisen. The First Consul, who was not called the President of the Republic, was, according to the constitution, merely a temporary magistrate, whose powers were limited to a period of ten years, and who shared the government with two colleagues, called, like him, consuls. But if we examine the state of affairs, what is Cambacérès, what is Lebrun, in comparison with the sun of which they are the satellites? In all the receptions and important functions Bonaparte is the only one who is looked at; everywhere and always, as the poet said later. Any one who wishes to get an idea of this man's ascendancy has only to consider what took place every fifth day at noon in the court-yard. It was the favorite spectacle of the Parisians, and the great attraction for the provincials and for-eigners who happened to be in Paris. In France nothing produces so strong an impression as the sight of the warriors who flatter its national pride and its warlike instincts. At the sight of such soldiers the whole people grew enthusiastic, and felt themselves capable of unheard-of prodigies. It seemed as if they could defy all Europe, and they were tempted to cry out, like their ancestors, the Gauls, "There is only one thing I fear: that the heavens will fall." They said to themselves, "We are a great nation."

All the regiments came in turn to Paris to take part in the reviews on every fifth day of the decade before the First Consul. They dazzled the capital, and the capital dazzled them. Parisians and soldiers got on very well together, and after the review retained very pleasant memories of each other. Thibaudeau shows us Bonaparte, one moment on foot, the next on horseback, going through the ranks to make acquaintance with the officers and soldiers, and to let them learn to know him, interesting himself in the pettiest details of their equipment, their armament, and drill, busying himself indefatigably with everything that concerned the welfare of his troops, welcoming his former companions in Italy, and addressing them with some flattering speech that drove them wild with enthusiasm. "It was interesting to see," says Madame de Rémusat, "how well he understood how to talk with the soldiers, how he would ask one soldier after another about his campaigns or his wounds. . . . I have heard Madame Bonaparte say that he was accustomed to study every evening, when he was going to bed, the army lists. He would sleep on the names of the corps, and on those of some

of the men who composed the corps, retaining them
in a corner of his memory; and in this way he had
the wonderful gift of recognizing the soldiers and of
giving them the pleasure of being picked out by their
commander. In talking with the men he assumed
a tone of good-fellowship which delighted them; he
addressed each one with *thou*, and recalled the feats
of arms they had performed together."

This was the time when, preserving some of the
republican familiarity, he wrote to the non-commissioned officer, Sergeant Léon Aune of the Grenadiers,
the following letter: "I have received your letter,
my dear comrade; you don't need to tell me what
you have done; I know very well you are one of
the bravest grenadiers in the army since the death of
Benezeth. You received one of the hundred sabres
of honor which I had distributed. All the soldiers
of your corps agreed that you were the one who deserved it most. I am very anxious to see you again.
The Minister of War sends you an order to come to
Paris." Never, except perhaps among the members
of Cæsar's legions, has there been seen such a fanatical love of military life. Second lieutenants would
not have given up their epaulettes for millions.
Every officer, every soldier, was proud of his uniform, of his regiment, of his colors. No one has
ever understood better than Bonaparte how to impress
the imagination of the soldier. He controlled him
with a word, with a glance, and appeared to him like
a supernatural being, like a demi-god. Even after

his defeats he preserved his authority; what must it have been when his comrades who had always seen him victorious thought him always invincible? Each one of the fifth day reviews was a new apotheosis for him. "If it happened to rain, or if the day was cloudy," says Thibaudeau, an eye-witness, "it often happened that at the moment Bonaparte appeared the rain stopped, the clouds broke, and the sun shone out. The multitude, always greedy of miracles, and the courtiers, always profuse in flattery, used to cry out, 'The First Consul controls the elements!'"

The wife of General Junot, afterwards the Duchess of Abrantès, describes one of these reviews which greatly delighted her. A little before noon, Josephine, her daughter, Hortense de Beauharnais, her sisters-in-law, a number of pretty women, of officials, of distinguished strangers, appeared at the palace windows. After the parade, sixteen magnificent horses, the gift of the King of Spain, were to be presented to the First Consul. The officers walked up and down among the soldiers, speaking to them from time to time, in a low voice, to correct a faulty position or some trifle in their dress. Every one was most zealous, for the First Consul must be satisfied. The trumpets sounded, the drums beat, and Bonaparte appeared on his white horse, Désiré. His soldiers gazed at him with an expression which seemed to say, "Yes, we will die that France may be great, and its name the first in the world. Whither shall we go? We are ready." He stopped beneath the window at which Madame Junot happened to be with some ladies, and turning to a young drummer who seemed to be about sixteen or seventeen years old, he said, " So, my boy, it was you who beat the charge at Zürich with a bullet through your right arm?" The little drummer blushed, and answered, " Yes, General." "And it's you, too, who showed great presence of mind at Weser?" The boy blushed more deeply, and answered in a lower voice, "Yes, General." " Well, I ought to pay the country's debt. You shall receive, not a drumstick of honor, but a sabre of honor. I appoint you a non-commissioned officer in the Consular Guard. Go on as well as you have begun, and I shall take care of you." Then the First Consul, with a pleasant smile, touched his hat to the ladies, who had been listening to him. The little drummer was as pale as death with emotion, but his face is eloquent. He may have grown pale before Bonaparte, but he would not turn pale before the enemy.

IV.

PARIS, in 1800, knew only two passions, — glory and pleasure. The once magic word, liberty, was now scarcely ever on men's lips, except as a matter of habit. The great city, always fickle in its tastes and emotions, was now thoroughly weary of politics, of parliamentary disputes, of clubs, news-papers, and outbreaks, and had become totally indif-ferent to all these things which a short time previous used to arouse it to fury. It scarcely remembered that it had been torn by a revolution. Edgar Quinet has described most admirably the state of feeling at the beginning of the Consulate, and he is borne out by all the contemporary authorities. "When men," he says, "after a heroic effort, are tired of the duties of freedom, and suddenly abandon the control of themselves, they experience a singular sensation of relief. There are many instances of this in anti-quity. After centuries of civil war, the Romans felt a profound peace, a happy satisfaction, in laying their conscience in the hands of a master. The French felt something of the sort after the events of the

18th Brumaire, which relieved them of the care of their own destinies. Doubtless this period is, except for the lack of dignity, one of the happiest in the memory of man." People began to say that, after all, the guillotine was not ornamental in a public square, and that a well-dressed, well-drilled regiment was far superior to a rabble of men with pikes; that, as its name implies, the Reign of Terror is the most disagreeable and alarming of systems of government; that Paris will never be a really austere city; that a good dinner is better than the black broth of Sparta; that a pretty woman who chats is far preferable to a speech-making tribune; people began to see some merit in the good old times; they acknowledged that social entertainments, life in the drawing-room, in the castles, that courtesy, gallantry, French gayety, songs, theatres, balls, and all the amusements which for centuries had been the joy and pride of the great capital were, after all, really indispensable. The re-action was as marked as the Revolution had been; and it was just because Madame Bonaparte was a woman of the old régime that she so well pleased Parisian society, which asked nothing better than to go back to the customs and pleasures of the past.

The official world set the fashion of festivity, and the winter was tolerably gay. Especially successful were the balls of Lucien Bonaparte, who occupied the sumptuous Brissac mansion, as Minister of the Interior. He was then in love with the fashionable beauty, Madame Récamier, the most charming woman in Paris. Since her first name was Juliette, he expressed his devotion under the pseudonym of Romeo: "Romeo writes to you, Juliette; if you should refuse to read him, you would be more cruel than our relatives, who have just become reconciled. . . . O Juliette! life without love is only a long sleep. The loveliest of women ought to be tender-hearted. Happy the man who shall become the friend of your heart!" It seems that Madame Récamier did not let herself be moved by Lucien, although she was much flattered by his attentions. Her husband, moreover, advised her to be gentle with the brother of the First Consul. So Madame Récamier was one of the principal ornaments of the balls given by the Minister of the Interior. The author of the delightful book, "Recollections of Madame Récamier," tells us that she produced a very great effect at a dinner, followed by a concert, which Lucien gave to his brother, General Bonaparte. "She was dressed in white satin, and wore a necklace and bracelets of pearls, as if she took a certain satisfaction in covering herself with things conspicuous for their whiteness, in order to efface them by the beauty of her complexion." Fouché, the member of the Convention, afterwards the Duke of Otranto, came behind the chair in which she sat, and said to her in a low tone, "The First Consul finds you charming."

At that moment Napoleon was holding the hand of one of Lucien's daughters, a little girl of not more than four, and in talking he thought no more about the child, who grew tired of her captivity and began to cry. "Oh! you poor little thing," said the First Consul, with genuine pity; "I had forgotten you." Lucien had gone up to Madame Récamier, and Napoleon, who knew all about his brother's devotion, said quite loud, "I should like to go to Clichy myself." (Clichy was where Madame Récamier lived.) Dinner was announced, and Napoleon went in first without offering his arm to any one of the ladies. He placed his mother on his right, and the place on his left remained empty, no one daring to take it. Then he turned towards the guests who were still standing, and said suddenly to Garat, the singer, "Well, Garat, sit down here." At the same moment Cambacérès took the place next to Madame Récamier, and Napoleon called out, "Ah, citizen Consul, next to the handsomest woman!" After dinner he asked Madame Récamier, "Why didn't you sit next to me?" "I should not have dared," she replied. He answered, "It was your place."

Madame Méchin, Madame Régnault de Saint-Jean-d'Angély, and Madame Visconti shone, even by the side of Madame Récamier, at the balls of the Minister of the Interior. The First Consul's three sisters were like princesses on those occasions. Josephine, in her seat at the end of the gallery, already assumed the bearing of a sovereign. The women all rose when she entered the ball-room and when she left. Besides the entertainments of official society, there were those of the great bankers, Messrs. Perregaux, Séguin,

Hainguerlot, Récamier, who renewed the traditions of the farmers-general. The Faubourg Saint Germain was not yet reconstituted, and the aristocracy gave no entertainments, but they amused themselves nevertheless; there were Garat's concerts, the theatre, dinners, Tivoli, Frascati, and the Hanoverian Pavilion. All classes of society were eager for pleasure, and dancing was especially the rage. "Next to money," says a contemporary pamphlet, "the dance has become the idol of the Parisians. With small and great, with rich and poor, it has become a universal passion. There is dancing at the Carmes, where the crowds are enormous; at the Jesuits' College; at the Seminary of Saint Sulpice; at the Filles Sainte Marie; in three or four churches; at Ruggieri's, Lucquet's, Manduit's, Wentzel's; at the Thelusson mansion."

The reopening of the Opera balls was the great attraction of the Carnival in 1800. For ten years the Parisians had been deprived of this favorite pleasure. In a period of furious hatred and of general slaughter, a masked ball would have been an impossibility. Under the rule of Robespierre the spies would not have respected the secrecy and security of a mask. The knife of the guillotine would have been the punishment of a witticism. And after the Terror, men were still so excited that those who wore a mask would have been exposed to the bitterest recriminations and the most violent abuse. Bonaparte, who was dreaming of the triumph of a policy of concilia-

tion and fusion, thought that under his government
the Opera balls had become once more possible, and
would even further the work of appeasement which
was part of his plan.   He was not mistaken: the reopening of the Opera balls seemed to him an event of'
real social importance.   Hence it was that he had
two long articles, which to-day are a real historical
curiosity, inserted on the first page of the *Moniteur
Universel*, in the numbers of the 8th and 9th of Ventose, year VIII. (February 26 and 27, 1800).   "The
Opera House is open," it is stated in the first of these
articles, "it is crowded; people arrive in dense crowds;
five or six thousand persons are massed in a space too
small to hold them.   Thousands of different disguises,
thousands of elegant, odd, or amusing costumes, call
forth jests and merry-making; satire has free scope,
and nothing is heard but laughter; all faces are lit
with joy and confidence; a leader of the riding-school,
without a mask, elbows a returned exile."   The official sheet, which saw in this ball a sign that the various parties were laying down their arms, adds with
keen satisfaction: "It is a curious and touching picture, less interesting for the times it recalls than for
those it foretells.   It shows that the revolutionary
leaven has ceased to ferment; that Frenchmen, tired
of hatred and fear, now only care to join hands and
forgive one another."

Enthusiastic over these happy results, the *Moniteur*
thus apostrophized the foes of the new régime : " Pu-
pils of Chaumette and Marat, go and count the receipts

at the opera; consider that the twenty-five or thirty
thousand francs, paid in at the door, will carry com-
fort and happiness in a hundred families of actors or
workmen connected with this theatre; calculate how
much the shop-keepers of Paris have made out of
those expensive costumes, those disguises hired for
large sums (it is estimated that dominoes were let
for twenty-five, thirty-six, and as much as forty-eight
francs), out of the carriages which were insufficient
in number to accommodate those who sought them."
Of course the *Moniteur* took pains to give Bonaparte
credit for all this: " When some of the persons of
the First Consul's family were seen at this entertainment, it was supposed that he had himself come to
look from a grated box upon the scene, which might
well have given him the sensation of noble vanity.
Every one who thought that he saw him would have
had a chance to say, ' Nobis haec otia fecit.'";

The other article, of the 9th of Ventose, expressed
the same satisfaction, although there are some re-
serves in regard to the unfamiliarity of some Parisians with masked balls: " These scenes of coquetry
have their rules which ought to be known, and a language of their own, which ought to be every one's
possession, but it must be said that among the Parisians of the present day, some have never known the
manners of a masquerade, and others have forgotten
them. A mask, moreover, implies a rôle; a rôle pre-
supposes an actor, and not every one is an actor, and
consequently among the crowd of maskers many

seemed to have forgotten their names and their characters. We saw a good many undignified Spaniards,
ungraceful dancing-girls, commonplace Orientals; we
saw discreet nuns, silent lawyers, solemn clowns, and
statue-like Harlequins."

The *Moniteur* consoled itself with the hope of
speedy improvement: " This is a misfortune," it says;
"but confiding in the native intelligence of the happy
Parisians, we feel sure that they will soon find once
more the talents required by these new sports: there
is no occasion for uneasiness."

Women of the highest society went in great numbers to the Opera balls. They wore masks and dominoes, and amused themselves with the men of their
acquaintance, who went in dress suits, without masks.
Madame Récamier, who was very timid when her
face was visible, became lively and sportive behind a
domino. Madame de Staël, on the other hand, as
soon as she was masked, lost her usual high spirits
and eloquence. In Paris, nothing was talked about
but the Opera balls which delighted every one. The
young were delighted to see an entertainment which
they had so often heard warmly spoken of, while
their elders hoped in the lamplight to go back ten
years, and liked to fancy that the horrors of the
Revolution were only a bad dream which vanished
at the sound of the joyous music.

While Paris was thus happy in feeling itself still
frivolous, and was trying to make up for time lost
in the way of distractions and pleasures, the émigrés

who were compelled to conceal themselves under false names, began to make their way back to the city where so many different things had happened since their departure. It was a great joy to them to see once more their native soil; but there was much sadness mingled with it. Chateaubriand has described his return. It was one Sunday, at about three in the afternoon, that the future author of the "Genius of Christianity" entered Paris on foot by the gate of the Étoile, after an absence of eight years. Poor and obscure, no one recognized him. "We have now no idea," he says, "of the impression that the excesses of the Revolution made upon the minds of men throughout Europe, and especially upon those away from France during the Terror. It seemed to me as if I were actually about to descend into hell." To his great surprise, he heard violins, horns, clarionets, and drums. As he passed down the Champs Élysées, he saw little halls where men and women were dancing. The Place Louis XV. seemed to him an accursed spot: "It was dilapidated, as melancholy and deserted as an old amphitheatre." Before the place where stood the scaffold of Louis XVI. he was overcome by profound emotion. " I was afraid," he says, "of stepping in the blood of which no trace was left. . . . I imagined that I saw my brother and my sister-in-law, with their hands bound, near the bloody instrument. . . . In spite of the merriment of the streets, the church-towers were dumb; I seemed to have got back on some day of great solemnity, like Good Friday."

In her Memoirs, Madame de Genlis has also well described her return, her emotion when she crossed the frontier and entered into France, when she heard the people speaking French, when she drew near Paris and made out from a distance the towers of Notre Dame, when she found how the city had changed during her absence. Everything seemed novel; she was like a foreigner whose curiosity stops her at every step. The names of the streets were changed. Cabs passed her which she recognized as confiscated carriages of her friends. She entered a little second-hand shop where were some twenty portraits. "I recognized them all, and my eyes filled with tears as I thought that three-quarters of the nobles they represented had been guillotined, and that the others, robbed of every penny and exiled, were perhaps still wandering in foreign lands."

What consoled Madame de Genlis for so many sorrows was the military glory of France. "I was glad to meet the son of one of my gamekeepers, now a captain, who had served in our successful armies with great distinction. His fine bearing and his martial air reminded me of what La Rochefoucauld had said: 'Vulgarity is never lost at court; it always is in the army.'" The émigrés who returned soon grew accustomed to the new régime. They used to talk calmly with the murderers of their relatives. Jacobins and the men of Coblenz used to meet every day in the theatres, in the promenades, and a sort of calm succeeded the paroxysm of wrath and hatred.

As Chateaubriand said, "Bonaparte put the Brutuses
and Scævolas into the police, and set about adorning
them with ribands, and degrading them with titles,
compelling them to betray their opinions and to dis-
honor their crimes.   Day by day there went on the
metamorphosis of the tyranny of all into the tyranny
of a single man."

V.

THE TWO NATIONAL FESTIVALS.

THE consular government was very strong in 1800, and yet it could not have survived a defeat; the baptism of victory was absolutely necessary to its existence. If the First Consul had been beaten at Marengo, all the recent framework of his power and glory would have fallen like a house of cards. He was well aware of this, and before he started for the second Italian campaign he said that he was staking everything for everything. In spite of an apparent truce the parties had not disarmed, and they awaited with impatience the course of events on the other side of the Alps. Royalists, Jacobins, bankers, speculators, wondered most anxiously what would be the result of Bonaparte's new challenge to fortune. His political foes pictured him already beaten, overthrown, perhaps slain, and formed a thousand plans, as if the succession were already open. All this agitation was of brief duration. Bonaparte left Paris May 6, 1800; he returned July 2. In less than two months he had accomplished great things.

As was usual with him, the conqueror had the gift

of setting his victories before the public. Everything
was arranged for arousing the Parisians, the modern
Athenians, for impressing their imagination. General de Ségur puts it thus: "We are all young, soldiers and generals. A third of our number were fresh
recruits. The oldest had had but eight years' experience. A threefold spring, — that of the year, of
our life, of glory, — the rivalry within us and about us,
inspired us." This imitation of Hannibal, the crossing of the Alps, a bold undertaking, an army defiling
man by man, one by one, by the goat-paths, over the
eternal snows; the artillery taken to pieces; the
cannon dragged by ropes; every soldier, every horse,
in danger of death at the least misstep; the Saint
Bernard, with its monks and dogs; the avalanches,
the precipices; the sudden entrance into the plains
of Italy; the day of Marengo, so hotly contested; the
heroic and touching death of the brave Desaix; Italy
won back in a campaign of a few days, — this new
heroic history worthy of antiquity was the general
subject of conversation, and aroused every one's
enthusiasm. Never, at any period of his life, was
Napoleon so popular, and yet he was not sated with
his glory. On his way to Paris, through Burgundy,
he said to Bourrienne, "Well, a few grand deeds like
this campaign, and I may be known to posterity."
"It seems to me," was the answer, "that you have
already done enough to be talked about everywhere
for some time." "Done enough!" said the hero of
Marengo; "You are very kind! To be sure, in less

than two years I have conquered Cairo, Paris, and Milan; well, my dear fellow, if I were to die to-morrow, after ten centuries I shouldn't fill half a page in a universal history."

Bonaparte passed through France amid ovations. At Dijon he was congratulated by a company of young women wearing flowers in their hair, who resembled the groups of women who, in the days of ancient Greece, used to dance about the victor in the Olympic games. At Sens he passed beneath a triumphant arch on which was inscribed the three historic words, "Veni, vidi, vici." When he re-entered Paris, in the night of July 2, the enthusiasm was indescribable. All, rich and poor, rejoiced, and the next day a vast crowd gathered in the Tuileries gardens.

Every one wanted to see the conquering hero. When the chief officials of the state came to congratulate him, he said to them: "Well, have you done much work while I was away?" And they answered, "Not so much as you, General." In the evening the whole city was illuminated, and without orders; every window, even to the garrets, showed a light. Twenty years later, at Saint Helena, Napoleon spoke of this day as one of the proudest and happiest of his life.

He was delighted to see Josephine again; not a cloud had at that time arisen between them, and their union was a real model of reciprocal affection. The hero of Marengo felt that this woman, whom he dearly loved, was his good angel. "Bourrienne," he said to his secretary, "do you hear the hurrahs of the populace which have not stopped yet? It is as sweet to me as the sound of Josephine's voice." As La Bruyère puts it: "The sweetest sound in nature is that of the voice of the woman we love."

Bonaparte's ambition had never been more satisfied, and never had the national pride of France been more flattered. "Military glory," to quote from Miot de Mélito, "was not yet a burden to the citizens, because the soldiers and officers came from all ranks of society without distinction, and returned to them without disturbance. The army belonged to the country, and its victories, in appearance at least, profited the country alone: it had not yet become the property of the Head of the State. What, then, was needed to assure this prosperity? What was lacking to give Europe the example of a great nation, regenerated, in the enjoyment of freedom without license, triumphant under skilful leaders, and yet not their slave? A Washington." And he adds sadly, "The man on whom our destinies depended professed to carry us back into the old paths; and unfortunately for him as for us, he was only too ingenious, and too much aided in this undertaking."

In 1800 Bonaparte, apparently at least, was still a Republican. Twelve days after his return to Paris occurred the national festival of July 14, the anniversary of the taking of the Bastille and of the Federation. This festival, one of the finest which had ever been seen in Paris, still preserved its democratic and military character. The people and the army joined hands. The Consular Guard, which had left Milan June 22, had been ordered to get to Paris in the morning of July 14. At Geneva it was invited by the authorities to a great banquet; and each officer found a laurel wreath under his napkin, with a poem by Madame de Staël, who did the honors. The Guard, to which had been entrusted the care of bringing the Austrian flags captured at Marengo, was exact at the rendezvous appointed by the First Consul. At ten o'clock in the morning of July 14, it was in the courtyard of the Tuileries, whence it departed for the Invalides, and then for the Champ de Mars. Prince Eugene, who belonged to it, says in his Memoirs, " The members of the Guard who had been left on duty in Paris presented a striking contrast, with their neat and smart appearance, to the troops just back from Italy, who were all gaunt, worn, and covered with dust. This contrast only redoubled the enthusiasm and respect of the Parisians, which the mere presence of the soldiers had evoked. It was one of the proudest moments of my life." Josephine was very happy to see her son taking part in such a triumph.

The celebration was held at the Invalides, the chapel of which was called the Temple of Mars. Lucien Bonaparte, as Minister of the Interior, made a speech, full of republican sentiment. Doubtless he remembered that at Saint Cloud on the 19th Brumaire he had sworn to kill his brother with his sword if he should ever lay a hand upon the liberties of France. He uttered a warm eulogy of the Revolution, and spoke of the capture of the Bastille: " The Bastille is taken, O France! Republic, cemented by the blood of heroes and martyrs, may Liberty, more precious for what it has cost us, and Peace, healer of every evil, be forever thy preserving deities!" By a singular association of ideas, the brother of the First Consul combined the 14th of July and the 18th of Brumaire. " The 18th Brumaire completed the work of July 14. All that the earlier day destroyed shall never be renewed; all that the later has built up is never to be destroyed. . . . Frenchmen, let us bear with pride the name of the great people ; let this name be an object of universal love and admiration, so that in the remotest ages the heroes of the 14th of July, the defenders and supporters of the Empire, may be held up to the respect of our descendants, and so that the Republic founded by their efforts may be as eternal as their glory."

The word *Empire* is, perhaps, a little startling in this passage. It sounds like a prophecy, but it must be remembered that in 1800 it was regarded as synonymous with state. The celebrated song, "Let us guard the Welfare of the Empire," was written by Republicans in the days of the Republic. It was a national hymn.

When Lucien had finished, three bands played simultaneously the "Song of the 25th Messidor"

(July 14), the words by Citizen Fontanes, the music
by Citizen Méhul.　It was the first time that the
experiment had been tried of a concert by three
bands at some distance from one another.　The solos
and choruses produced a great effect.

> O glorious destiny !
> Applaud, people of France !
> Soon, crowned with palms,
> Victory will establish peace.
> The brow of the Alps humbles itself :
> We have crossed its ice ;
> And all the forts of Italy
> Open a second time to our soldiers.

Solo.

You die, brave Desaix, you die !　Ah, can you believe
That the glory of your name expires with you ?
The Arab, in the desert, recounts your glory,
And his children will tell it to their children for all time.

According to the *Moniteur* there was great emotion
at this moment.　All turned towards the monument
raised in his honor, which was topped by his bust,
the work of Citizen Dupaty.

Chorus of Warriors.

> O Condé, Dugommier, Turenne,
> It is you whom I hear, whom I see ;
> You seek the great captain
> Who has outdone all his exploits.
> The sons are greater than their sires,
> And your hearts are not jealous.
> France, after so many sufferings,
> Rises again better worthy of you.

A great century ends, a great century begins.
Glory, virtues, fine arts, arise with it!
O God! see this great people bowed at thy feet.
The conquerors of Europe invoke thy aid.

OLD MEN.

From infancy and youth
To love work and good morals.

YOUNG MEN.

Give peace to the aged.

YOUNG WOMEN.

Grant to all happier days.

GENERAL CHORUS.

Immortal Being, by thy light
Let France advance henceforth,
And to warlike merit
Add all the virtues of peace.

When the choral was over, the First Consul went
into the courtyard, behind the dome, where he visited
the disabled soldiers. The five whom their companions had picked out as most worthy of national
reward, were presented to him, and he gave them
gold medals inscribed with their name, age, birth-
place, and exploits. Then he went to the Champ de
Mars, where the troops were waiting for him under
arms. Every bit of high ground was densely crowded,
and all the windows of the Military School were
packed with spectators.

The Minister of War presented to the three Consuls the officers who carried the captured battle-flags.

Every one wanted to get a nearer view of these trophies of the heroes who had deserved so well of their country, of the victorious general who had accomplished so much. They left the high ground and rushed into the Champ de Mars in the midst of the troops. Nothing could oppose them. No orders, no obstacles, stopped this irresistible throng. Every one shouted, "Long live the Republic! Long live Bonaparte!" "These two names," said the *Moniteur*, "are equally dear to the French. Let the friends of liberty rejoice; so touching a spectacle was never seen. . . . What a people is this! Happy is he who can serve it and win its love!" The celebration ended with all sorts of amusements: foot and horse races, a balloon ascent, illuminations, music and dancing in the Champs Élysées, fireworks, and a concert. At the grand dinner, at which Bonaparte was present with the principal officials of the Republic, were to be seen the disabled soldiers who had that morning received the medals at the Temple of Mars, and with them two of their comrades, one aged one hundred and four; the other, one hundred and seven. The First Consul proposed this toast: "To the 14th of July and the French People, our sovereign!"

The celebration of the 1st Vendémiaire, year IX., was also a Republican festival; it was the anniversary of the foundation of the Republic; it introduced, however, some monarchical memories. The First Consul wished to make combination of all forms of glory. The festival of the 1st Vendémiaire, year IX., was preluded, as it were, by that of the fifth complementary day of the year VIII. On that day the remains of Turenne, with his sword and the bullet that killed him, were transported in great pomp to the Temple of Mars (the Chapel of the Invalides), where Carnot, the Minister of War, made a speech.

The former member of the Convention spoke in the highest praise of the great general of Louis XIV. " On the tomb of Turenne the old man will every day shed tears of admiration; thither the young man will come to test his talent for a military life. . . . In our days Turenne would have been the first to spring into the path which our Republican phalanxes have followed. Words cannot describe our feelings here. What have I to say of Turenne? There he is himself. Of his victories? There is the sword which his victorious arm wielded. Of his death? There is the fatal bullet which tore him from France, from all humanity."

In the evening of the same day there were free performances in the theatres. The First Consul and his wife went to the Français, where the " Cid " and " Tartufe " were given. In the morning, Turenne; in the evening, Corneille and Molière.

Another reminiscence of Louis XIV.: On the 1st Vendémiaire it was in the Place des Victoires, the spot where that king's statue had been placed that Bonaparte laid the corner-stone of the monument to

Kléber and Desaix. In the middle of the square
there had been put up a building like an Egyptian
temple with a dome, beneath which stood the busts
of the two heroes. The windows, balconies, even
the roofs of the houses, were crowded with spectators, who burst into frantic applause the moment the
First Consul appeared.

Bonaparte afterwards went to the Invalides, where
he found inscribed in gold letters on marble tablets
the names of the men who had received arms of
honor. In the Temple of Mars was given the "Song
of the 1st of Vendémiaire," with words by Esmenard
and music by Lesueur, a Republican hymn, in which
this stanza was noted : —

> Liberty, banished from the walls of Romulus
> Far from the degraded Tiber, fleeing from tyranny,
> Hastens at your voice ;
> And on the happy banks which the Seine fertilizes,
> It comes to raise again, for the happiness of the world,
> Its altars and its laws.

Lucien Bonaparte, the Minister of the Interior,
then spoke in the Temple of Mars, in honor of the
establishment of the Republic. "Though but just
born," he said, "Republican France, stronger than
all thrones, advances with a giant's stride, visiting
and forming again the old boundaries of ancient
Gaul. The sceptre of Henry IV. and of Louis XIV.
rolls shattered in the dust : at once the government
of the sovereign people seizes all the sceptres of
Charlemagne. So eight years of our era have filled

our annals with more victories and wonders than
eight hundred years of the rule of kings. To our
Revolution alone belongs this gigantic and wonderful character; the evils which afflicted us belong to
all. Happy is the generation which sees a revolution
begun under a monarchy ended by the Republic."
He ended with this lyrical outburst: "It seems to
me as if upright on a broken statue or on the ruined
tomb of an old king of France, the century just ending takes its flight, and says to the beginning century:
'I leave you a grand heritage. I have augmented
all branches of human knowledge; I have been called
the age of philosophy. I disappeared, and the storms
re-enter with me into the night of time. . . . Preserve peace and liberty; do not disappoint the hope
of sages' . . . ." And then, at the height of his
enthusiasm: "The century that begins will be the
grand century. I swear by the people, whose instrument I am, by the wisdom of the first magistrates, by the union of citizens. The great destinies
of Republican France are accomplished."

When the orator had ceased, cries of, "Long live
the Republic!" resounded from all parts. The liberal promises of the consular government still inspired
confidence; and it was in thus piously uttering the
name of Liberty, in exalting the capture of the Bastille, in celebrating with pomp the Republican holidays, that the preparations were laid for the speedy
re-establishment of absolute monarchy.

VI.

WE have just seen Bonaparte and Josephine in all the brilliancy of official life in the palace of the Tuileries, surrounded by all the pomp of real sovereignty. Let us now study them in their rustic life, in an agreeable, modest country-house. The husband and wife appear without formality, showing their domestic qualities, and one soon grows interested in the slightest details of their lives. We are almost like their guests, and we may learn to know them as if we had spent years in their company. We should study them especially at Malmaison, for no other mansion is so rich in memories of them. By going through it as it is to-day, deserted and empty, it is possible to imagine it as it was in 1800. Some day, perhaps, it will be torn down, the victim of some revolutionary mob; now, however, while it is still standing as it existed in the beginning of the century, it is easy to give each room its old physiognomy, to recall its former animation, to renew its past.

On the left bank of the Seine, close to the village of Rueil, at the foot of the charming amphitheatre

topped in the distance by the aqueduct of Marly,
stands the famous mansion amid dense verdure. I
walk up the avenue of palm-trees to the castle gate;
passing through this, I enter the main courtyard,
with gravel paths intersecting the grass-plots and
flower-beds as in old times. I gaze at its front with
its three stories, its two wings, its slate roof; everything is as it was in 1800. Under a tent-shaped ve-
randa, surmounted by gilded crescents, I enter the
great hall paved with squares of black and white
marble. This runs through the mansion, giving a
view of the park beyond. The roof above is vaulted,
and is upheld by four stucco columns. To the left
of the hall are the dining-room, the council-chamber,
the library; to the right, the billiard-room, Josephine's *boudoir* and drawing-room, the picture-gallery.

The dining-room is decorated with six nymphs, in
black and white, on a stucco ground. In old times
there was a large window of plate-glass between the
hall and the dining-room, through which Josephine
used to watch the children coming to receive toys
and sweetmeats. On the mosaic floor I see a rose
which marked the place where she used to sit at table.
Then there is the council-chamber where so many
important deliberations were held, the library with a
door on which are painted two helmets and two in-
scriptions from the Greek and from the time of chivalry. This was the taste of the time — reminiscences
of antiquity and of the Middle Ages. There is not a
single book on the shelves, but I notice the medal-

lions of Plutarch's heroes and the mahogany arches separated by windows. I picture to myself Bonaparte in this room, studying, reading, meditating, and unfolding his maps. From the library there is a passage into the garden, over a little bridge across the moat, which on this side lies close to the castle. In 1800 this bridge was covered by a canvas tent which gave the First Consul another room. He used to have his table carried thither, and would work there alone, stepping every moment from the bridge out into the garden, and from the garden back to the bridge. "When I am in the open air," he used to say, "I become conscious that my ideas expand more freely. I can't understand men who can sit by the stove and work without any view of the sky."

Retracing my steps, I return by the library, council-hall, and dining-room to the hall, and pass through it to the billiard-room, which is wainscoted with wood painted light green. I see the billiard-table, or rather its frame, for in 1870 the Prussians took away its cloth and the bed. I then look at the *boudoir*, which is perfectly bare, and go into the drawing-room, which is equally empty. The mantelpiece, into which were set mosaic medallions, a present from the Pope, has been damaged, but the arabesques, which represent flowers and birds in gold on a white ground, have not been destroyed. It was in this room that Josephine used to hold her levees, and here, a few days before her death, she received the visit of the Emperor Alexander. The mirrors which reflected so many beautiful faces, so many gorgeous uniforms, are broken; but one would say that the graceful shade of Josephine wanders silently through this drawing-room of which she was the central figure. On one side is the gallery where the musicians used to stand, and where Garat and other great artists sang, where Queen Hortense, who was a charming composer and performer, used to play the harp and sing, — the gallery where were many pictures and objects of art, now all dispersed.

We have examined the ground floor, and will now ascend the staircase opening on the billiard-room, and go up to the first floor. To the right an anteroom leads up to Josephine's bed-chamber, a round room. In old times it was hung with red. We can still make out the painting on the ceiling, a blue sky with clouds and a few dashes of gold on the woodwork. The place where the bed stood is empty. Napoleon and Josephine occupied this room for a long time, and it was of this period of his life that Napoleon said at Saint Helena, "Not one of my thoughts, not one of my actions, escaped Josephine; she followed, grasped, guessed everything, — a fact which sometimes inconvenienced me in my occupations." It was there that she wrote to her mother, who had stayed in Martinique, "You ought to love Bonaparte; he makes your daughter very happy; he is kind, amiable, in a word, a charming man." This room was also the scene of her unhappiness. To it, when driven from the Tuileries, she returned to sleep

the evening of the day when her divorce was pronounced. In it she drew her last breath; and there,
after his return from Elba, he locked himself up to
muse in solitude. The next room was his retiring-
room during the Consulate. Another room and a
bathroom completed their private apartment. At
the other end of the castle were the rooms which
Hortense occupied after her marriage.

In the middle of the first floor is a long corridor,
lit by eight windows opening on the courtyard. It
leads to the little rooms which are generally assigned
to guests. During the Consulate they were simply
furnished. The aides-de-camp and visitors used to
occupy them.

Descending the staircase to the hall, we may go
out into the garden, over a little bridge decorated
with two obelisks of red granite, a reminiscence of
the campaign in Egypt. Here is the broad lawn
where, in 1800, they used to play prisoners' base, and
where they dined in pleasant weather. It is covered
with clumps of trees, and by streams flowing from a
spring over which stood a little temple hidden by
the trees. In the gardens there were places for all
sorts of games to amuse the aides-de-camp and the
young people of the family and the court. Like
Marie Antoinette's Little Trianon, Josephine's Malmaison had its summer-houses, its sheepfolds, its cot-
tages, its exotic trees, its rare plants, belvederes, its
greensward, its little lakes with swans both white
and black, its Temple of Love. The temple still

exists; I see its Ionic columns of red marble, but the god is no longer there; I do not find the statue of Eros, who, on a pedestal garlanded with roses, held his bow to wound another conquest with his dart: my eyes seek in vain Voltaire's famous distich: —

> Whoe'er thou art, thy master see;
> He is, or was, or soon shall be.

In 1800 Malmaison was the resting-place, the favorite resort, of the First Consul. Thither he went for distraction from the cares of power and the fatigue of greatness. There in the springtime he used to take what he called his furlough; that is to say, the evening of the ninth day, the whole of the tenth day, and the next morning. In summer, after his return from Italy, he used to spend many days every week in this dear Malmaison where Josephine had established herself. There the great man was amiable, familiar, and kind. He was more than informal; he was companionable. He used to take part in the games with all the zest of a young man. He would make jokes and admit discussions, and he told stories with astounding brilliancy and wit. As host he was considerate, affable, entertaining, and he left his guests perfect freedom. The entertainments were likewise informal and merry. Those about the first magistrate of the Republic did not suffer from the wearisome formality, the servile refinements, the insipid flattery, the childishly intricate etiquette which

MALMAISON

became so onerous under the Empire. Bonaparte, who had not yet abandoned republican ways, was not yet intoxicated by the monarchical incense. His meals were simple; he sat scarcely half an hour at table. After dinner, when he was in a good humor and the weather was fine, he was free to steal a few minutes from his work, and he used to play prisoners' base with all the eagerness of a schoolboy.

Let us watch these sports. Here is the First Consul, the hero of Arcole, of the Pyramids, of Marengo, who takes off his coat and runs about like a boy of fifteen. Among the women I distinguish his three sisters, Elisa, Pauline, and Caroline; Madame Campan's two nieces, Églé and Adele Auguier (one of whom became the wife of Marshal Ney, the other Madame de Broc); Madame Cochelet; Sophie de Barbé-Marbois (afterwards the Duchess of Piacenza); Miss Clarke; Mesdemoiselles de Lally-Tollendal, Victorine Victor, Isabey; Elisa Monroe, the daughter of the future President of the United States; and above all Hortense de Beauharnais, Hortense, who is everywhere the first in the games, in study, and in society. Among the men, the First Consul's three brothers, Lucien, Louis, and Jerome, then the future Prince Eugene, Lauriston, Isabey, Didelot, Lucay, Rapp, Savary, and finally Bourrienne, who thus describes the merrymaking: " The game begins, and two lines of prisoners start from the two sides, but the number is equal and the victory uncertain; it is the moment for a bold stroke, the guard is about to yield. Bonaparte springs forward with most eager activity, and chases Hortense; she dodges him most actively, but he is close behind, and about to catch her, when his foot trips on a root hidden in the grass, and he falls at full length on the battle-field; all utter a cry, but Bonaparte gets up laughing, and surrenders himself to the victors." Bourrienne adds that almost always unexpected falls would stop the illustrious player in the midst of his triumph.

Is not this a miniature representation of what was to happen to him afterwards in more serious matters? Unexpected falls at the moment of triumph, is not that Napoleon's destiny? But the falls at prisoners' base are attended only with innocent pleasantry, while those of the successful general will be followed by deep anathemas. "Then came the exchange of prisoners, which was always the source of hot dispute; Hortense was always considered equal to two, for her boldness knew no bounds. In point of fact, these differences formed the only aristocracy at the Malmaison." But soon the progress of etiquette interrupted these sports, which were thought too democratic; tumbles on the grass seemed to lower the dignity of the head of a state, and one was averse to thinking that the First Consul could be captured by his aides-de-camp. The games continued in the summer of 1801, but in 1802 they stopped; they disappeared, like many other things, with the republican simplicity.

The game finished, they would walk in the park,

enjoying the cool evening air. In the moonlight, beneath the huge trees, the women, in their white dresses, resembled graceful phantoms. Nothing pleased Bonaparte more than the sight of a pretty woman, wearing gracefully a white dress; and Josephine, knowing this, almost always wore dresses of white India muslin. Later they would return to the house, and in the ground-floor rooms the First Consul used to display his marvellous talent as a talker. The Revolution, philosophy, the East, were his favorite subjects. His emphatic manner, his highly imaginative language, his novel and bold ideas, which were always original and poetical, aroused interest, surprise, and admiration. As for Josephine, her mind was nothing extraordinary, but no one understood better than she did how to do the honors of a drawing-room. Bourrienne said of her, "I have never seen a woman carry into society such an equable character, or such a spirit of kindness, which is the essential quality of an amiable character."

At that time Josephine was rejoicing in her happiness. She did not yet see the vision of divorce rising before her, she no longer gave Bonaparte any excuse for jealousy, she rather treated him with the tenderest, most affectionate solicitude. At Malmaison she was really happy, for there she led a life after her own heart. No palace, however splendid, could appear to her preferable to this simple country-house. Yet she was uneasy; and while she was enjoying this agreeable leisure, plots were weaving

against her husband's life.   When she was expecting
his arrival she would start and tremble at the slightest sound.   In 1800 the neighborhood of Malmaison
was not secure.   People coming from Paris were
often fearful of attack from thieves hidden in the
quarries between Chant du Coq and Nanterre.   But
there was no attempt at Malmaison; Paris was the
scene of Ceracchi's conspiracy and of the explosion
of the infernal machine, before the end of the year
1800, which had begun so brilliantly and happily.

VII.

THE INFERNAL MACHINE.

THE extreme partisans on both sides who had at first hoped that Bonaparte would be their man, and who saw him working for himself alone, were exasperated by their disappointment and staked their last hope on crime. Not being able to conquer the First Consul, they determined to kill him. Thus a twofold and permanent conspiracy, — that of the Red Terror and that of the White Terror. The fierce revolutionaries, who had never forgotten the passions and hatred of 1793, used to meet in secret and, with fierce imprecations, swear that he, whom they called the tyrant, should die. On the other hand, the Royalists in the pay of England used its money to hire a real legion of thieves and assassins. The famous Georges Cadoudal, an irreconcilable Chouan, from his mysterious retreat at Morbihan used to direct the bands of highwaymen who stopped the stage-coaches on every road, and he sent to Paris bravos to kill the First Consul. There was from that moment a perpetual struggle between the police and the conspirators, with new suspicions, new denunciations, new fears.

Bonaparte was continually surrounded by ambushes, and, tired and impatient at the numberless reports which exposed a new peril at every step, he was sometimes tempted not to read them, but to trust quietly to the grace of Providence. Sometimes the plan was to stab him, at another to shoot him with a gun or a pistol; sometimes to kill him at the theatre, again to abduct him between Paris and Malmaison. Josephine, who was very timid and impressionable, lived in a continual state of alarm. She thought she saw a snare in every clump of trees, an assassin at every turn of the road. Malmaison seemed to her a nest threatened by vultures.

First, there was the conspiracy of Ceracchi and Arena. Ceracchi, a Roman and a fanatical Republican, could not forgive the First Consul for protecting the Pope. Arena was a Corsican, the brother of one of the members of the Council who, on the 19th Brumaire, escaped through the windows of the orange-house at Saint Cloud. The two men had for accomplices Demerville, a former clerk of the Committee of Public Safety; Topino-Lebrun, a painter, a pupil of David; and a certain number of Italian refugees who desired a republic in both Rome and Paris. They determined to assassinate the First Consul at the opera, where it was announced that he would be present October 10, 1800. But the police got wind of the plot, and such precautions were taken that Bonaparte thought that he could go to the performance without danger. Before starting from the

Tuileries, at the moment when, after dinner, Josephine was dressing, Bessières entered with Eugene de Beauharnais. He went up to them and said, smiling, " Well, you don't know that they want to assassinate me this evening at the opera." Eugene and Bessières exclaimed with horror, and at the same time expressed their surprise that he persisted in going to the performance. " Calm yourselves," he said ; " the police have taken all the necessary precautions." Bessières, who was in command of the cavalry of the guard, ordered Eugene de Beauharnais to start at once for the Opera-house with a picket guard, and to protect the First Consul. When he reached the Opera-house, Eugene made half his men dismount, and after giving his orders to the rest, entered the building, fifty paces in front of Bonaparte, and himself preceded by his men, thus making the people in the passage-way think that he was the First Consul. Suddenly he halted his men, faced them in two lines, stepped aside, and Bonaparte passed quietly through the double line into his box. A few minutes later Ceracchi and Arena were arrested in the house. This attempt had failed, but it was soon followed by another and a more formidable one.

This time the Republicans were not concerned with it ; it was a Royalist conspiracy, organized by three cut-throats of Georges Cadoudal, named St. Réjant, Limoëlan, and Carbon. The first-named of these had acquired, as a naval officer, some familiarity with artillery, and he was about to put it to a terrible use.

One Chevalier, a former workman in the arsenals under the Convention, was arrested when working at a machine which was doubtless intended for an attempt on the First Consul's life; it consisted of a barrel of powder and grape-shot, to which was fastened a gun-barrel. This implement of destruction gave St. Réjant his idea of the famous infernal machine. He confided his secret only to his two accomplices, and, evading the suspicions of Fouché's police, he wove with terrible skill the threads of his conspiracy.

Whenever the First Consul drove out from the Tuileries, towards the rue de Richelieu and the boulevards, he always took the rue Saint Nicaise, a long, narrow street, no longer existing; it started from the rue des Orties, which ran along the quay of the Louvre, and continued at the other side of the Place du Carrousel until it reached the rue Saint Honoré, to the left of the rue Richelieu, in which stood the Opera-house. St. Réjant chose the rue Saint Nicaise for the execution of his plan. Then he hired a stable, calling himself a pedler, and in it he put a horse and cart, — a cart which was destined to be the infernal machine. He calculated the time which the First Consul's carriage would take to go from the Tuileries to this place, and arranged to have the machine explode at the moment determined. He knew that Bonaparte was going to the Opera-house the 3d Nivôse (December 24, 1800), on Christmas Eve, to hear the first performance of an oratorio of Haydn, and he chose this day for his crime. The machine was shaped like a cart, and it contained a barrel of powder. St. Réjant placed it in front of the house, where the First Consul would have to pass, and he was brutal enough to have the horse held by a young girl only fifteen years old, who might have been killed by the explosion. He arranged to receive word from his two accomplices of the moment when the carriage of the First Consul would arrive, then he would start the fire in the barrel and take the necessary precautions for his own safety. The police were in absolute ignorance of the conspiracy, and the three wretches fancied themselves sure of success.

Let us now turn our attention to the Opera-house as it appeared in the evening of the 3d Nivôse. Haydn is the fashionable composer, and every one is talking about his oratorio, "The Creation." It is Garat, the unrivalled Garat, the modern Orpheus, music made man, who with Madame Walbonne and Madame Branchu, two excellent singers, is to bring out the new oratorio. The orchestra is larger than usual; the choruses have been doubled, those of the Théâtre Feydeau having been added to those belonging to the opera. The hall is as bright as day. Every place has been taken for this performance, to which all the officials, all the people of fashion, and all the artists mean to come. The women are in full dress, and all the fashionable beauties take good care not to miss such a festivity. The oratorio is about to begin; the musicians are tuning their instruments

amid the hum of the crowd which always precedes
the first performance of a long-expected piece. Already people are turning their opera-glasses towards
the distinguished people. It is known that the First
Consul and Madame Bonaparte mean to come, and
that is an additional attraction.

Meanwhile what is going on at the Tuileries?
Josephine, Hortense, and Madame Murat were very
anxious to go to the theatre, and to reach it in good
season so as not to lose a note of the oratorio. But
Bonaparte was less eager for this pleasure; he had
been working hard all day, and worn out, he had
just fallen asleep on a sofa. He was awakened with
difficulty, and at last agreed to go to the Opera-house.
His hat and sword were brought, and he got into the
first carriage with Lannes, Bessières, and his aide
Lebrun. An escort of mounted grenadiers follows
him. Josephine was to take the second carriage with
Hortense, Madame Murat, and Rapp. A trifling
incident, to which perhaps these four persons owed
their preservation, delayed their departure for a few
moments. Josephine was going to wear for the
first time a magnificent shawl which she had received
from Constantinople; she had thrown it on her shoulders, when Rapp said to her in an outburst of frankness, " Let me make a suggestion, madam; you have
not put on your shawl as becomingly as usual."
Josephine then asked Rapp to fold it into the shape
that Egyptian women wore it, and while he is doing
this they heard the First Consul's carriage driving

away. "Hurry, sister," said Madame Murat, impa-
tiently; "there's Bonaparte going."

The three went down the staircase of the Pavilion
of Flora and got into the carriage. Josephine and
Madame Murat took the back seat, and Hortense
and Rapp the other. They were going through the
Carrousel, and the First Consul was already in the
rue Saint Nicaise, when a loud explosion was heard.
Afterwards, at Saint Helena, he recounted how, having left the Tuileries half-asleep, he had dozed off
again, and he suddenly opened his eyes, dreaming
that he was drowning in the Tagliamento. At the
time of his first campaign in Italy he had insisted on
crossing this stream in the middle of the night, having no notion how deep it was, and he tried to drive
throughout in his carriage, with an escort of men
carrying poles and torches. He came near paying
very dear for his imprudence; his horses lost their
footing, and he narrowly escaped being ingulfed.
The memory of this incident was haunting his
dream when the infernal machine exploded with a
tremendous report. Lannes and Bessières, his companions, were very anxious to stop. "To the opera,"
Bonaparte shouted; and the coachman, who was
drunk, and thought the explosion was a salvo of
artillery fired in honor of his master, and did not
know until the next day what had happened, continued on his way at full speed. In a moment the
carriage reached the door of the Opera-house; and
the First Consul entered his box without a sign of

emotion. Not one of the spectators had any idea of what had just happened. The performance went on. To be sure, a faint noise had been heard above the music, but it had aroused no anxiety. But Junot had said, "What a singular hour to be firing cannon!"

What had become of Josephine, Hortense, and Madame Murat? Were they hurt? Bonaparte did not know. At the moment of the explosion they screamed with terror. Hortense was slightly cut in the arm by a piece of glass when the carriage-windows were broken by the concussion, and Josephine nearly fainted. Rapp got out to see if the First Consul was safe and sound. He made his way through the corpses and ruins in the rue Saint Nicaise to the Opera-house. Meanwhile Josephine's carriage went on by another street, and the three women arrived at the theatre. They entered the First Consul's box, which was to the right of the stage, between the two columns which separated the balcony from the stage boxes. Josephine was trembling with emotion, and Hortense had wrapped a handkerchief about her arm. Although near her confinement, Madame Murat remained impassible, with all her brother's firmness. When Bonaparte saw his wife, his sister, and his step-daughter, he greeted them with a smile, then he asked for a programme, and continued to look at the audience with imperturbable calmness.

Suddenly the news of the attempt spread through

the hall. The Prefect of Police brought all the details that he could pick up: more than fifteen persons killed, more severely wounded; forty houses seriously damaged; the First Consul and his wife saved by a miracle. At that moment, as if moved by an electric current, immense applause arose from the pit, the orchestra, the amphitheatre, and the boxes. All eyes were turned towards Bonaparte; every hand was clapping. It was a strange mingling of indignation and enthusiasm, of wrath and joy, of hate of the criminals and of love for the man of destiny who had just escaped their machinations.

The First Consul did not stay long at the theatre. On his return to the Tuileries he found many officials, who had gone there to congratulate him. Then his anger, which he had hitherto restrained with difficulty, broke out. "It's the work of the Jacobins!" he exclaimed. "It's the Jacobins who tried to assassinate me. There are no priests, no nobles, no Chouans, in this thing. It's the men of September, the rascals covered with mud, who are in open revolt, in continual conspiracy, in solid line against every government that has established itself. Not three months ago you saw Ceracchi, Arena, Topino-Lebrun, De-merville, try to assassinate me. Well, this is the same thing. They are the blood-drinkers of September, the assassins of Versailles, the brigands of the 31st of May, the conspirators of Prairial, the authors of all the crimes against the governments. If they can't be chained up, they must be crushed. We must clean France of these disgusting dregs; we must have no pity on such rascals!" Bourrienne, who recounts this scene, adds, "One must have seen Bonaparte's animated face, his rare but impressive gestures, have heard the sound of his voice, to get any idea of the wrath with which he uttered these words."

For several days the First Consul maintained that it must be the Jacobins who were at the root of this crime; the evidence alone convinced him that it was the work of the Royalists. Both parties, however, were pursued indiscriminately; and although in the conspiracy of Ceracchi and his accomplices there was no overt act, they all were sent to the scaffold, like the makers of the infernal machine which had made so many victims. Public indignation did not distinguish between the criminals; punishment, even if excessive, was demanded. The men of the old régime said that if Bonaparte were dead, the guillotines of 1793 would be set to work again at once; and the friends of the new ideas imagined that he alone prevented the triumph of the counter-revolution and of the foreigners. Hence there was general joy. For many days the attempt was the sole subject of conversation. The Parisians crowded to look at the place of the disaster, at the pieces of chimneys, bricks, tiles, and slate; and then, at the sight of the ruins, they denounced the men who had done this thing. The day after the explosion people gathered in a mass from the gates of the Louvre, well into the

courtyard of the Tuileries; and when the band of
the Consular Guard began to play the celebrated air,
" Where is One better off than in the Bosom of One's
Family ? " frantic applause greeted the First Consul.
Fervent gratitude was expressed for the coachman,
who, the rumor ran, had saved his life by his skill.
Three or four hundred cab-drivers gave him a dinner,
for he had become the hero of their profession. For
a long time there was sung in the streets a song, of
which numberless copies were printed, containing
these crude couplets : —

> An infernal machine
> Of new invention,
> By its explosion
> Wrought unheard-of devastation,
> Overthrowing all about it,
> Men and houses.

> The Consul in his carriage
> At that moment was passing;
> He was going to the opera.
> He it was, for certain,
> That they tried to kill;
> But it was a vain attempt.

> The swiftness of his horses
> Had forestalled the blow;
> But, suddenly stopping,
> He hastens to make enquiries.
> Without fearing this black design,
> He pursued his way.

> His wife, all in tears,
> Wishes to share his danger.

But they come and reassure
About the horrible uproar,
Saying to her, " He has got by;
The Consul is not wounded."

The incident of the infernal machine made a deep
impression on Josephine, not merely by the horrid
nature of the attempt, but still more from fear of the
consequences it might entail.   One would have said
that by the light of this fatal flame, at the sound of
this explosion, she had seen the apparition of what
she dreaded most — divorce.   Her enemies were now,
in fact, to take the occasion of this plot to advance
their pretended ideas of what was needed for the
public safety, the national security, and the future of
the country, for the advantage of the supporters of
hereditary succession.   Napoleon's brothers, who had
always been hostile to Josephine, were already trying
so to mould public opinion that the First Consul,
having become almost a sovereign, should be obliged
to divorce his barren wife; and Lucien, who had so
often and so ostentatiously declared his republican
faith, was now, under the Republic, going to start
the discussion of a dynasty.   Josephine already saw
the misery and anguish, for her husband as well as
for herself, which were poisoning destinies apparently
the most enviable.   When she saw this officer of fortune, this Corsican, absolutely six years earlier, and
now by means of marvellous events, the equal of the
highest potentates, yet never contented, and always
menaced, she might have well meditated these words

of the "Imitation of Christ," a book on which history throws light and which throws a light on history: "Men say to the weak, What a happy life this man leads! How rich he is! How great! How powerful! But consider heavenly joys, and you will see that all these temporal advantages are nothing, that they are not stable, that they are rather a burden, because no one can possess them without fear and uneasiness."

VIII.

IN general, unsuccessful conspiracies have no other effect than to consolidate the powers they attempted to destroy. The main result of the infernal machine was to add to the prestige of the First Consul, and to give him a pretext to smite his enemies, white or red. A few weeks later, the peace of Lunéville filled the public with joy. The Empire of Germany recognized the natural boundaries of Republican France, and the existence of the Batavian, Helvetic, Ligurian, and Cisalpine Republics. The warlike nation had become peaceful; after dreaming of nothing but victories, it was dreaming of nothing but treaties. Diplomacy, from a thing despised, became the fashion, like many other old-fashioned things; foreigners, recently abhorred, were received with every attention, and from all parts of Europe they hastened to Paris as the centre of elegance and pleasure. Foreigners of distinction made no secret of their surprise. What! this superb city, this magnificent capital, is the spot which the émigrés said was a savage den, a brigand's cavern! This Head of the State is the man they called an ogre, a veteran, a bandit! This brilliant and witty society is what the men of Coblenz called the leavings of the galleys and the slums! They were astounded at the wild exaggerations of partisans when they saw in amiable, gracious, hospitable France, drawing-rooms worthy of the old régime, and a Republican court which in splendor surpassed many courts of powerful kings. As General de Ségur said, "The new society was more attractive to the foreigners than the old. And in fact, so varied was its composition, that it offered more liberty, variety, and originality, and yet with no real loss of the urbanity and desire to please which the French character and the example of the old court had spread among all the ranks of the cultivated and intelligent middle classes." No one thought any more about the guillotines, or red caps, or of the "Marseillaise," or asked of impure blood to moisten our furrows. The god of battles appeared bearing an olive-branch. The officers tried to pass for men of society. Balls took the place of the bivouac. The young officers of even the lowest birth imitated the manners and speech of the young noblemen of the Versailles court. Bonaparte said of his military companions, "What supports them is the idea they have that they have taken the place of the old nobility." The Marquis Colbert de Chabanais, in his interesting memoirs of his grandfather, General Colbert, said very truly: "The society which was rising at that time was animated by but one thought, to re-

place the old nobles ; and in the reaction against the
manners of the Revolution, every one was trying to
recover the tone, the ways, the dress of the old
régime. The Jacobin, who had been most bitter
against certain ways of dressing as the insignia of
an aristocracy, was now the first to adopt them, and
as anxious to wear silk stockings as he was later to
seize the titles once rejected and scornfully pro-
scribed."

It is possible to see a sort of monarchical advance
from the beginning of the Consulate to the establishment of the Empire. Every day there was a step
backwards in habits, fashions, and institutions. The
Tuileries grew more and more like a royal palace.
The Faubourg Saint Germain filled up. The Republican phraseology disappeared by official order ; the
new calendar was never formally abolished, but the
old one gradually reappeared, and Sunday took the
place of the *décadi*, or tenth day. The church festivities were celebrated. The giving of presents on
New Year's Day, the costumes of Carnival and Lent,
the masquerades of Shrove Tuesday, oratories, the
promenade at Longchamps, Easter eggs, — all these
things began to reappear. The theatres resumed
their former appearance. There was a return to
1788. Dinners, balls, festivals of every sort, supported the shopkeepers of Paris. The émigrés, on
their return from exile, began to accustom themselves
to the new order of things. Chateaubriand has said,
speaking of this time, " Order began to reappear ;

the cafés and the streets were deserted, and people stayed at home; scattered families were reunited; they gathered the fragments of their inheritance, as the troops assemble after a battle and find out how many are lost." The melancholy author of "René" at last discovered the charms of consular France which at first had filled him with horror. "Gradually," he tells us, "I began to enjoy the sociability which is a characteristic of the French, the delightful intercourse, the swift and easy exchange of intelligence, the absence of stiffness and prejudice, the indifference to wealth and title, this natural levelling of social distinctions, this equality of mind, which makes French society unrivalled and atones for our defects. After a few months' residence with us one cannot live anywhere except in Paris."

The First Consul's three sisters, Madame Elisa Bacciochi, Madame Pauline Leclerc, and Madame Caroline Murat, were at the head of society and were rivals in luxury. The first had literary aspirations, and her intimate friend was Monsieur de Fontanes, the official leader of literature. The second, renowned for her elegance and her whims as a pretty woman, was a wonderful beauty. The third, also handsome, was already noted for her ambition. Madame de Staël, by her wit, knowledge, and eloquence, continued to be the queen of the Parisian drawing-rooms. She did not lose courage in the advances she made to Bonaparte, but she inspired him with a sort of instinctive repulsion, as if he knew that this

brave woman's soul would oppose his power. Madame Récamier aroused a more and more general
enthusiasm. Her husband had bought the Necker
mansion in the rue Mont Blanc, where she gave
grand parties. In summer she installed herself close
by Paris, in the Castle of Clichy, which enabled her
of an evening to go to the Opera or to the Théâtre
Français. After the performance, she would drive
out to the country. She was not exclusive in her
friendship, and she gathered about her, besides men
of letters like La Harpe, Lemontey, and Legouvé,
men of all parties who must have been astonished at
finding themselves in the same company: thus men
of the old court, like the Duke of Guignes, M.
de Narbonne, Christian of Lamoignon, Adrien and
Mathieu de Montmorency; and people of the new
régime, like Lucien and Joseph Bonaparte; members
of the Convention, like Barrère and Fouché; and
revolutionary generals, like Masséna, Moreau, and
Bernadotte.

Nor were the arts forgotten. Garat the singer
aroused the most enthusiastic admiration. He was
called the modern Orpheus, and wherever he sang
there was always to be seen in the front row, watching his every movement, languishing, weeping, sobbing, even fainting from rapture, a lady of distinction,
a foreigner, who had been prominent in Paris during
the last days of the Monarchy, and who had just
returned to the capital. In his interesting book about
her, the bibliophile Jacob describes her as more than

once, before three or four hundred spectators, throwing herself into the enchanter's arms and falling at his feet as if to worship him. This lady was the Baroness de Krüdener, the future prophetess, the future spiritual guardian of the Emperor Alexander. Who would have thought, on seeing her adoring Garat, that she would become the soul of the Holy Alliance, and Napoleon's most implacable foe? Like Madame de Staël, she made advances to him and was repulsed. The hero of so many battles had occasion to repent his indifference to these two women, whom Josephine, with more tact, knew how to manage. If it had not been for Madame de Krüdener, probably the Allies in 1814 would have treated with the Empire, instead of restoring the Bourbons.

But to return to 1801. The drawing-rooms were brilliant, the theatres crowded. There were many great actors, of whom the greatest was Talma, whom the First Consul regarded as a personal friend. As Chateaubriand puts it, " What, then, was Talma? Himself, his own time, and antiquity. He was profoundly and intensely moved by love and patriotism. He had the fierce inspiration, the savageness of the Revolution through which he had passed. The terrible sights he had seen were repeated in the remote and mournful accents of the choruses of Sophocles and Euripides. . . . His mere entrance on the stage, the mere sound of his voice, were intensely tragic. His face expressed suffering and thought; they showed themselves, too, in repose, in his poses, his gestures, his gait." With actors of the highest merit, the Théâtre Français soon regained its old fame. The Théâtre Feydeau was equally admired. Here sang the delightful tenor Ellevion, the excellent bass Martin, and Madame Dugazon, who gave her name to parts of a certain style. The opera was the favorite resort of the fashionable world, who made the boxes as much of a spectacle as the stage. A company of Italian singers had just taken the Olympic Hall, a little theatre in the rue Chantereine, where prominent beauties used to display their gorgeous dresses.

Josephine was very happy in this vortex of pleasures, in this life of the drawing-room and the theatre. Every first performance, every ball, every grand dinner, was an excuse for ordering a new gown, for wearing her jewels. She was delighted to receive the distinguished foreigners who were thronging to Paris, and to renew the habits of the old régime, for which she was admirably suited.

She was much gratified by the visit to Paris, in May, 1801, of the Infant of Parma, Louis, the son of a sister of Marie Antoinette, and of his wife, a daughter of Charles IV., King of Spain. The treaty of Lunéville conceded to this young prince, Tuscany, which had been made the Kingdom of Etruria, and before entering his new realm he went to Paris in order, as it were, to receive his investiture from the hands of Bonaparte. Josephine was much flattered at receiving, or, rather, at protecting, the nephew of the martyred Queen and the daughter of the King of

Spain. Since she had always continued to be a Legitimist, even in the Republican drawing-rooms of the Directory, she was enchanted at an opportunity to be agreeable to a Bourbon prince, and it was especially at such a time that she congratulated herself on having married the soldier of fortune to whom she was indebted for these great privileges.

Although the King and Queen of Etruria were travelling under the style of the Count and Countess Leghorn, they were received with all the honors due to crowned heads. They were entertained with splendid entertainments. Bonaparte was more and more convinced that, in spite of the Revolution, the French had always remained unchanged, that they liked luxury, titles, show, fine equipages, rich liveries, decorations, and all the trinkets which pamper and tease human vanity. His monarchical plans grew stronger, and possibly he began to dream of the day when he should have Talma, his favorite actor, play before an audience of kings. The Legitimists were simple enough to fancy that the First Consul was working in their behalf, and the creation of the Kingdom of Etruria was but the prelude to the restoration of the Kingdom of France.

Those who thus imagined were very ignorant of Bonaparte; he had the character of Cæsar. Doubtless he would have preferred the first place in a village to the second in Paris. In spite of the hopes of the Faubourg Saint Germain, he declined with scorn the sword of the Constable of France. What he wanted was the sceptre. What do I say? One sceptre was not enough for him. He was inwardly entertained by the credulity of the Royalists, and Josephine's zeal for the Legitimists, far from influencing him, only made him smile.

The visit of the King and Queen of Etruria gave him an opportunity to test public opinion. It showed that even the Republicans were not annoyed by the sight of this prince and princess. Just as the great Roman Republic liked to make and unmake kings, so the French Republic, which had created sister-republics, took a certain satisfaction in making a kingdom. Bonaparte, who had some very aristocratic traits, was secretly proud to appear as the protector of a descendant of Louis XIV. He thought, and truly, that the visit of a Bourbon to France was a striking proof of growing calmness. Only seven years before, Marie Antoinette had laid her head on the block, and now her nephew was crossing the place of her execution on his way to Malmaison to pay his respects to the First Consul!

The King and Queen of Etruria entered Paris in old carriages of the time of Philip V., drawn by mules covered with bells, and stopped at the Spanish Embassy, in the rue Mont Blanc. The day after their arrival they were taken to Malmaison by the Chevalier d'Azara, the Spanish ambassador. The First Consul received them with military honors, and returned their visit the next day.

A succession of brilliant entertainments was given

in honor of the royal guests. That of M. de Talleyrand, then Minister of Foreign Affairs, in his castle
of Reuilly, was a model of elegance and good taste.
It was in summer; the weather was propitious; nature and art combined to make the entertainment a
success. In the illuminated gardens the moon and
the stars rivalled the brilliancy of the Bengal lights.
The party began with a concert, and when the end
of the gallery was opened, there was disclosed a scene
representing the place in front of the Pitti palace at
Florence. Dancers and singers, dressed as Tuscan
peasants, played and danced, while they sang couplets in praise of their Majesties. An Italian impro-
visator, named Gianni, pronounced a tolerably long
ode in honor of the young King, who was delighted
to hear his native tongue. The new sovereign had
been somewhat chagrined when, on paying his respects in Italian, the First Consul had replied in
French; he then said, " *Ma, in somma, siete Italiano,
siete nostro* "*;* and Bonaparte answered dryly, " I am
a Frenchman." At M. de Talleyrand's the King and
Queen of Etruria might have imagined themselves in
their new kingdom. When they went out into the
garden, they were surrounded by a band of pretty
Tuscan peasant girls, who offered them flowers.
Supper was served in the orange-house. The tables
were placed around the orange-trees, which rose like
epergnes; from the branches hung baskets full of
sweetmeats. Fireworks and a ball closed the entertainment.

The fête given a few days later by the illustrious Chaptal, at that time Minister of the Interior, was no less successful. It took place in the Brissac mansion, in the rue Grenelle Saint Germain. A scene represented the city of Florence illuminated; a Tuscan village had been built, peasants sang in chorus, others recited passages from Petrarch and Tasso. Hidden musicians played and sang in every direction. A temple was seen on the top of a little hill, and there Apollo and the Muses celebrated the arts and glory. After supper the company entered the large gallery, where nymphs and shepherds from the opera danced quadrilles. One of the girls gave the King a bouquet which in his hands, as if by magic, took the shape of a crown, holding verses by the poet Esmenard. The Duchess of Abrantès in her Memoirs describes the First Consul's enjoyment of the evening. " I have seldom seen him so much interested by anything of the sort, and he expressed his satisfaction not only that evening, but long afterwards. He spoke of the songs and music from the concealed performers, which filled the gardens as if by enchantment."

June 25, the anniversary of the battle of Marengo, there was another entertainment, given by the Minister of War, Berthier. There was a much-adorned representation of camp life. Supper was served in the garden under tents; bivouac fires lit up the groves; panoplies and trophies adorned the dancing-rooms. Officers in uniform, standing behind the ladies at table, were their cup-bearers. A balloon was sent up in the dark night, which, as it rose, disclosed in flame the name Marengo.

Madame de Montesson also entertained the King and Queen of Etruria at her house in rue du Mont Blanc, next door to the Spanish Embassy. Charlotte Jeanne Béraud de la Haye de Riou, Marchioness of Montesson, was certainly one of the most remarkable of the ladies of the consular society. Born in 1737, she was at that time sixty-four years old; a widow since 1769, she had made a morganatic marriage in 1773 with the Duke of Orleans, who was the father of Philippe Égalité and the grandfather of the King Louis Philippe; he died in 1785. During the Revolution she had been most devoted to Louis XVI., who treated her like a relative when the number of his courtiers was dwindling day by day. She was a charming woman, well educated, witty, very polite, a survival of the manners of the old aristocracy. Being a great admirer of the First Consul, in whom she saw the restorer of society, she was devoted to him and to his policy. Bonaparte, who was much flattered by this attitude of so distinguished a woman, had restored her property and was glad to see her the mistress of a house which he regarded as a model of refinement and real elegance. Whenever she invited Josephine to breakfast, Bonaparte urged his wife to accept, and he himself was often the guest of the widow of the Duke of Orleans. The Marchioness of Montesson's Wednesday dinners were renowned.

On that day, in Lent, she used to have a dinner with
meat for the majority of her guests, and one without
for ecclesiastics and those who remained faithful to
the laws of the Church. All the old nobility in Paris
would meet in her drawing-room, and her very magnificent ball recalled the most splendid entertainments
of the Monarchy.

At the Théâtre Français there was a special performance of the " Œdipe." The theatre was crowded;
for nothing could gratify the Parisians more than to
see Bonaparte doing the honors of Paris to a Bourbon. When the actor who played Philoctetes recited this line, —

I have made kings; but would not be one,

the audience turned towards the box where the Head
of the Republic was sitting with his royal guest, and
burst into the wildest applause. A few days later
the King and Queen of Etruria left for their new
kingdom, where they were installed by Murat, and
the Queen, who was a wise and intelligent woman,
kept up a friendly correspondence with Josephine,
whose gracious reception had charmed her.

Hardly had the young King left Paris when after
the royal festivities came the Republican holiday,
the 14th of July, the anniversary of the capture of
the Bastille. It had been regarded as important that
a Bourbon should not be present at this celebration;
but there was nothing very marked about it. A
temple of Victory was built before the Palace of

the Corps Législatif, with a portico supported by six columns and four monuments, dedicated to the commemoration of Desaix, Joubert, Hoche, and Kléber. In the middle of the temple there was a piece of sculpture representing Victory offering peace to France. In the middle of the Place de la Concorde there was a column built in honor of the army.

The most impressive of the national festivals of the year 1801 was undoubtedly that of the 18th Brumaire (November 9). It was known as the Festival of General Peace. At this happy moment every one was talking of universal peace. The month before, arrangements had been made which settled every difficulty. The preliminaries of peace with England had been signed in London, October 1, and the news, which reached Paris two days later, had aroused most unprecedented satisfaction. On both sides of the Channel there was the same wild enthusiasm. In London the populace had unharnessed the horses from the carriage of Colonel Lauriston, the First Consul's aide-de-camp, and drew it with their own hands. In the same month, treaties or settlements of some sort had been made by France with Portugal, the Porte, the regencies of Tunis and Algiers, with Bavaria and Russia. Joseph Bonaparte, who had been appointed by his brother general peacemaker, and who had had the distinction of signing the treaty of peace with America at Morfontaine, with Austria at Lunéville, was going to sign the English treaty at Amiens. Meanwhile, the English plenipotentiary, Lord Cornwallis, reached Paris to take part in the festival of the 18th Brumaire, and on that day his was the only carriage allowed to be driven. One would have said that the First Consul had as strong a desire for peace as he had had for war.

The Place de la Révolution had become the Place de la Concorde. The 18th Brumaire, it was decorated with porticos and covered with dance-halls. On the left bank of the Seine, between the Pont Royal and the Pont Neuf, there had been built a temple of Commerce. A fleet of launches and barges, decorated and dressed with flags, with crews representing the different nations of Europe, ascended the river from Chaillot to this temple. Scarcely had they arrived when songs and dances in honor of peace began. A balloon was sent up bearing the flags of all the friendly powers, and from it there started a parachute which covered a descending Mercury. A huge theatre had been put up in the Place de la Concorde. In it were enclosed the famous horses of Marly, where were given performances illustrating the horrors of war and the benefits of peace. First there was a representation of the bombardment of two cities; afterwards there appeared temples dedicated to Peace, to the Arts, to Industry, which opened and disclosed the men whom the war had spared. At the end of the platform of the Pont Neuf stood a triumphal arch bearing Bonaparte's name. At the Salm mansion, now the Palace of the

Legion of Honor, a colossal statue represented a hero sheathing his sword in token of peace.

Napoleon at Saint Helena once said in reference to this happy period of his life: " I really thought that the fate of France, of Europe, and my own were settled, and that there would be no more wars. But the English Cabinet kindled everything anew, and to it alone Europe owes all its subsequent troubles; it alone is responsible. For my part, I had intended to devote myself solely to the government of France, and I think I should have produced wonders. My fame would have been as great, and I should have been much happier; I should have made a moral conquest of Europe, such as I came near making with arms. What glory they have robbed me of!" In 1801 France was at peace and radiant with joy. Any one who would have predicted the terrible catastrophes which were about to burst forth within a few years would have been called a madman. It was a period of intoxication, of enchantment, the traces of which are preserved in all the contemporary Memoirs. France was happy because it aroused the envy of all the other powers. Perhaps the most necessary thing for its ardent and impressionable character is the gratification of its pride. Without this it is sad, agitated, uneasy. It is a nation which cannot endure mediocrity or misfortune. Without glory it is out of its element.

IX.

IN the summer of 1801 and the spring of 1802 Malmaison saw its fairest days. At that time Saint Cloud was not then the First Consul's country-seat; Malmaison, in its new splendor, had no rival. It was known as a favorite resort of great men and celebrated women. One would have said that it had an air of its own, and that the very stones were conscious of their importance. It was not a palace, and yet it was something more than a castle. It was plain that it would in time belong to history, and that its furniture would be a matter of interest to every one. The place inspired a sort of attentive and respectful curiosity.

Fontaine, in his unpublished manuscript Memoirs, which might well be called the Journal of an Architect, wrote under date of December 10, 1800: " The First Consul ought really to come to Malmaison only to rest and to forget once a week the affairs of government; but in fact people make formal calls, ministers come out to report, and officers to pay their respects, and everything is too small for such a multitude. They are enlarging the stables and offices. They have added to the park all the land lying between the road, Mademoiselle Julien's house, and the garden. Trees are set out everywhere." Great changes and improvements were made in the park and in the house between 1800 and the summer of 1802. To the park was added the whole plain separating it from Rueil. The view was then bounded by the Côte d'Or, a large hill, on the west, and by the wood Saint Cucufa in the far southwest. The park was divided into two distinct parts, united by gentle slopes. The first was a smooth, flat stretch of about a kilometre behind the castle; the other was more picturesque and showed greater variety, lying as it did on the slope of a hill. In the first was the large grove watered by the brooks which started from the Temple of Love. These little streams wound among the flower-beds and clumps of trees towards a little lake, into which they fell in a series of cascades; another stream flowed into the lake from the other side. This lake lay in the lower part of the park, surrounded by plane-trees and poplars. From it started the brook which Delille had sung; it ran into the garden through two rows of venerable chestnut-trees. On the right of the lake was a shepherd's hut, and in the middle of the wood a Swiss dairy.

Josephine did not like the French gardens, such as Le Nôtre designed, with their majestic quincunxes, their square grass-plots, their clipped yews, their

shrubs set in a bed of Procrustes. She cared only
for English gardens, which had been made fashionable by the Prince of Ligne at Bel-Œil; by Horace
Walpole at Strawberry Hill; by the Marquis of
Caraman at Roissy. Fontaine wrote about her as
follows, in December, 1800: "Madame Bonaparte is
much distressed at our making some straight paths.
She wants everything done in the English fashion.
An avenue set out to lead straight from one place to
another seems to her a barbarous infringement of the
laws of gardening, and it is only at the cost of the
good opinion she had of our talents that we have
succeeded in getting for the main approach and for
the road to the stables a dispensation from the rule
demanding winding ways." Fontaine wrote again
on this subject in September, 1801: "Our heresy in
regard to the present fashion of gardens has much
injured us in Madame Bonaparte's estimation. To
speak about order and regularity in a garden was
sheer blasphemy. They wanted nothing but groups,
effects, contrasts, and, above all things, sentiment."
The park contained an abundance of surprises and
contrasts: here was Love, in his temple; there a statue
of Saint Francis in Capuchin dress, in a grotto; here
a colossal Neptune, Puget's masterpiece, a Neptune
overlooking the lake, and brandishing his trident
between two rostral columns of Sérancolin marble;
there, under a weeping willow, was a tomb with
a bas-relief carved by Girardon. Close to the castle was a large and fine conservatory, designed by

M. Thibaut of the Institute. It was lofty enough to contain the longest exotic shrubs. In the middle a portico, upheld by two marble columns with gilded bases and capitals, opened into the drawing-room, whence one looked out into a circle of rare flowers and plants spreading on both sides. Josephine, the poetic creole, the pearl of the Antilles, seemed a beneficent fairy reigning over this charming and mysterious empire.

The inside of Malmaison, as well as the park, had been much beautified. The decorations of the hall, the dining-room, the council-chamber, the library, the billiard-room, the boudoir, the drawing-room, the gallery, left nothing to be desired. In September, 1800, the architect Fontaine wrote: "The decorators have finished the ceilings of the library and the frieze in the room of the First Consul, on the first floor, above the drawing-room. Madame Bonaparte takes a lively interest in everything we do. She is ordering some new decorations, and wants us to give our attention to the gardens, the waters, the hot-houses, in short to everything which can make this place more agreeable, for she regards it as her own private property." A bathroom was put in the first floor, near the First Consul's room, by the side of the door, and on the other side, a dressing-room and a little sleeping-room. Two small staircases were built, one leading from the First Consul's room to the gallery on the ground floor; the other, from the first floor to the library and the council-chamber.

"We are very sorry," writes the architect, "that the old shape of the house and the previous changes do not let us place the First Consul's rooms over the library; as it is, if he wishes to go from his chamber to his study or to the council-chamber, he has to pass through the whole width of the house, whether he goes through the corridor on the first floor, or comes down into the gallery and passes through the rooms on the ground floor."

We cannot leave Fontaine's manuscript Memoirs without citing what he says of the little theatre built for amateur performances. "It is now some time," he wrote, March 22, 1802, "since a love of theatrical performances began to appear in the household of the First Consul. . . . We had made a sort of portable theatre which was set up for this purpose in the gallery, near the drawing-room. Then we had contrived to construct a little hall by taking a corner of one of the largest rooms in the north pavilion on the second floor; but this last plan, although it gave more space, was less commodious, for it required that the spectators should leave the drawing-room, go up two pairs of stairs, to sit in a narrow room which was neither large nor handsome. At last, the First Consul has yielded to long-continued supplications, and has commissioned us to build as cheaply as possible a little theatre, entirely isolated, in the courtyard on the side of the farm. He has given us a month to do it in, and we shall set to as soon as he has approved the cost. Yesterday we made a plan and an estimate, and gave them to M. Bourrienne who, with Madame Hortense, Madame Bonaparte's daughter, is one of the most enthusiastic actors." The architect promised to build in thirty days, for the sum of thirty thousand francs, in the farmyard, near the gallery of the ground floor, a theatre of wood, with no pretentions to monumental solidity and no external ornaments; and he kept his word. In shape it was polygonal, and it was covered with slates. It held easily about two hundred spectators. The ceiling was decorated with printed calico. It contained a pit, a row of boxes, a gallery, an orchestra, and two little greenrooms. The floor was built above the ground, to avoid dampness, and made to serve as a ballroom on occasion.

Since the building was isolated, a gallery of canvas led to it from the ground floor. It was inaugurated May 12, 1802, not by amateurs, but by some Italian actors, who gave the "Serva Padrona." "The hall was very satisfactory," says the architect, "and if the piece played had been better adapted to the taste of the spectators, they would have been more amused."

A word is necessary about the amateurs who used to play in this theatre, and who might be called the actors in ordinary to the First Consul. The Duchess of Abrantès says in her Memoirs: "Mademoiselle de Beauharnais had been so successful at Madame Campan's in 'Esther' and the other plays in which Mesdemoiselles Auguier and Mademoiselle Pannelier also

showed remarkable talent, that she was obliged to
appear on the stage at Malmaison. Eugene de Beauharnais acted remarkably well; I am not prepossessed
when I say that Junot had really great talents; M.
Didelot made a capital Crispin. I got through my
parts very tolerably, and General Lauriston made a
noble Almaviva, or any other lover in court dress.
But the best of the company was M. Bourrienne; he
acted serious parts to perfection."

This is the way Bourrienne speaks of the actors of
Malmaison: "Hortense acted admirably; Caroline
(Madame Murat), only tolerably; Eugene, very well.
Lauriston was a trifle heavy; Didelot, passable, and
I may say without vanity, that I was not the worst
in the company. If we were not very good, it was
not for lack of good advice and good instructions.
Talma and Michot used to come to make us rehearse
together and separately. How many lessons I have
received from Michot when walking in the beautiful
park! And, if I may mention it, it gives me to-day
great pleasure to return to these trifles which are so
important when one is young, and so marked a contrast to the greater stage on which we did not represent fictitious characters." Bourrienne adds that the
company owned a rich collection of properties. The
First Consul had given each one of the amateur
actors a collection of plays, richly bound, and as the
protector of the company, he had had expensive and
elegant costumes made for them. "Bonaparte," con-
tinues Bourrienne, "took great pleasure in these

performances; he liked to see comedies acted by his friends; sometimes he even complimented us. Although I liked it as much as the others, I was obliged to tell him more than once that my occupation left me very little time for learning my part; then he would assume his caressing way, and say, 'Oh! nonsense; you have such a good memory! You know what pleasure I get from it; you see how these plays light up Malmaison; Josephine is very fond of them. Get up earlier.' 'And I sleep so much, as it is, don't I?' 'Come, Bourrienne, do it to please me; you do make me laugh so! Don't deprive me of this pleasure; I haven't too many, as you know.' 'Indeed I won't deprive you of any. I am delighted to be able to give you any entertainment.'" And thereupon Bourrienne would set about learning his part.

Napoleon, whose administrative genius busied itself with trifles as well as with great things, looked after the details of the theatre at Malmaison with the same solicitude that he showed for the condition of his soldiers. He was, moreover, well read in dramatic literature. From his infancy he had studied and committed to memory the French tragedians, and especially Corneille, whom he warmly admired. He liked to declaim the principal passages. In 1795, before the 13th Vendémiaire, when he was yet unknown, Talma gave him tickets to the Théâtre Français. He was interested in the new plays, and used to examine them with care, commenting upon them with great intelligence and originality. Most great statesmen have been interested in the theatre. Napoleon, in this respect, had the same tastes as Richelieu and Louis XV. There is nothing strange in this. Is there not a certain resemblance between the ruler of a state and the manager of a theatre? Do not both have to do with leading men, supernumeraries, optical illusions, a pit, hired applauders, newspaper notices, and a public which applauds one day and hisses the next? Are not great men actors in the drama of history? And is not human life a tragic comedy, in which they play the principal parts? Was not Napoleon all his life an incomparable manager, the manager of his own glory? He did not need to look to Talma for lessons in the art of posing so as to impress the popular imagination; he had already a wonderful knowledge of scenic effect. Victorious or beaten, all-powerful or a prisoner, he knew how to arrange the incidents of his career to resemble the events of a colossal drama. Who understood better than he how to select, for those actions of his that would one day become historical, the stage and the setting that would best suit them?

In the hands of an organizer like Napoleon, the performances at Malmaison could not fail to succeed. At first the list of their plays was very small. They did not dare try the great plays at first, with natural distrust of their powers. But soon, after playing a number of gay and amusing short pieces, like the

" Héritiers," the " Étourdis," the " Rivaux d'eux-mêmes," and " Défiance et Malice," at the request of the First Consul, they ventured to try more important plays.

On the evenings of their performances there was always a very brilliant company at Malmaison. After the play the ground-floor rooms were crowded. The performance was followed, either by a concert, where were to be heard the best singers and the most skilful musicians of the time, or by a small ball, or rather a dance, three or four quadrilles going on at the same time in the spacious room. The First Consul himself did not disdain to dance with untiring energy ; and on such occasions he would ask the musicians to play the old tunes which reminded him of his boyhood.

The Duchess of Abrantès gives a vivid description of these pleasures, in which she liked to take part. " There was nothing more delightful," she says, "than a ball at Malmaison, at which the women who composed what was really, though without the name, Madame Bonaparte's court took part. All were young, many were pretty ; and when they were dressed in their white crape gowns, carrying flowers, and wearing garlands as fresh as their young, laughing faces, radiant with gayety and happiness, it was delightful to see them dancing in the hall in which were the First Consul and the men with whom he was weighing the fate of Europe." Bourrienne also recurs to the same memories with a certain tenderness, when he says, "Away from the cares of government, which, so far as possible, we left behind us at the Tuileries, we were sometimes very happy in our colony of Malmaison; and then we were young, and what does not youth beautify?" And he adds, recalling the drawing-rooms after the performance of a play in the little theatre, "There the conversation was most animated and varied; and I may say with truth that gayety and freedom were the soul of the conversation, and made its whole charm. There were refreshments of every sort, and Josephine did the honors with such grace that every one could feel that she had been more occupied with him than with any one else. After these delightful entertainments, which generally closed at midnight, the guests would return to Paris."

Hortense was the leading star of the theatre of Malmaison. She made a great hit as Rosina in the "Barber of Seville." The other parts were thus cast: Almaviva, General Lauriston; Figaro, M. Didelot; Basile, Eugene de Beauharnais; Bartholo, Bourrienne; l'Eveillé, Isabey, the artist. It will be remembered that the same play had been given a few years before on another, equally remarkable, amateur stage at the Little Trianon. Beaumarchais's piece was played there August 19, 1785, at the very moment when the incident of the "Diamond Necklace" occurred. It was Marie Antoinette who took the part of Rosina; Almaviva was Count de Vaudreuil; Bartholo, the Duke of Guiche; Basile, M.

de Crussol; and the Figaro was the Count d'Artois, the future Charles X.

The memory of Marie Antoinette was still very fresh at the Consular Court, and Madame Campan, who had brought up, in her boarding-school at Saint Germain, a good many of the young women of this new court, had instructed them in the traditions of the old régime. The country balls of the Little Trianon, the taste for pastorals and idyls, the sheep-folds, the Swiss chalets, the fashion of wearing white dresses, the English gardens, the rustic life, — all these things reappeared at Malmaison. Like Marie Antoinette, Josephine delighted in a park with retreating paths and winding walks, with the greensward covered with daisies and violets. Like the Queen she was full of feeling, kind, generous, sympathetic with the suffering, sometimes gay, but generally sad and melancholy. Like the Queen she had the love of flowers which is shared by almost all pretty women. May it not be because there was an analogy between their fate and that of flowers? Like the flowers, they charm the eye, delight with their beauty, and, alas! fade in a day, and are soon forgotten even where they once shone in all their beauty!

Many things have changed at Malmaison. The park, mutilated, cut up, and reduced to the proportions of a simple garden, is but the shadow of what it was. The avenue of chestnut-trees is destroyed, — a magnificent avenue of trees, centuries old, in which Napoleon liked to walk, musing as he listened, at

the hour of the Angelus, to the distant sound of the
church-bell at Rueil.   There are no traces left of
the fine hot-house which contained so many rare
plants and exotic shrubs.   There is not the least
fragment of the pretty little theatre where Hortense
used to act.   Malmaison survives ; I see the shrine,
but where are the divinities ?

How Josephine loved this blessed spot !   People
travel far from Paris to look at landscapes which are
certainly less fair.   All about Malmaison there are
many spots to tempt an artist.   There are, too, many
excursions for the lady of the castle.   In a few minutes one can reach Butard, a hunting-house with a
charming pavilion in the style of Louis XV., which
the First Consul bought.   There it is delightful to
float in a little boat on the pond of Saint Cucufa.
There is an agreeable promenade on the superb terrace of Saint Germain, that graceful and majestic
amphitheatre which looks out on a fairy-like panorama, and the aqueduct of Marly lends a classical
air to the horizon, recalling Poussin's most beautiful
landscapes.

Josephine preferred Malmaison to all her other
residences.   In comparison with this favorite abode,
the Tuileries seemed like a prison, and in fact about
this royal palace, now destroyed, there was even at
the time of its greatest splendor something sad and
gloomy.   Malmaison, on the other hand, was cheerful ; only the gentle and happy side of life appeared
there.   There was no rigid rule of etiquette, but

every one breathed freely and took pleasure in living. Josephine was right in wishing to remain there. Napoleon had quite as much fame in this comparatively modest residence as beneath the gilded canopies of Saint Cloud, Compiègne, or Fontainebleau. At Malmaison he still preserved some of that Republican simplicity which was so well suited to the origin and character of his glory, which was very great, but of recent growth. As for monarchical splendor, was not the Tuileries enough in the winter, and was it necessary to install himself in the old royal residences in the summer? Palaces are gloomy places to those who have not been born in them; they are the home of illusions; they nourish the optimism which is often the forerunner of a downfall. At Malmaison the First Consul still heard the truth. At Saint Cloud no one will dare to tell it to him. He will have no friends; he will have courtiers.

Josephine had a presentiment of all this. She would not have wished a larger, a more magnificent residence than this Malmaison which she had selected, bought, and prepared to receive her husband on his return from Egypt. It was her ideal. *Hoc erat in votis.* September, 1801, Fontaine the architect wrote: " The castle of Malmaison, in spite of all we have spent, and all the additions, is too small for the First Consul, who requires a country-house. He has thought of taking Saint Cloud and having it put into condition. . . . Madame is averse to giving up Malmaison, which she regards as her own property, which she is

having decorated, and which she prefers to any spot
on earth." She looked on this place as her own, as
her work, and she wanted to stay there; for a secret
instinct told her that the palaces would bring her
misfortune. If Bonaparte had listened to her, he
would never have established himself at Saint Cloud.
But under the spur of his gigantic ambition he began
to find a house which had previously belonged to
private owners, unsuitable to his lofty rank. He
demanded a court, a military and a civil establishment, a complicated system of etiquette, imposing
pomp. Even country life demanded some of the
show of royalty. He demanded henceforth to be
everywhere, and at all times, on the same footing as
the kings and emperors, his future brothers, and
Saint Cloud appeared as necessary to his advance to
sovereignty.

X.

OF all the young girls of the Consular Court
the most remarkable and the most gifted
was Josephine's daughter, Hortense de Beauharnais.
Amiable, courteous, witty, with the figure of a nymph,
light hair, and a brilliant complexion, she was the
poetic image of France at that time, in all its youthful loveliness, force, and confidence in the future, of
that France, lit up by the light and glowing dawn.
Everything seemed to smile on the charming young
girl, who was endowed with the rarest and the richest
qualities. Yet, like almost all women of exceptional
intelligence, talents, and beauty, she was predestined
to an unhappy life. When she was married, early in
1802, she had already had experiences of sadness,
grief, and disappointment. Her infancy had been
clouded by deep tragedy. Born in Paris, April 10,
1783, she had, when five years old, started for Martinique with her mother, who was returning home to
escape the miseries of her unhappy marriage, and they
were nearly lost in a fierce tempest at the mouth of
the Seine. Returning to Paris in 1790, she was an eye-

witness of the horrors of the Revolution, her father,
General de Beauharnais, being one of its noblest victims.   In obedience to a law requiring the children of
noblemen to learn a trade, Hortense became a dress-
maker's apprentice, and her brother a joiner's, while
their parents were in prison.   Their former governess
carried them, dressed like working-people's children,
to the Carmelite Prison, where their mother was
locked up.   Alexander de Beauharnais was guillotined, and only Robespierre's overthrow saved Josephine from the same fate.   Hortense was eleven at
the time, and these terrible events left a lasting impression on her sensitive character, stamping it with
a melancholy which nothing could dispel.   In her
happiest moments she was not free from sadness, and
her smile was not far from tears.

In September, 1795, she was entrusted to the care
of Madame Campan, formerly a lady-in-waiting to
Marie Antoinette.   At that time Madame Campan
kept a boarding-school in which were revived all
the social and religious traditions of the old régime.
Hortense's companions were Caroline Bonaparte, the
future Queen of Naples; Stéphanie de Beauharnais,
the future Grand-duchess of Baden; Léontine de
Noailles, daughter of the Duke of Mouchy; Renée
Leclerc, later the wife of Marshal Davout; Elisa
Monroe, daughter of the Minister of the United
States to the Directory, who afterwards was Presi-
dent; Mademoiselle Hervas, who married Duroc;
Emilie de Beauharnais, famous in 1815 for her devo-

tion to her husband La Valette ; Mademoiselle Cochelet, who subsequently became a reader at the Dutch
court. Hortense, who was very fond of her companions, continued her intimacy with them even after
she became Queen. At the school, her room-mates
were Madame Campan's nieces, Adèle and Eglé
Auguier, one of whom became Baroness de Broc,
and the other the wife of Marshal Ney, Duchess of
Elchingen, and Princess de la Moskowa. At this
period of her life when, to quote her teachers, she
had not " the honor, or the good fortune, or the misfortune to be a princess," Hortense was comparatively
happy. In her devotion to study and the fine arts,
she found more solid joys than in the pomp of greatness, and she certainly preferred that modest and
obscure asylum, the boarding-school at Saint Germain, to the splendor of the Dutch palace.

After her mother's marriage to Bonaparte, Hortense soon perceived the power of his genius. She
conceived for him a feeling of intense admiration
and affection. Bonaparte, too, was as fond of her as
if she had been his own child. " He who generally
had a low opinion of women," says Madame de Rémusat, " always expressed his respect for Hortense, and
the way in which he spoke of her and treated her
disproves the accusations which have been brought
against her. In her presence his language was always more reserved and decorous. He often appealed
to her to decide between her mother and himself, and
listened to advice from her which he would not have

received from any one else. 'Hortense,' he used to say, ' makes me believe in virtue.' " When Bonaparte, after his return from Egypt, wanted to separate from Josephine, it was she who succeeded in calming his wrath. But she was none the less pained by the suspicions of which her mother was the object, and her uneasiness and distress, though for a moment dispelled, soon reappeared.

Yet Hortense knew some happy moments at the Tuileries and at Malmaison. Her stepfather's triumphal entrance into the royal palace, the reviews, the universal joy over the battle of Marengo, the enthusiasm and national pride which fired France, — all these things thrilled her young soul. She was thoroughly patriotic, and worshipped glory. Her songs and poems reflect her character. She was like the mediæval heroines, the women who inspired knights and troubadours. The ideas and sentiments of chivalry were what fed her heart; the harp, the lute, the sword, were always in her thoughts. She might have presided at a tournament, or have been the lady-love of the bravest paladins. At the time of the Consulate there was still poetry in women's hearts. The love of money, which since then has done so much harm to society, had not yet polluted the spring of noble actions. The spirit of sacrifice, heroism, the ideal, were still believed in. It is women who mould the character of men; if they are selfish, avaricious, self-interested, if they prefer in their lovers money to courage, to beauty, to intelligence, to all the qualities of the heart, men necessarily become prosaic, vulgar, low. We who live in a practical, positive time cannot readily form an idea of the generous enthusiasm, the noble unselfishness, the patriotic pride, the contempt for danger, the thirst for adventure, which existed at the beginning of the century in a generation hardened by such bitter experiences, and made bold by the brilliant destinies it saw before it. It was a time when the country, at the sight of great events which seemed to happen by a miracle, possessed a vigor, a fire, a confidence in the future, an audacity which overcame all obstacles and blotted from the dictionary such a word as "impossible." Men and women had the same inspired passion, glory. After the storms of the Revolution, after the bloodshed of the Terror and the war, peace seemed to smile again, and doubtless Hortense de Beauharnais nourished happy dreams as she moved among the band of warriors, writers, and artists who formed the train of the hero of Marengo. Could she have foreseen her dark future, the death of her children, the woes of her mother, the soil of France polluted by foreign armies, her happiness would have been marred; but those things were providentially hidden.

Hortense had noticed among the fellow-soldiers of the First Consul his aide-de-camp, Duroc, a handsome officer, loyal and chivalrous. At that time young women often fell in love with officers whose sword was their sole fortune, and not with the thought that by this sword they might become princes or kings. Their affection was only warmer because it was disinterested. To Hortense it seemed perfectly natural to prefer Duroc to the richest bankers or the grandest nobles, and at first Bonaparte did not oppose his stepdaughter's choice. He was very fond of Duroc; and since he had married two of his sisters to officers, there seemed to be no good reason why he should not do the same with Hortense. But Josephine was absolutely opposed to this marriage, which seemed to her a very unsuitable one. She wanted to marry her daughter either to some man of the old régime, or to a Bonaparte. For a moment she thought of giving her daughter to M. de Mun, an émigré who had just been permitted to return, and was the possessor of a considerable fortune. But this plan having fallen through, owing to Hortense's opposition, on the grounds that he had been Madame de Staël's lover in Germany, Josephine was only anxious to marry her daughter to Louis Bonaparte. The wife of the First Consul was then tormented by the vision of divorce, which filled her with terror and despair. She thought that by this marriage she could firmly unite the Bonapartes and the Beauharnais. More than that, she thought that even if she were childless, her daughter might not be, and that her grandson might one day rule over France; which is, in fact, what happened.

Louis Bonaparte, who was born at Ajaccio, September 2, 1778, was then twenty-three years old. He

had already attained high honors. Since he was fourteen, he had been on his brother's staff, and he had
served creditably in Italy and Egypt. Made colonel
of the 5th Dragoons in 1800, he had distinguished
himself at Marengo and had taken part in the expedition to Portugal. He was not only a brave and
cool officer; he had received a thorough education,
and displayed an aptitude for literature. His appearance was agreeable; he seemed gentle and modest.
So far as appearances went, he promised to make an
excellent husband.

Madame Campan, as well as Josephine, did her
best to give Hortense a good idea of Louis Bonaparte
and to persuade her to make a match which seemed
in every way desirable. She began with gentle hints;
and knowing that her pupil had no fancy for Louis,
she appealed to her reason rather than to imagination. Suspecting Hortense's interest in Duroc, she
congratulated her in advance on resisting this infatuation: "You must say to yourself," she wrote to her,
"that, after the most rigid examination, you are satisfied with yourself. I sincerely admire your wisdom,
my dear child, and I shall not be afraid to say to the
First Consul that, out of twenty ordinary girls whom
he may place in the society of a staff composed of
young men who share his military occupations and
his glory, who have every soldierly virtue, twenty
will be moved by the respectful glances and attentions of these young men. That is the way his two
sisters made their choice. Apparently, to judge

from what your mother has said, that is what he feared for you."

Without mentioning Louis Bonaparte by name, Madame nevertheless referred to him : " You promise me to keep your heart free and ready to accept any proposal that shall not arouse an unconquerable repugnance. In your decision do not decide from appearances alone, but with due regard to qualities and sweetness of disposition." But Madame Campan did not yet feel sure of gaining her cause, as these lines show : " If your heart is free, you will weigh the advantages and the disadvantages ; but if you have any prepossessions, you will see merit only in the one you have chosen. A woman of intelligence finds the same quality in the man she loves, however stupid he may be. His ugliness is a charm that outrivals more regular beauty. In a word, the illusion of love passes away, and the indissoluble tie remains ; the husband is seen as he is, and he is not to blame, for he is not changed. It is wrong to find fault with him ; the fault lies in the eyes and the prepossessions of the wife's heart." Obviously, to a young, poetic, romantic, enthusiastic girl like Mademoiselle de Beauharnais, such cold and prosaic advice could hardly have been agreeable.

Madame Campan went on ; she appealed to motives of interest and ambition, I might almost say to reasons of state, and ended thus : " Act in such a way that your conduct and Eugene's shall please the First Consul and suit his views about establishing you

both. You are one of the closest ties between him
and your mother; and if you fall into disgrace, you
must not think that you would readily find consolation. One may live in a humble position, or even
feel that it is pleasant to be obscure; but it is painful
to descend, and this, I assure you, is true."

This crafty reasoning had but little weight with
the young girl, who used to say with melancholy,
"My stepfather is a comet, and we are only the tail:
we must follow him wheresoever he goes, whether it
be to good or to evil fortune." She did not let herself be intoxicated by the brilliancy of her destiny,
and she never forgot the stern lessons of her early
experience. One day at Malmaison she was late for
dinner, and the First Consul had sat down without
waiting for her. Josephine went up to her daughter's room, and seeing that she was busy finishing a
drawing, asked her if she expected to have to support herself by her skill, since nothing could tear
her from her work. "Mamma," answered Hortense,
seriously, "who can say what may not happen in
times like these?"

Greatness had no attraction for this girl, who
judged human dignities for what they really were.
The idea of marrying a man who was almost a
prince and would become a king, did not tempt her
in the least. But the First Consul was slow at
coming to a decision. He had nearly promised the
hand of his adopted daughter to Duroc; and had it
not been for Josephine's entreaties, — for she was

most anxious to have Louis Bonaparte for son-in-law, — Duroc would have been successful. Towards the year 1801 the First Consul had sent to him by special messenger his commission as general commanding a division. This reached him in Holland, on his way to St. Petersburg, whither he had been sent to congratulate the Emperor Alexander on his accession. Bourrienne tells us that during his absence the correspondence of the young lovers passed through his hands by their consent. He adds that almost every evening at Malmaison he used to play billiards with Hortense, who was expert in the game. When he told her in a low voice, "I have a letter," the game stopped, and she ran to her room when he gave her the missive. Then the girl's eyes would fill with tears, and it was long before she would come down to the drawing-room. She still was hopeful. The First Consul said, "It makes no difference what my wife does; they suit each other, and they will marry. I like Duroc; he is of good birth. I gave Caroline to Murat, and Pauline to Leclerc; and I can give Hortense to Duroc, who is a capital fellow." But Josephine managed to alter everything. Bourrienne, who was an eye-witness of her wiles, tells us how she brought over the First Consul to her opinion by her entreaties, her skill, her caresses, and all the devices which she well knew how to move.

Perhaps Duroc would even then have succeeded, in spite of Josephine, if he had insisted more strenuously. But he was modest, with what was really exaggerated delicacy; he was fearful of being thought an ambitious schemer; he was averse to sowing dissension in the household of his chief, his benefactor; and this dread of annoying the hero he worshipped prevailed over every other feeling. Besides, Bonaparte had given him to understand that if he married Hortense, he should be appointed to the command of the 8th Military Division, and that on the day after the wedding he should leave for Toulon with his wife. The First Consul had added, "I don't want any son-in-law in my house." This threat singularly cooled Duroc's ardor; for he could not bear to think of separating himself from a chief for whom he had a boundless admiration which was almost idolatry, and, rather than leave him, he abandoned his aspirations to the hand of Mademoiselle de Beauharnais.

The girl, who expected a stronger feeling on the part of the man she had chosen, was naturally piqued by his determination. She felt that she was not loved with a fervor equal to her own, and this deception added to her pain. Deprived of Duroc's support, she at last, in despair, yielded to her mother's prayers, and her marriage with Louis Bonaparte was settled.

XI.

PARENTS who persuade their daughter to a marriage of interest or convenience, with no concern for her feelings, assume a heavy responsibility. They should never forget that, while love often departs, it never comes, after marriage. What more painful than to see a young girl sacrificed to calculations against which the soul revolts? There are abundant felicitations, and the girl is covered with flowers like the victim in ancient sacrifices. But during all the festivities, even at the altar, she suffers keenly. The music of the ball, the hymns of the church, sound to her like a funeral march. In her eyes the flowers she wears on her head are already as faded and withered as her illusions. Under her bridal veil she hides her pallor, perhaps her tears. She answers the compliments that are offered her with a forced smile. The customary compliments sound like irony; and when the last note of the organ has sounded, and the altar candles are put out, and she is alone, it is not the jewels, or the robes, or a fine-sounding name, or a coronet upon her presents,

140

— mere empty trifles, — that can soften the bitter agony of disappointment.

Madame Campan wrote to Mademoiselle Hortense de Beauharnais: " You are about to form a tie which all Europe will applaud, as I do. I have some slight knowledge of character and of similarities. . . . I have noticed in you both a conformity of tastes which assures your domestic happiness. . . . You will unite two families which ought to form one, and both are dear to France. I am sure that you will love each other much and always. Louis was not too much disposed to matrimony. The First Consul, who knows how to remedy every evil, has chosen for him the woman who cannot fail to make him happy by the qualities which he admires, and one can only praise the man who desires such qualities in his wife. Soon, my dear friend, I shall cease to write to you letters of advice. You will have a competent guide. Now the teacher can only rejoice in her work. A marriage based on a similarity of position, education, and tastes, such as all the world sees here, must be the happiest union possible."

Unfortunately Madame Campan was mistaken. Hortense well knew that her old teacher was wrong in thinking that she understood a girl's heart. Prophecies destined to be cruelly disproved did not at all deceive the sad young woman who resigned herself to her fate in silence. Possibly she was afraid to confide to her stepfather her repugnance to the projected union. Bourrienne tells us that she felt a respectful timidity before the First Consul, and that she always trembled when she spoke to him; whenever she wanted to ask anything of him, it was done through Bourrienne; and if there was any difficulty, he used to say that Hortense had asked him to make the application. "Little goose!" Bonaparte would reply, "why doesn't she ask me herself? Is she afraid of me?" Yes, Hortense was afraid of the First Consul, and that is why she did not ask him to release her from the union he proposed. Besides, Josephine, who was not always accurate in her statements, had at last persuaded her husband that Hortense and Louis were in love, and at Saint Helena he still thought that for a moment there had been a feeling of this sort between the two young people. As for Louis Bonaparte, as soon as he saw that this marriage had been determined by his all-powerful brother, he did not even try to oppose it. Every wish of the First Consul was regarded as a command. Yet he had no more interest in Hortense than Hortense had for him. He wrote in his Memoirs, in speaking of his marriage, "Never was there so gloomy a ceremony; never did man and wife have a stronger presentiment of a forced and ill-assorted marriage." At the same time all the numerous courtiers of the First Consul and his wife were speaking with enthusiasm of a union which flatterers were praising in busy rivalry.

The civil ceremony took place January 3, 1802, at the Tuileries, in the presence of the Bonaparte and

Beauharnais families. Mass was not yet said in this palace, and it was in the house in the rue de la Victoire, where Josephine lived when she married Napoleon, that the marriage took place. In the beginning of 1802, before the Concordat, the church ceremonies were always celebrated in private houses, where unsworn priests officiated. This mansion had been chosen for the residence of the young couple, and there it was that Cardinal Caprara, who was arranging the terms of the Concordat with the French government, gave the nuptial blessing. General Murat and his wife Caroline Bonaparte, who had been civilly married two years before, had not yet had the ceremony solemnized before a priest. They took this opportunity to have their situation legalized by the Church, and on the same day as Louis and Hortense, in the same house in the rue de la Victoire, they received the nuptial blessing from Cardinal Caprara.

There was another woman, too, who would have gladly enjoyed the same privilege: Josephine. Strangely enough, when the First Consul was busying himself with the interests of religion and the re-establishment of the Church, he set the example of the violation of one of its main laws, and, from a religious point of view, his union with Josephine was an unholy one. She was very anxious to put an end to this state of things; but Bonaparte, whether it was that he dreaded to call the attention of the public to the nature of the bond which attached him to his wife, or whether he wished to have a ready excuse

for divorce whenever he should wish it, obstinately
refused to accede to her wishes. This was a mor-
tification to her which only added to her daughter's
distress.

Young women have by instinct the art of conceal-
ing their emotions ; in this respect they outdo trained
diplomatists. No one who saw Madame Louis Bonaparte in the festivities that succeeded her marriage
could have guessed the secret torments that agitated
her. At the ball given in her honor by Madame de
Montesson, the widow of the Duke of Orleans, she
had a most enthusiastic success. It was a magnificent
entertainment, at which all the splendor of the old
régime reappeared. This assemblage of eight hundred persons of the highest aristocracy, the brilliant
uniforms, the rich dresses, the many diplomatists, the
powdered footmen in silk stockings and scarlet livery,
the profusion of flowers on the staircase and in the
rooms, the great abundance of candelabra and chande-
liers, of diamonds and other precious stones, brought
back the memory of festal evenings at Versailles.
The young bride, with her sweet, intelligent face,
her sensitive mouth, her kindly expression, her fine
blond hair, her brilliant complexion, her combination
of creole indifference and French vivacity, aroused
the admiration of the crowd who gathered about her.
She wore a peplum over a long tunic ; and when she
danced with the exquisite grace that marked all her
movements, she was like one of the Hours painted on
the frescos of Herculaneum. Intelligence, inspiration,

beauty, shone from her blue eyes with an undefinable charm. As one of her contemporaries said, she pleased *imperatively*. The First Consul was delighted with the Marchioness de Montesson's ball. For a fortnight nothing else was talked of in the Tuileries drawing-room; it set the tone for the consular society.

Every one there imagined Hortense perfectly happy, but she was suffering in silence; in silence, for she had too much tact, too much dignity, to complain. She went to one party after another, always agreeable, always pleasant and admired, with a smile on her lips and sadness in her heart. She was not yet wholly wretched; but that she soon would be, she clearly foresaw. Her misfortunes were certain to grow with her advance in position. She knew that the higher she rose, the more she would suffer. In comparison with the period which she spent on the throne of Holland, the first few months of her married life were a happy time. At least she was in her own country, among her friends, near her mother and brother. Later her queen's crown would be heavy on her brow, and every palace she would inhabit would be but a new place of exile. Those who saw her at the Consular Court, of which she was the fairest ornament, preserved a tender memory of her irresistible charm, as the Memoirs of her contemporaries testify. Few women have had to the same extent the gift of pleasing.

In 1802 and the beginning of 1803 Louis Bonaparte, who stood in mortal terror of his brother, did

not dare to show his whole jealous and quarrelsome
character.   He did not dare to manifest his evil suspicions of the First Consul, and he permitted his wife
to live at Malmaison, to do the honors there with
Josephine, or even alone when Josephine was at
Plombières, and to act in the little theatre by the side
of the gallery.   Madame Louis Bonaparte, as Rosina
in the "Barber of Seville," was really admirable.   It
was said of her that "if she had been the wife of the
First Consul's aide-de-camp, she would always have
been applauded for her perfect acting."   She was
very graceful and charming as the young Andalusian
girl, with her sweet, saucy air, her bright eyes, and
her thick black curls beneath a black velvet hat
decorated with long pink feathers.   After one of the
performances of the "Barber of Seville," the First
Consul wrote to his wife at Plombières, July 1, 1803:
"I have received your letter of the 10th Messidor.
You say nothing about your health or the effect of
the baths.   I see that you mean to come back in a
week, and that is a great pleasure to me, for I much
miss you.   You must have seen General Ney, who is
leaving for Plombières; he is to be married on his
return.   Hortense played Rosina yesterday in the
'Barber of Seville' with her usual intelligence."

Madame Louis Bonaparte sought in study, in painting, and in music, consolation for the sorrows of an
uncongenial marriage; but in the arts she saw only
their melancholy side.   She was naturally affectionate, and with a husband capable of understanding and

esteeming her, she would have been perhaps a model wife; instead, she was the companion of a man ill in body and mind, morose, discontented, uneasy, and suspicious. According to Madame de Rémusat, she took untiring pains to please the husband whom she had the misfortune not to love; she was gentle, submissive, deferential. But her husband, instead of being grateful, was only annoyed. " She is practising on me," he used to say, " in order to deceive me." He let her see his aversion to his stepsister and mother-in-law, Josephine, whom he regarded as an enemy of the Bonapartes, and whom he did not hesitate to represent to Hortense in the most odious light. Hortense, who had warmly loved her mother, and had remained a Beauharnais at heart, was deeply wounded by her husband's remarks, when he would say to her, " You are now a Bonaparte, and our interests ought to be your interests; those of your family don't concern you any more," and when he went on to say, that he was determined to take every precaution necessary to escape the common fate of husbands, and that he should not be duped by any attempt to avoid him, or by any pretences of affection that were designed to blind him.

These odious suspicions filled with indignation Hortense's haughty and sensitive soul. Her brow darkened as she saw the cloud gathering, and her surprise at the heartlessness that threatened her, filled her with disgust for honors that were purchased at so high a price. Then terrible insult awaited her:

she was tortured by hearing that her pure and noble affection for her father-in-law had been misinterpreted, and that the First Consul was accused of an unholy passion for her, which she returned. This detestable calumny only added to Louis Bonaparte's suspicions, and henceforth he was placed in a painful and difficult position in regard to his brother. This is what Madame de Rémusat says: " The Bonapartes, and especially Madame Murat, who had opposed this marriage with some violence, because, since Joseph's children were all girls, it was evident that if Louis had a son, who would be Josephine's grandson, he would at once be a very important child, spread abroad the detestable rumor of the intimacy of the First Consul with his stepdaughter. The public heard it with delight. Madame Murat confided it to Louis, who, whether he believed it or not, only redoubled his precautions. Servants were taught to spy, letters and notes were opened, all acquaintances were frowned on, even Eugene was regarded with jealousy; there was a series of violent scenes; the poor woman knew no rest."

October 10, 1802, Madame Louis Bonaparte gave birth, at Paris, to a son, who was to die at the Hague, May 5, 1807. Madame Campan at this time wrote to the mother about the way in which Louis, in accession of amiability, had celebrated the birthday of his first-born. " You were moved by it; your tender heart must have been moved. But, — I know you well, — did you show it? I am well aware that

simple, pure souls, that have been well trained, despise all demonstrations, but sometimes with the best
motives errors are made." How could Hortense be
happy, even by the side of her child's cradle, when
she knew that calumny did not spare even this little
being? when every mark of Napoleon's interest in
the infant was to the public additional proof of her
degradation?

Bourrienne, who is generally severe, and especially
towards the First Consul, denounced these vile insin-
uations most severely. "I am glad," he says in his
Memoirs, "to be able to give the most formal and
positive lie to these infamous suppositions. They lie
in their throat when they say that Bonaparte had
any other feeling for Hortense than that of a stepfather for his stepdaughter. The whole disgusting
story is a lie, and yet it spread not only throughout
France, but into every corner of Europe. Is there
no way of escaping vile gossip?"

Napoleon was much concerned at these reports, and
Josephine was horrified. Their happiness at the
birth of the child was poisoned by the prevalent
rumor. "Poor Josephine," says Bourrienne, "paid
a high price for her glory. Knowing the groundless-
ness of these reports, I tried to console her by telling
her how I tried to show their wickedness and falsity.
But Bonaparte, under the influence of the affection
of which he was the object, only augmented his wife's
grief. He was deluded enough to imagine that the
whole thing was due to the desire of the country to

see an heir; consequently, when he tried to console
her as a mother, he pained her as a wife, and the
vision of a divorce returned.   In his wild illusion,
Bonaparte imagined that France wanted to be gov-
erned by a bastard, which is a curious way of establishing a new legitimacy." Hortense was not ambitious.   All the plans formed about her baby's cradle
only annoyed her.   She thought that such calculations only lessened the natural feelings, by altering
its poetry and sanctity.   Private life seemed to her
preferable to that of a queen, and she hated to think
that in France, or elsewhere, he might become the
heir to a throne.

Even at Saint Helena Napoleon recalled these unhappy calumnies, and in his "Memorial" may be
found this curious passage: "Louis was a child
spoiled by reading Jean Jacques Rousseau.   He
could not be long satisfied with his wife.   A good
deal of unreasonableness on his side and of lightness
on hers, these were the wrongs on each side." And
then he once more defends himself, saying that criminal intimacies of that sort suited neither his ideas
nor his habits, and any one who had the slightest
knowledge of the Tuileries, would understand how
impossible would be such a revolting crime.   "Louis
knew what value to set on such rumors; but his vain,
capricious character was shocked, and he made use
of them as pretexts."

Josephine, who was jealousy incarnate, at times
thought her husband guilty, possibly her daughter.

The Bonapartes made the most of these sources of
dissension, for even under the Republic there flour-
ished all the intrigues and low ambitions of a court.
Hortense, who was naturally sentimental and romantic, felt herself a stranger amid such surroundings. She missed the happy dreams of her youth
and her swiftly vanished happiness. Very early and
precocious experience had taught her all that was
vilest and most cowardly in human nature. This
generous young woman, whose aspirations had been
most noble, with her passion for art, her love of the
ideal, woke from these lofty visions to find herself
in a low, malicious world. Her health was affected,
and she needed all her resignation and generosity to
avoid reproaching her mother for having thus sacrificed her. Later she will be guilty of unpardonable
faults, but in defence of these may be pleaded ex-
tenuating circumstances, because she will yield to
affection and not to calculations of interest. That
is the reason for the sympathy that was shown to her
by her contemporaries of all parties, even when her
errors were most notorious. Not merely the friends
of Imperialism, but even the bitterest foes of Napoleon respected her. In 1814 the Emperor Alexander
treated her with regard and devotion. At about the
same time, Madame de Krüdener wrote to Mademoiselle Cochelet about the then unthroned Queen :
·" What news of this angel whom you love so much,
and to whom my heart nourishes respectful devotion?" And later, Chateaubriand became the courtier
of this lady in exile, when she was sanctified by grief.

XII.

MADAME JUNOT, who, a few years later, became the Duchess of Abrantès, was a brilliant figure among the young women who formed the Consular Court. Her high birth, her intelligence, her beauty, her marriage, all placed her in the front rank. She was the daughter of a very beautiful woman, Madame de Permon, a great friend of the Bonapartes, and was born at Montpellier in 1784. The Permons were a Corsican family, of Greek origin, who also bear the name of Comnenus, tradition saying that they belonged to the line of the Eastern emperors. Madame de Permon, who at Ajaccio had been a neighbor of Madame Letitia Bonaparte, always loved her as a sister, and it was at her house at Montpellier that Charles Bonaparte, the brother of the future Emperor, died. After the Revolution she established herself in Paris, in a pretty house in the Chaussée d'Antin, and there she received those people of the old régime who had survived the general ruin. The young Napoleon Bonaparte, whom she treated as a boy, asked her to marry him, although she was a good

152

many years older than he: but she was far from accepting his suit; she merely smiled at it. During the Directory, Madame de Permon, who was intimate with what remained of the society of the Faubourg Saint Germain, was one of the most conspicuous women in Paris. She might have been taken for the sister of her daughter Laure, the future Duchess of Abrantès, a charming girl whose grace and precocious intelligence delighted every one.

After the 18th Brumaire, Laure de Permon married one of the bravest and most brilliant of the First Consul's fellow-soldiers, the young General Junot, who was born at Bussey-le-Grand in 1771. He was as chivalrous and adventurous as a knight of the Crusades, madly reckless of his money and his life, devoted to women, war, and glory. As governor of Paris, he occupied a magnificent house, a present from the First Consul in the rue des Champs Élysées (now the rue Boissy d'Anglas). Their first child, a daughter, born in 1801, had for sponsors at its baptism Bonaparte and Josephine. Her godfather gave her a beautiful pearl necklace; and her godmother, one hundred thousand francs for furnishing the house in the rue des Champs Élysées. In the spring of 1802 Junot and his wife, for a housewarming, gave a ball which was honored by the presence of the First Consul. He examined the house from cellar to garret, and, pleased to see his companion, thanks to his munificence, so comfortably established, he stayed at the ball till one o'clock in the morning.

That evening Josephine wore in her hair a crown of vine-branches with bunches of purple grapes, and her dress, embroidered with silver, was trimmed with bunches of grapes like those in her hair. Her daughter, Madame Louis Bonaparte, danced like a sylph. She wore a classical dress, a peplum of crape embroidered with silver, and on her head she wore a crown of roses.

In spite of the kindness of the First Consul to Junot, Madame de Permon, who continued to think herself of higher birth and social position than the Bonapartes, assumed a protecting attitude towards them, and she was not fascinated by the hero of Marengo, whom she had known poor, obscure, and young. She was not sparing of her criticisms, doubtless wishing that he would pay his court to her as he had already done. She was annoyed, for example, that he did not leave his card after spending an evening in company at her house, and to soothe her feelings her son said, "But he's a very great man." "Well, what difference does that make? Marshal Saxe was a great man too, but yet he used to make visits."

Madame Junot inherited her mother's independent and somewhat caustic character. In conversation she was able to cope not only with the First Consul's sisters, but even with himself, as we may see from this anecdote taken from her Memoirs.

The scene is at Malmaison, where Bonaparte was alone, Josephine having gone to Plombières on ac-

MADAME JUNOT

count of her health. Her husband still writes to her
affectionate letters, but he is certainly less deeply
in love than he was in the Italian campaign. He
writes: "We are rather gloomy here, though Hortense does the honors of the house admirably. . . .
I love you as much as I ever did, because you are
kind and especially lovable. . . . A thousand good
wishes and many kisses." In fact, the First Consul
readily consoled himself for Josephine's absence.
He liked to be at Malmaison, and he discharged his
duties as host with much charm; he was pleasant,
happy, and full of animation. Madame Louis Bonaparte, to console him, had brought together a number
of young and pretty women, among whom was
Madame Junot, who had been recently married.
The husbands of these ladies were for the most part
detained by their duties in Paris. From time to
time they came out to Malmaison to dine with the
First Consul, leaving for Paris the same evening.
Their wives stayed at Malmaison, occupying the
little guest-chambers which opened on the long cor-
ridors on the first floor. Junot stayed at his post as
governor of Paris and left his wife peaceably under
the protection of Madame Louis Bonaparte.

One morning Madame Junot, who had been sleep-
ing soundly, awoke with a start. Judge of her surprise, whom did she see near her bed? She fancied
herself dreaming, rubbed her eyes, and then burst
out laughing. "Yes, it is I," said Bonaparte; "why
are you so surprised?" It was evidently very early,

and Madame Junot held out her watch before the
First Consul's face; it was not yet five o'clock.
"Indeed," said Bonaparte, "is it no later than that?
Well, so much the better; we can talk." Then he
pushed an easy-chair up near the bed, sat down
calmly, and instead of talking ran over a huge bundle
of letters, on which she saw written in large characters: "For the First Consul himself, for him
alone; personal." For a whole hour he went through
his correspondence. The clock sounded. "The
deuce! six o'clock. Good-by, Madame Junot."
Then through the bedclothes he pinched her foot,
and with his papers under his arm went off, hum-
ming some little song horribly out of tune.

The next morning the same thing happened. At
the same hour the First Consul had the maid open
the door, sat down by Madame Junot's bed, without
apologizing for waking her so early, ran over his
letters and papers, pinched her foot through the bedclothes, bade her good-by, and went off singing. As
soon as he was gone, Madame Junot called her maid
and said, "I forbid your opening the door when any
one knocks at such an early hour." "But, ma'am, if
it's the First Consul?" "I don't want to be waked
up so early by the First Consul or any one else. Do
what I tell you." That evening Madame Junot
repeated her orders, and went to bed somewhat disturbed, wondering if it was advisable for her to stay
at Malmaison. She loved the First Consul as a sister
loves a brother but what were his feelings?

The next morning at six she heard steps in the corridor, and some one knocked at the door. No one opened it. He knocked again. The maid said, "I can't open the door; Madame Junot has taken the key." He went away without any answer, and Madame Junot breathed again. In a few moments she had fallen asleep, but she was soon aroused again, for the door was opened, and Bonaparte, who had entered with a pass-key, appeared: "Are you afraid you will be murdered," he said. "We hunt at Buttard to-morrow, you know. We shall start early, and to make sure that you are ready, I shall come myself to wake you. Since you are not among a band of Tartars, you need not lock yourself up as you have done. Then, too, you see that all your precautions against an old friend don't prevent his getting to you. Good-by!" And he went off, but this time he did not sing.

Madame Junot was in despair. The First Consul left her room at the moment when the servant-women were passing through the corridor about their work. What would they say about a young woman who receives visitors at that hour of the morning? It would be more than imprudent to stay at Malmaison; but to leave would offend the First Consul, distress Madame Louis Bonaparte, arouse Junot's suspicions, and give rise to malicious comments. The poor young woman was sadly perplexed, when suddenly she felt two arms embracing her tenderly and heard a well-known voice saying, "What

is the matter, Laure?" This time it was not the
First Consul, but Junot, who had come out to pass
the day at Malmaison, and was much surprised to
find his wife so agitated. "My dear, I want to go
away; I want to go back to Paris." "Oh, you may
be sure that as soon as Madame Bonaparte returns
from Plombières, I shall take you away." "But
why not now?" "Now? Before she gets back?
Nonsense, my dear child." Madame Junot did not
insist. Her plan was made.

That evening Junot dined at the table of the First
Consul, who was most gay and agreeable, and after
dinner he took leave to return to the city; for as
governor he was unable to be absent a single night.
Before leaving he went up to his wife's room for a
moment, and she, by dint of entreaties and endear-
ments, succeeded in persuading him, in spite of
orders, to spend the night.

The next morning Madame Junot awoke just as
five was striking. Everything was calm and silent
in the beautiful light of early morning; and as she
gazed at her husband, and saw the glorious scars
upon his brow, she felt safe, and thought to herself,
"I don't fear anything; he will protect me."

At that moment the door was opened violently.
"What, still asleep, Madame Junot, when we are
going hunting!" She recognized the voice of the
First Consul; and he came forward, pushed aside
the bed-curtain, and stood motionless with surprise
as his eye fell on his companion-in-arms. Junot

started up, quite as much surprised. "Heavens, general! what are you doing in a lady's room at this hour of the day?" The First Consul answered in the same tone, "I came to wake up Madame Junot in time for the hunt. . . . I might find fault, for, M. Junot, you are here in disobedience to orders." "General," said the governor of Paris, "if there ever was fault that deserved to be pardoned, it is this. If you had seen this little siren for a full hour last evening trying to persuade me to stay, I am sure you would forgive me." "Well, I pardon you completely," answered Bonaparte; "and to show that I am not angry, I will let you come to the hunt with us." And with these words he left the room. "Upon my word," said Junot, arising, "he is an excellent man. What kindness! instead of finding fault, or sending me back to Paris. You must confess, Laure, that he is really far above ordinary mortals."

When they were starting for the hunt, and keepers, horses, dogs, and carriages were all assembled before the castle, and Junot was choosing a horse, his wife got into a small barouche with the First Consul. Soon they were off, and the following dialogue took place: "Madame, you think yourself very intelligent, do you not?" "Oh! not extraordinarily intelligent; but I don't think I am a fool." "A fool, no; but a goose. Can you tell me why you made your husband stay?" "My explanation will be short and clear, general. He is my husband; and there is no offence, I suppose, in a husband's staying with his wife." "Then you had no other reason than your affection for him when you asked him to stay?" "No, general." "You are not telling the truth. . . . I know why you did so: you distrusted me, as you should not have done. Ah, you see you don't answer!" "And if I had another motive than this distrust of which you speak; if I knew that your visits at such an hour in the room of a woman of my age would compromise me in the eyes of those who are here with me, and if I had taken this means to stop them"— "If that is the case, why didn't you speak to me? Have I not in the last week shown friendliness enough to deserve your confidence? The next step would have been, doubtless, to tell Junot what you had imagined." "Heavens, general! how could such an idea occur to you, knowing him as you do? He is as violent as Othello. If I had told Junot all that has happened in the last week, neither he nor I would be here this morning." "Won't you, then, believe that I mean you no harm?" "Certainly, general; I am so sure that you do not mean me ill, that I can assure you that my attachment for you, which dates from my childhood, and my admiration, are not in the least diminished; and there is my hand in token."

After a moment's hesitation the First Consul took off his glove and held out his hand to Madame Junot, saying, "You must believe in my friendship for you; it depended only on you to make it something solid. And yet you wish to leave Malmaison?" "Yes, general, after the hunt. I have persuaded Junot to take me away." "And when shall you be back?" "When I am needed for the play, general; but you can dispose of my room; I shall not occupy it any longer, I assure you." "As you please. Besides, you are right in going away this morning; after this stupid business you and I could have no pleasure in meeting." And, opening the door of the barouche with his own hand, Bonaparte sprang out, got on a horse, and galloped away. That same afternoon M. and Mme. Junot were back in Paris.

This adventure at Malmaison, thus recounted by Madame Junot, makes an admirable pendant to the adventure at the camp at Barlogue, told by Madame de Rémusat. At heart both of these ladies were glad to carry the impression that Napoleon felt a tender interest in them, and with a little coquetry they could have made a conquest of the conqueror. They insinuate that their virtue alone forbade this victory. However this may be, if we suppose that the First Consul's affection for Madame Junot was purely fraternal, — paternal I cannot say, for Bonaparte was then but thirty years old, — we must confess that were he another Scipio, his conduct was not prudent, and that his choice of working-room exposed him to a temptation to which even a consul might succumb. Madame Junot did well to leave Malmaison. Some people pretend that this incident is the reason why her husband was never made a Marshal of France, but it seems incredible that Napoleon should not be above such petty spite. At any rate, the Duchess of Abrantès and the Countess de Rémusat show us how Napoleon treated women, with a mixture of rough-ness and amiability; gallantry he never showed. In fact, he feared them more than he loved them; it touched his pride to think that he might be subject to their influence. If Madame Junot had fallen in love with the First Consul, she would not have been his mistress; he would have been her master. He might have had a caprice for her; he would never have loved her.

A few days after the incident recounted above, Madame Junot went out to Malmaison to make a visit to Josephine, who had just returned from Plombières. She stayed to dinner, and at ten o'clock asked for her carriage. Just as she was about to start, a terrible thunder-storm arose. "I sha'n't let you go, in weather like this!" said Josephine, "I will go and have a room made ready for you"; and she started to the door to give her orders. Madame Junot stopped her, on the pretext that she had no clothes and no maid. "I will lend you one of my nightcaps, and everything that you want," replied Josephine, "and one of my maids shall wait upon you. Come, you will stay, won't you? Besides, how could you get through the woods at this hour? It wouldn't be safe. You know how dangerous the Bonjéval woods are." Meanwhile, the First Consul was standing by the fireplace, busily arranging a log with the tongs, and taking no part in the conversation. As Madame Bonaparte renewed her entreaties, he said, still holding the tongs, " Don't torment her any longer, Josephine: I know her; she won't stay."

If we have dwelt perhaps too long on this anec- dote, it has been to give a definite notion of the way in which these Memoirs of the Duchess of Abrantès are written. Doubtless they bear traces of the haste in which they were composed; they contain many errors, and are inexact; many of the conversations are more fictitious than real, and belong to romance rather than to history; there is a good deal of pad- ding, and much ore by the side of the gold. But in spite of these faults, there is a charm and abundant life and animation in this collection of the pictures of so many illustrious persons. The Duchess de- scribes a play that she has seen from the boxes. When she describes the Parisian drawing-rooms, of which she was one of the main ornaments, she can say " et quorum pars magna fui." If her Memoirs had been more formally written, they would have been less agreeable reading : their faults, their care- lessness even, only add to the charm. They are like an easily flowing conversation, in turn serious and idle, sad and gay, ironical and enthusiastic. That is the way a great lady talks whose smile and tears are always charming, who makes delicate fun of absurdities, and is eloquently indignant with petti- ness and meanness. The reader perceives her love for everything fine, for letters, for love, for glory.

Like Madame de Rémusat, she was an eye-witness

of the reaction in Parisian society against the glories
of the Consulate and the Empire, but she reacted
against this tendency. Her friend, the great novelist
Balzac, but for whom, it is said, she would never
have written the Memoirs, strongly urged her to
remain faithful to her Memoirs, and sometimes to rise
into the region of poetry. Hence the pages of real inspiration that intersperse the pages of trifling anecdotes and boudoir gossip. And when the Duchess
recalls the springtime of her life, those happy hours
when France was great and glorious, her language
glows with the fire of enthusiasm. " My country,"
she writes, " my beloved country ! My country !
There is a magic charm in the letters composing this
and which is like the name of the being we love. . . .
When I recall those glorious days — the laurels where-
of were fed with the blood of him whose name I bear
— my soul, overwhelmed by so many disasters, both
public and private, my heart, wearied by the long
silence of songs of war and victory which I heard in
my cradle, in my youth, in all my life until the days
of our shame, — my soul, my heart, I say, are moved
anew, and I glow with the pride which used to make
us raise our heads and say, ' I too am French.' "

Is not this fitting language for a noble woman,
who, in 1814, when completely ruined, could have
secured for her eldest son the very rich succession of
Aeken, if she had agreed to make him change his
nationality, but who, preferring for him the name of
" Frenchman " and poverty, refused ? Junot had

been in possession of an income of more than a million of francs, and his widow was penniless; nothing was left her but her intelligence and her pride. Why is there not a new edition of the eighteen volumes of her Memoirs and of the six volumes of her "History of the Parisian Drawing-rooms," which abound with original and amusing anecdotes, and with sketches and portraits drawn by a firm and graceful hand? Madame Amet, the worthy daughter of the Duchess of Abrantès, who was born at the beginning of the century, and remembers Napoleon and Josephine, her godparents, could better than any one prepare the notes and the Introduction which would recall her mother's charming person. At once an artist and a fine lady, a woman of letters and of the drawing-room, generous to a fault with her money and her intelligence, as cheerful in poverty as in wealth, as much admired by Parisian society in the humblest apartment as in her splendid mansion of the rue des Champs Élysées, a noble nature, rising above vulgar ambitions and petty calculations, the Duchess of Abrantès occupies a place apart in the company of the celebrated women of the Consulate and the Empire. It is with real emotion that one reads the verses which Victor Hugo dedicated to her memory. The woman who inspired that poet, Balzac, and so many great writers with such devoted friendship, was certainly no ordinary woman.

XIII.

MEN'S decisions often rest on many grounds; and often when they are thought to be moved only by calculation, they are moved quite as much by sentiment. This was the case, if we are not mistaken, with Napoleon, when he brought about the restoration of religion in 1802. Above all things, he was a politician; but besides being a politician, he was a Christian. Doubtless his faith was not very profound; he did not observe the forms of religion, and he felt the influence of the eighteenth century and of the Revolution. But in spite of Voltaire, he had learned in his infancy to respect Catholicism: perhaps he was not perfectly sure that the Roman Church was true; but he was less certain that it was false. The feeling which led him to say on his death-bed: "Not every one who wants to be, is an atheist," makes itself clear with more or less distinctness, as the circumstances determine, throughout his career. As Thiers said, "It is intelligence that discovers intelligence in the universe; and a great mind is better capable than a small one of see-

ing God in his works." Bonaparte was not simply
a deist; there was in his character a deep stamp of
Catholicism. "When we were at Malmaison," says
Bourrienne, "and used to walk in the avenue that
led to Rueil, the sound of the village church-bell
often interrupted our conversations. He would stop
in order not to lose a bit of the sound, which delighted him. It used to move him so deeply that he
would say: 'That reminds me of my early years at
Brienne. I was happy at that time.' Then the bell
would stop, and he would resume his mighty reve-
ries." The sound of the bell at Rueil was not without its influence on the Concordat.

According to the "Memorial," Napoleon said at
Saint Helena: "It would be hard to believe the resistance I met to restoring Catholicism. I should have
met with less opposition if I had unfolded the banners of Protestantism." Edgar Quinet considers that
an erroneous assertion. He says that if the First
Consul had tried to introduce into France any religious innovations, he would have been in direct and
open contradiction with himself; and that Catholicism alone agreed with the form and the logical cohe-
rence of his plans. "Examine closely his thought,"
adds Quinet, "and you will observe that his ideal was
the Empire of Constantine and Theodosius, and this
tradition he inherited from his ancestors, like all the
Italian Ghibellines. So far from inclining towards
the religious emancipation of the individual conscience, he always had a vision of a pope whose

emperor and master he should be, — a conception which is exactly that of the Ghibellines and the commentators of the Middle Ages. From this combination of the Italian and the French genius grew the extraordinary logic by which he so easily drove back France to the political institutions of Charlemagne. . . . This man, who, in so many respects, was extremely modern, in others resembled a ruler of the Middle Ages, a Carlovingian."

It is certain that he started from the idea that France having become great by the cross and the sword, it was by the cross and the sword that it was to preserve its greatness. And is it not, indeed, an absolute law of history that a people preserves its force only by remaining faithful to the principles by which it attained it?

"Every society," says Thiers, "demands a religious belief and form of worship. . . . What better thing, then, can a civilized society demand than a national religion, founded on the true feelings of the human heart, in harmony with the rules of high morality, consecrated by time, and which, without intolerance or persecution, brings together, if not all, at least the great majority, of the citizens, at the foot of an ancient and revered altar?" And he goes on with fervor: "It existed, this religion which had brought under its dominion all civilized peoples, had formed their morals, inspired their songs, furnished the subjects for their poetry, their pictures, their statues, left its stamp on all their national memories, marked with

its sign their banners in turn vanquished or victorious. It had disappeared for a moment in a great
storm that swept over men's minds; but when that
storm had passed, the necessity of belief returned,
and this was again found in every soul, the natural
and indispensable faith of France and of Europe. . . .
What more necessary, more inevitable, in 1800, than
to lift up the altar of Saint Louis, of Charlemagne,
and of Clovis, which had been for a moment overthrown ? "

Yet the First Consul needed rare perseverance for
the accomplishment of such a task. There are periods
when hypocrisy is the fashion, but there are others
when the opposite quality prevails — I mean the fear
of man. This was the case with a large part of
French society. The country people remained Christian and Catholic; but in the aristocracy, in the
middle classes, and especially in the army, Voltairian
ideas had made great ravages. It needed all Bonaparte's authority to silence the sarcasms of his generals; and it was not by persuasion, but rather by a
discipline of iron, that he collected them about the
altar of Notre Dame, as if for a review or a parade.

No resistance could discourage the First Consul,
because he was convinced that Catholicism, so far
from being dead, as some people imagined, was still
living in the habits, the civilization, and the inner
life of some who called themselves its bitterest enemies. He did not think its principles incompatible
with those of the Revolution, as it began, while still

unstained by excesses, and he remembered that **Pope Pius VII.** had said in a homily, December 25, **1797**, when he was only Bishop of Imola : " Be good Christians, and you will be good democrats. The early Christians were full of the spirit of democracy." Pius VII. sent to Paris Cardinal Consalvi, who, after long and laborious negotiations, concluded with Joseph Bonaparte, aided by Crétet, Counsellor of State, and Abbé Bernier, the Concordat of July 15, 1801. It was presented to the legislative bodies along with the laws concerning the Catholic worship, and the various Protestant forms, April 8, 1802, and was adopted without discussion. Ten days later, on Easter Sunday, the First Consul determined to have a great religious ceremony take place at Notre Dame, and one which also had its worldly side.

Bonaparte wished on the same day to ratify at the Tuileries the treaty of Berlin, and to be present, at Notre Dame, at the mass and *Te Deum* for the establishment of the Concordat. He left his palace in great pomp. Officials of all kinds and a brilliant staff escorted him. Josephine, who accompanied him, was also numerously attended by the prettiest and most fashionable ladies of Paris. The troops formed two lines between the palace and the cathedral. Everywhere the crowd assembled to see the First Consul, whose red coat attracted every eye. On reaching Notre Dame, he descended slowly from his carriage, and was received at the door by the Archbishop of Paris, who presented him with holy water,

and led him under a canopy to the place reserved for
him in the choir, near the high altar. Behind him,
the generals, in full uniform, stood throughout the
long ceremony. The members of the Senate, the
legislative body, and the Tribunate, were placed on
each side of the altar.

At that time there was in Notre Dame a superb
roodloft, of Gothic construction, and most picturesque. It was from this that Madame Bonaparte and
her suite witnessed the ceremony. There were about
eighty of these ladies; more than two-thirds of them
were under twenty, many were not over sixteen. A
great number were very pretty. The Duchess of
Abrantès recalls this solemn day with great satisfaction in her Memoirs, and describes it as one would
do it nowadays. "I still remember," she says, "Madame Murat's dress, with her pink satin hat, surmounted by a tuft of feathers of the same color, and
how fresh, rosy, and spring-like her face appeared
beneath it. She wore a dress of India muslin, with
wonderful openwork embroidery, and lined with pink
satin matching her hat. Over her shoulders was a
mantilla of Brussels lace, with which her dress was
trimmed. No mundane festival was more magnificent than this religious one; and while the thoughts
of the pious turned to their Creator, it was in His
creatures that the free-thinking generals most interested themselves, and many of them, standing behind
the First Consul, and so in no dread of his eyes,
acted unbecomingly.

"Many young women," the Duchess goes on,
"took their degrees in beauty on that day. There
were many who were known to be pretty and charming, but there was also a large number who could
scarcely be distinguished at the vast entertainments
of Quintidi [the fifth day of the decade], while at
Notre Dame, with the sun blazing through the colored glass, these young faces shone with marvellous
beauty; nothing was lost. The First Consul noticed
it and spoke about it that same evening." The roodloft of Notre Dame, April 18, 1802, is a subject that
may be recommended to an historical painter.

The ceremony was really magnificent, as became
a nation which is both religious and warlike. The
clatter of arms, the sound of the organ, the salvos of
artillery, which from daybreak had rattled every
window, the chants which rose beneath the vaulted
roof of the old cathedral, the smell of powder mingling with that of the incense, the gilded uniforms by
the side of the rich chasubles of the priests, — all this
pomp delighted the populace of Paris, which is always
eager for great shows. It was observed that luxury
and elegance had made great strides since General
Bonaparte had made his solemn entrance into the
Tuileries. Then there had been in the procession
almost nothing but cabs with their numbers hidden
by bits of paper, and now there were handsome private carriages, as fine as those of the old régime,
following the First Consul's coach. The servants of
the principal officials were for the first time in livery;

and the crowd, instead of denouncing this return to monarchical ways, took a childish delight in it. That evening the members of the Diplomatic Body dined at M. de Talleyrand's, the Minister of Foreign Affairs; there was an illumination and a concert in the Tui̇-eries garden, and in the palace Cardinal Caprara, the Archbishop of Paris, and the highest ecclesiastics dined at the table of the First Consul, who had a long and friendly talk with the First Consul, congratulating himself on the great success of the day.

There was only one flaw, and that was the attitude of a great many of the officers. Paris was full of them; they found the calm of peace unendurable; and since they were still faithful to the principles of the Revolution, they were indignant with the reaction which was led by Bonaparte. This was the feeling of especially the old officers of the Army of the Rhine, who had always been jealous of the Army of Italy, and who had gathered around the discontented generals, like Moreau. The venerable General de Ségur has left in his Memoirs traces of the impression made upon him and many of his comrades by the events of April 18, 1802. " I heard the clamor, but without sufficiently disapproving its malignity; at Notre Dame I saw their indignation on the occasion of the *Te Deum* for the Concordat. On that day I did not sufficiently condemn Dalmas's retort to Bonaparte: ' Yes, it was indeed noble mummery! The only pity is that there weren't present about a thousand of the men who got killed in overthrowing what you are re-establishing.' The brutal impertinence which was uttered by many other generals at the Tuileries, and even within Napoleon's hearing, displeased me without doubt, but less than it should have done. I acknowledge that in the cathedral my attitude was not the most reverent, and I remember that as the procession was passing the Palais Royal on its way home, near a group of officers with whom I was standing, our disdainful bearing in response to the repeated salutes of the First Consul could not have satisfied him."

Bonaparte was not made uneasy by these signs of opposition, for he had determined to crush any show of resistance. Congratulatory addresses on the Concordat reached him from every quarter. "You will see," he told Bourrienne, "how much I shall get out of the priests." The Royalists lost their only claim to popularity, and the hierarchy of the Church was formally placed in the hands of the authorities. There appeared at this time in the windows of every bookshop an engraving representing the triumph of religion in France over the atheism of the Revolution; the cross was upheld by Bonaparte's sword, and below was this inscription: "The 28th Germinal, year X. of the French Republic (April 18, 1802), Easter Sunday, by the triumphant arm of Napoleon Bonaparte, First Consul of France, religion arises from the abyss into which impious atheists had hurled it; Cardinal Caprara, legate, with plenipotentiary powers from the Pope, to the French government,

celebrated mass in the cathedral church of Notre
Dame, in presence of the three Consuls and all the
regular authorities." At the same time a sonnet was
circulated, which ended thus: —

> He restores to France a solemn harmony,
> Makes peace with all the world besides,
> Placing it in triumph at the feet of the Eternal.

The followers of Voltaire had retorted by secretly
circulating a caricature of the First Consul, representing him as drowning in a basin of holy water,
with bishops pushing him back into the water with
their crosiers. In spite of these isolated sarcasms,
the religious reaction was complete; the offices were
empty on Sunday; the Archbishop of Paris celebrated
mass at the Tuileries; the Bishop of Versailles, in
the presence of the authorities, solemnly consecrated
the chapel of the School of Saint Cyr; and advantage
was taken of the moment to inaugurate a monument,
already constructed, to Madame de Maintenon, with
this pious inscription: —

> She established Saint Cyr, to the edification of France;
> Her tomb was destroyed, her corpse insulted.
> Youth laments this, and gratitude
> Raises a new tomb to her avenged shade.

The clergy harmonized with the government; and
the First Consul presented to a number of bishops
an episcopal ring, in token of his satisfaction with
the return of peace.

Chateaubriand's "Genius of Christianity" appeared

at the moment when the Concordat was announced, and, as M. de Villemain has said, " No book has ever appeared at a happier moment, or was ever helped by more varied influences, by the political situation, by blind faith, by interest, or by more conflicting passions." Later, in his edition of 1828, he said, " The 'Genius of Christianity' was full of the spirit of the old monarchy; the legitimate heir lay, so to speak, beneath the sanctuary, the veil· of which I lifted, and the crown of Saint Louis hung above the altar of the God of Saint Louis." This phrase did very well for the reign of Charles X., but certainly Chateaubriand would not have written it in 1802 or 1803. Then, he dedicated his book to Bonaparte, and to Bonaparte he addressed this enthusiastic eulogy : " In your destiny we see the hand of Providence, who had chosen you from afar for the accomplishment of his mighty plans. Whole peoples are regarding you ; France, augmented by your victories, has placed its hope in you, since it is on religion that you establish the State and your own prosperity. Continue to hold out a helping hand to thirty million of Christians who pray for you at the foot of the altars you have restored to them." Bonaparte said that he had never been better praised.

So the First Consul appeared to France and to Europe in the light of the protector and restorer of religion; but, strangely enough, at the moment when he was so much occupied with matters of the Church, talked theology like a doctor, and was trying to give

peace to men's consciences, he made no attempt to
bring his own situation into conformity with the rules
of the Church, and notwithstanding his wife's earnest
solicitations, his marriage continued to be merely a
civil one. While Josephine appeared with the majesty of a queen in the roodloft of Notre Dame, she
was, from a religious point of view, not his legal
wife. Does not this state of affairs show the con-
fusion which the Revolution had wrought, and the
very strange anomalies resulting from it? Madame
Bonaparte was not very pious, but she was not without religious feeling; and she suffered as a Christian
and a woman. The ceremony at Notre Dame, recalling, as it did, the memories of her happy infancy,
filled her with apprehensions regarding her present
situation, which seemed so enviable.

XIV.

AT the present time the Faubourg Saint Germain has lost its ancient character. Its famous mansions have disappeared; boulevards run through it in every direction. The great families who used to control it have made numerous alliances with the middle classes. They have broken away from their traditions by giving allegiance to Napoleon I., to Louis Philippe, and to Napoleon III., and with their prejudices they have lost the feeling of caste which was their strength and their pride.

At the beginning of the century, the French nobility presented a very different aspect. It remained standing on a heap of ruins. But a few years separated it from the period of its greatest prosperity and splendor, and it had shown abundant energy amid the catastrophes and terrible trials it had passed through. As General de Ségur has put it, what other body, attacked in the same way, beaten and scattered, could have shown itself so compact, so persistent in its sentiments, and have displayed an equally firm resistance to such misfortunes?

178

To return home under false names or with false passports, to be obliged to solicit repeatedly the removal of their names from the list of émigrés, to find their houses and lands in the possession of strangers, to pass every day the spot where their relatives and friends had been put to death, was surely a sad fate. But the nobles, if they were unhappy, did not think themselves humiliated. Their sufferings raised them in their own estimation. Their magnificent mansions in the Faubourg Saint Germain no longer belonged to them, but they were uninjured, and every one pointed them out as the property of their old owners. Always proud and convinced of their rights, they regarded the Revolution as a passing evil, and the purchasers of the national property as thieves. They said that their emigration, so far from being a crime, had been their only safety; and they added that if those who left had been robbed, those who stayed at home had been put to death. As to the words liberty, the rights of the people, they only sneered at them, and all the more because the government treated as fanatics the men who still fanned the passions of the Revolution.

Unable to use their swords or their rapiers, the émigrés returned to France, with sarcasm on their lips, and avenged the work of the executioner's axe by their dexterity with a light but deadly weapon, — ridicule. Ruined as they were, they yet preserved in their distress the privilege of setting the fashion. They ironically compared the rude ways of the new men with the graceful and delicate manners of the old régime, and pursued with their jests the Turcarets of the Revolution, the upstarts, the men who, to employ Talleyrand's expression, did not know how to walk on a waxed floor. The First Consul and the army itself were not spared in their sarcasm. In their eyes, as General de Ségur said, the immortal exploits of the Republican soldiers were nothing but triumphs of brute force, a sort of savage, false, illegitimate glory, a usurpation of old and imprescriptible rights. "Such," he adds, "were the perfectly natural feelings of the survivors of this cruelly decimated class. Their influence was diminished, but they preserved the feeling of caste which is the most persistent and the most powerful of all forms of party-spirit; for family and social relations, hereditary habits of rule, and a sensitive regard for points of honor, pride, and pretensions to exclusiveness, become a second nature, composed of all the interests and all the passions which most surely control men's hearts."

In spite of their haughtiness, the émigrés were obliged to draw nearer and nearer to Bonaparte; but in 1802 they contented themselves with paying their court to Josephine, in obtaining through her the restitution of all or part of their property, or permission for a relation or friend to return to France. Women like to protect, and to confer rather than receive a kindness. It was with keen pleasure that Josephine found herself sought after by people of the old régime, who still refused to bow before her hus-

band, and who used to come to call on her in the
morning, in her apartment on the ground floor of the
Tuileries, at the same time boasting that they had
never set foot on the grand staircase of the palace.
These delicate distinctions are amusing, and it was
clear to every intelligent observer that the nobility
was anxious to move slowly, but that soon it would
be very glad to appear in the rooms of the powerful
dispenser of places' and wealth.   Bonaparte might
have taken umbrage at the attitude of these people,
who undertook to draw a line between his wife and
him ; but he knew men, and he foresaw all the flattery and obsequiousness of the Empire after the
Concordat.   Already men of the most diverse parties
met within the walls of the Tuileries, on the ground
floor, — the members of the old régime, the great lords
and fine ladies of the court of Versailles ; on the first
floor, the generals, the ministers, the members of the
Convention, the men of the Revolution.   The time
was drawing near when they all were to meet in the
same vestibule and ascend the same staircase.   Bonaparte was convinced that soon he should be able to
mingle in his palace marquises with regicides, and
establish a rivalry of interested homage and flattery
to be rewarded by gold and honors.   Hence he permitted Josephine to pass her time with Royalists,
and congratulated himself on this aid to his plans of
fusion and unity.

In fact, there were two men in Bonaparte, — the
aristocrat and the democrat.   By birth, education, and

his start in the army, he was an aristocrat; later, he became a democrat, more from policy than from conviction; and if not really, at least apparently, he had identified himself with the most ardent Republican enthusiasm. This double nature betrayed itself in his words and his deeds. Jacobins and Royalists were successively the object of his anger. The Legitimists filled him alternately with sympathy and with contempt. In the presence of great nobles he remembered his coat-of-arms; when with his soldiers, he used to say, "My nobility dates from Arcole and Marengo." In his heart he dreaded the Bourbons, and had an instinctive fear of their return. The former royal pupil, the officer of the armies of his very Christian Majesty, recalled the white flag amid the triumphs of the tricolor. Louis XVIII., forgotten, poor, abandoned, as he was, disturbed him; and the omnipotent First Consul would have gladly treated with this Pretender, whose only weapon was a principle. He was proud of his relations with the Bourbon monarchies of Spain and Naples, and he was flattered by the thought that he had set a descendant of Henry IV. and Louis XIV. on the throne of Etruria. Just as a tribune often exults in the conquest of a great lady, so this Republican general gloried in his victory over the French nobility.

Yet there were in the Faubourg Saint Germain many causes of uneasiness. If he was less in awe of the men because he could readily punish them, he feared the women, for they could more easily defy his power. An outbreak would not have disturbed him, but the opposition of a drawing-room was a more serious matter. He stood more in fear of a woman of character like Madame de Staël than of a legion of demagogues. A thousand swords were less alarming than one fan. Already he had a close watch kept on the few newly opened drawing-rooms of the Faubourg Saint Germain, notably on that of the Duchess of Luynes, whose husband, a few years later, gladly received his nomination as senator.

As for Josephine, she was never more at her ease than in the society of the émigrés, for with them she felt a harmony of ideas and hopes. She liked their manners, their language, even their prejudices. She was flattered by their respect and devotion, and felt herself rehabilitated in the eyes of good society by her sympathy with the adherents of the white flag. Thiers has said that she ought rather to have crushed them beneath the weight of her pride; but how could she have done this when she had shared their feelings, their grief, their sufferings, and but for the 9th Thermidor would have died on the guillotine?

The Legitimist opinions of the former Viscountess of Beauharnais were at once a matter of feeling and of calculation. By her childish and youthful memories, by the horror with which the crimes of the Revolution filled her, by the terror she had felt of perishing on the guillotine like her first husband, Josephine was a Royalist. In her mind all authority other than that of a king was, if not precisely usurpation, at any rate a perilous risk. A Monk seemed to her greater than a Cromwell, or even than a Cæsar. She would have been delighted to be the wife of a Constable and to become a Duchess by the will of Louis XVIII. A stool would have pleased her better than a throne, because she thought a stool firm, and a throne frail. As the wife of a Constable, and a Duchess, she felt that she would be in no danger of divorce, and she would not be told that since she gave her husband no heir, she was imperilling the future security of France. She would not be tormented by all sorts of dynastic ideas and by family rivalries which her adversaries encouraged in order to ruin her. She would not fear attempts like the plot of the infernal machine; the priests would give their blessing to her marriage, and before God and man she would enjoy in peace her husband's glory and a position safe from all perils of war and revolution. Hence she yearned to see her husband restore legitimacy as he had already restored religion.

Bourrienne said in his Memoirs: " Under the consular government, the Royalist committee was not in a state of active conspiracy; it confined itself rather, if I may say so, to persuasion. All its efforts tended to the circumvention of the persons who were supposed to have the most influence with the First Consul, in the hope of inducing him to desire the return of the Bourbons. It was especially against Madame Bonaparte that the batteries were directed." The émigrés knew Josephine's character, and they

appealed in turn to her vanity, her feelings, her interest, and her imagination. They told her that by
persuading her husband to bring back the King she
would do a great deed, that she would be the protect-
ress, the guardian angel, of the heir of Saint Louis;
that the throne and the altar would owe her everything, that she would place on her head an undying
aureole, and that Bonaparte would be the greatest of
men. Lamartine expressed the same thought in his
celebrated ode.

Josephine lent a ready ear to these persuasions,
but Bonaparte laughed in his sleeve at those simple
beings who fancied that a man of his character would
be contented with the second place. He had, moreover, arranged a plan for controlling the nobility.
As Madame de Staël has said, he took good care not
to put an end to the uncertainty of the émigrés by
laws defining their privileges. "He restored one
man to his property; from another he took them for
all time. A decision in the restoration of estates
reduced one to poverty, while to another it gave
even more than he had owned. Sometimes he gave
the property of a father to a son, that of an elder
brother to a younger brother, in accordance with his
confidence in their devotion to his person. He made
his favor of importance, not for any frivolous pleasure
it might give, but for the hope of seeing one's country
again, and of recovering at least a part of one's possessions. The First Consul had reserved to himself
the power of disposing on any pretext of the fate
of all and each."

The Senatus-consultum of April.26, 1802, had, it is true, proclaimed an amnesty to the émigrés; but an exception was made against those who had accepted positions in hostile armies, or who had remained in the service of French princes, as well as against the ecclesiastics who had refused to tender the resignation required by the Pope. The same act had guaranteed the national property to its purchasers. But a question had arisen in respect to the property of émigrés, which had not been sold after confiscation, and remained intact in the hands of the government. To this class belonged a quantity of woods and forests of enormous value. It was decided that these unsold properties, instead of returning to their owners, should vest in the State. It was by restoring or keeping them, as he might choose, that Napoleon did what he pleased with the French nobility. The nobles who submitted to his government were enriched; the others remained poor. This result accorded with his general policy. He protected the Faubourg Saint Germain, a school for his chamberlains. He was aristocratic and religious, but in order to control the aristocracy and the clergy. He was a monarchist, but on one condition — that he should be the monarch.

XV.

THE END OF THE TEMPORARY CONSULATE.

IT is not Bonaparte who courted Fortune; it is rather she that made all the advances and yielded to him. He sneered at the hot demagogues who so speedily abjured their political principles, and it was with malicious satisfaction that he said to Bourrienne, " All my virtuous Republicans have only to put a little gold lace on their coats, and then they are my men." Everything was ready for the rule of the new Cæsar. He made a pretence of refusing the diadem, and said at a reception, to a deputation of the Tribunate, May 7, 1802, " I desire no other reward than the love of my fellow-citizens. . . . Death itself will have no terrors for me, if my last looks may see the happiness of the Republic as secure as its glory." Would not one who heard him imagine that he was making a sacrifice in assuming the supreme power? The Republic, which was so sincerely loved by the army, which had called forth such generous devotion, so many heroic efforts, on the field of battle, now existed only in name. Bonaparte was a real monarch, absolute and acknowledged. With more justice than

Louis XIV. — for since the day of that King centralization, the great force of absolute power, had made enormous advances — he could say, "The State, it is I."

The senators, whose servility was to weary him as that of the senators of ancient Rome wearied Tiberius, were eager to know his secret heart. What did he want? A prolongation of his powers? Consulate for life? A king's crown? An emperor's diadém? He had but to say the word, and it would be the law of France. Since he affected a modesty which was far from his thoughts, the Senate decided to win his gratitude by prolonging his powers for ten years, and he pretended to accept this offer most thankfully. In reality, however, he could not understand their want of perspicacity, unimportant as it was; for their decision was made May 8, and two days later the Council of State, paying it no attention, declared that the French people should be consulted on this question: "Shall the First Consul be made Consul for life?" Any offence that the Senate might take with such a procedure was to be allayed by sending to that body the results of the voting. It should have the pleasure of announcing the issue of the plebiscite — what more could it ask?

Bourrienne tells us that when all was completed for the Consulate for life, except the voting, which could have but one result, Bonaparte went to Malmaison the middle of May to spend a few days. "That was his habit," adds his secretary, "after any

event outside of the usual course of government.
There he used to reflect on what he had done; and
since, in some mysterious way, his boldest acts were
always crowned by success, he acquired more confidence in his good fortune and became more enthusiastic in the sort of worship he offered to audacity. So
long as he was moved by passion, he saw only the end;
but that once reached, he examined all the obstacles
he might have met." Now when he was about to
obtain the Consulate for life, which he had so ar-
dently desired because it seemed to him the only
step yet to be taken before ascending the throne, he
strolled through the paths of Malmaison, thinking of
the incredible results which justified his dreams. In
this moment of pride and omnipotence, we must believe that his mind was haunted by the vision of the
legitimate monarchy. Louis XVIII., without a treas-
ury, without an army, without resources of any sort,
the importunate and despised guest of the crowned
heads of Europe, made him uneasy. He would have
paid enormous sums, have made the greatest sacrifices, to get from this Pretender the renunciation
of rights which seemed to him formidable, as if he
already had a presentiment of 1814 and 1815. The
head of the house of Bourbon had written to him,
September 7, 1800: "We can assure the peace of
France. I say *we*, because I need Bonaparte for
that; and he, too, cannot do it without me." And
to this Bonaparte had replied: "Sir, I have received
your letter. I thank you for the kind things you

say. You ought not to wish to return to France;
you would have to step on half a million corpses.
Sacrifice your own interest to the peace of France;
history will give you credit for it. I am not insensible to the misfortunes of your family. I will gladly
contribute to the easing and soothing of your retire-
ment." But in spite of addressing the descendant
of Louis XIV. simply as sir, and of his protecting
tone to the heir of so long a line of kings, he was at
heart annoyed by the existence of this exile. This
is clearly shown in the following conversation between the First Consul and his secretary in the park
of Malmaison in May, 1802: " 'Bourrienne, do you
think that the Pretender to the crown of France
would give up his rights, if I were to offer him a
large indemnity, or even a province in Italy?' 'I
don't think he would. In fact, it is extremely un-
likely that the Bourbons will come back into France
so long as you are the head of the government, but
they must regard their return as probable.' 'Why
so?' 'The reason is simple. Don't you see every
day how your prefects conceal the truth from you,
and flatter your wishes, in order to get influence over
you? and are you not angry when at last you get at
the truth?' 'Well?' 'Well, it must be just the
same with the agents of Louis XVIII. in France. It
is in the order of things and in human nature, that
they encourage the Bourbons with the hope of a return, if for nothing else, to show their skill and use-
fulness.' 'That is true. But don't be uneasy; I am

not afraid of them. Yet there may be something to do about it. I shall think of it; we shall see.'"

Meanwhile Josephine was in serious distress. She remembered not without alarm the prediction of a sorceress: "You will sit on a throne, but not for long," and the height she reached made her uneasy. In May, 1802, she said to a Councillor of State: "I do not approve all the plans that are projected, and I said as much to Bonaparte, who listened attentively to me, but his flatterers soon made him change his mind. The generals say that they did not fight against the Bourbons to set up a family of Bonapartes in their place. I do not regret that I have given no children to my husband, for I should tremble for their fate. I shall remain devoted to Bonaparte's destiny, however perilous it may be, so long as he has the regard and friendship for me which he has always shown. But the day he changes, I shall withdraw from the Tuileries." As Thibaudeau has said in his Memoirs: "In France and in Europe everything conspired for the sacrifice of the rights of the people in favor of the First Consul. At court one woman still resisted the mighty current; she alone was not blinded by all the illusions of greatness. She was incessantly pursued by the wildest alarm and the gloomiest forebodings. Indeed, Madame Bonaparte perhaps foresaw her fall in her husband's elevation to the throne; but a delicate instinct, which in women often takes the place of perspicacity, prevented her seeing without horror a man reigning over the ruins of the Republic who owed to the Republic his greatness and glory."

Amid the obsequious senators who were busily flattering the new Cæsar, Josephine perhaps feared the dagger of a Brutus. Saint Cloud, to which she was soon to move, was not an agreeable place for her, and she regretted leaving that charming spot for new palaces and castles full of gloomy memories. Had not Saint Cloud brought unhappiness to Henry III., to Henrietta of England, to Marie Antoinette? And why should she assume a crown? Josephine said to Rœderer, " Bonaparte's true enemies are those who fill him with ideas of a dynasty, of hereditary succession, of divorce, and a second marriage." She was as modest and disinterested as Bonaparte's sisters were haughty and ambitious; in her heart there was no place for anger or pride. The part she played was not that of a Lady Macbeth; for a year and a half she had been entreating her husband not to let himself be tempted by the crown. At first he had reassured her; and once when towards the end of 1800 she sat in his lap, and said tenderly, " I beg of you, Bonaparte, don't be King," he answered, laughing, " You are absurd, Josephine. It's all those old dowagers of the Faubourg Saint Germain, and especially Madame de La Rochefoucauld, who got up those stories; you tire me, leave me alone." But she had not influence enough to stem the course of destiny, to stop the chariot of the triumphant hero. Bonaparte thought that the duty of a woman was to spin and knit, and he sent her to her domestic cares, while he went on in his proud and victorious career. Fouché, who was stoutly opposed to these monarchical plans, said to her: "Madame, keep quiet. You will only annoy your husband, to no purpose. He will be Life Consul, King, or Emperor, — whatever any one can be. Your timidity wearies him; your advice wounds him. Let us stay in our place, let things happen which neither you nor I can prevent."

How slight is human wisdom, and how right Persius was when he exclaimed, "Oh, the cares of men, and the emptiness of things!" (*O curas hominum, O quantum est in rebus inane!*)

Bonaparte's fame exceeded that of the greatest. France was at his feet; he called forth from the whole world a long cry of surprise and admiration, and yet he did not suspect with what truth he answered in a somewhat melancholy train the congratulations of the senators. "Fortune has smiled upon the Republic, but Fortune is fickle, and how many men on whom she has heaped favors have lived a few years too long! The interest of my glory and that of my happiness would seem to have marked the limit of my public life." These words are very touching. Let us imagine Bonaparte dying as he uttered them. What a flawless hero! what incomparable glory! No murder of the Duke of Enghien! No war with Spain! No retreat from Russia! No continental blockade, resulting in the English control; no persecution of the Pope, ending

in the triumphal entry of the Sovereign Pontiff into
the eternal city; no seas of blood turned out, not for
the aggrandizement of France, but, alas! for its
diminution; no invectives, no imprecations, no flight
in the disguise of an Austrian officer; no foreigners
encamped in Bois de Boulogne or on the hill of
Montmartre; no Waterloo, no Saint Helena; but
France all-powerful, invincible, defying the jealousy
of the kings of Europe, and amid a glorious peace in
enjoyment of its natural frontiers, — that is what
would have happened if this man, who was looked
upon as indispensable, had died at the dawn of his
power and glory. I well remember the closing lines
of the " King Œdipus " of Sophocles: —

> From hence the lesson learn ye,
> To reckon no man happy till ye witness
> The closing day; until he pass the border
> Which severs life from death, unscathed by sorrow.

But in 1802 who could predict 1812, 1814, 1815,
1821? Bonaparte was illustrious; his retinue more
magnificent than that of the former kings. His colleagues, the other Consuls, did not dare sit in the
same carriage. When he went to preside at the
Senate, he was alone, majestic in a state carriage
drawn by eight horses. He breathed an odor of
incense which intoxicated him. Joyous and triumphant, he declared that " the liberty, the equality,
the prosperity of France, shall be secure from the
caprices of fate and the uncertainty of the future;

that the best of people shall be the happiest, as it deserves; and that he, satisfied with being called by order of those from whom all power emanates, to restore justice, order, and equality, will see the approach of his last hour without regret and without fear of future generations." Henceforth he is called by that magic name, Napoleon! He chooses for his festival the festival of the Virgin Mary, as if he wished his glory to gain some of the splendor of the Queen of Heaven, and to be a sort of Assumption. August 15, 1802, he let his star shine above the towers of Notre Dame, forty feet above the two platforms. In the middle of this symbolic illumination shone the sign of the Zodiac, under which is the birthday of this predestined man, and all night his bright star shone over the buildings of the great capital.

PART II.

THE CONSULATE FOR LIFE.

I.

THE PALACE OF SAINT CLOUD

RUINS seen by moonlight or in the dim light of a dark, rainy winter day, are perhaps less sad than when seen embowered in green at the dawn of a bright day. Then it seems as if nature, in its serene calm, was smiling at men's vain plans, and protesting in its immortal majesty against their follies and their miseries. This is what I felt August 15 last. The weather was superb, the sun magnificent, the sky without a cloud. I had decided to walk out to Saint Cloud, and I remembered that it was there where long ago the 15th of August was the ruler's holiday. At that time the courtyard of the palace was full of fine carriages adorned with coats-of-arms; powdered lackeys were running about; valuable horses were pawing the ground; and within the palace there was a continual coming and going of officers, diplomatists, chamberlains, equerries, and officials, all brilliant in uniforms and decorations. In the evening the palace and the park were illuminated; at a distance lay the great capital, like a giant sunk in floods of light. There was no lack of protestations

of devotion, of flattering speeches so ingenious that
they seemed sincere; for there are many who know
how to give to the wiles of ambition and interest the
appearance of a natural expression.

All is changed within a very few years. Who
thinks now of the Emperor's festival? Two or three
hired carriages brought to the palace gate a handful
of foreigners, of tourists, who, guidebook in hand, and
a field-glass over their shoulder, came to look, with
perhaps more scorn than pity, at the ruins which bear
witness of our misfortunes and our discords. At a
distance, there is a certain illusion about the palace;
a nearsighted man would never suspect the ravages
of fire and petroleum. But what a sight greets one
on getting near the red and damaged walls! One of
the guards uttered some sad reflections on this mansion which he had seen so magnificent and which is
to-day so gloomy and so devastated: it is the difference between a woman brilliant with youth, beauty,
glory, and the skeleton of the same woman. One
would say that buildings really have a soul, and that
when they are a mere stone corpse, their soul yet survives. Ruins call forth the same thoughts as a
tomb.

The park is as fine as ever; the old trees are as
majestic, the flower-beds as lovely, the turf as green,
the shrubs as delicious, the waterfalls as musical, as
in other days. The birds still sing; but one misses
the music of the bands, the bugle-calls, and the roll-
ing of the drums.

I sat down on a stone bench and thought of all that had taken place in the palace in ruins before me. In the full blaze of noonday the phantoms of the past appeared as if it were black midnight. I thought of Henrietta of England, who was so rich in graces, and died, "like the flower of the field," in the night of June 30, 1670, "a disastrous, a terrible night, when suddenly there came, with a burst like a clap of thunder, this astounding news: Madame is dying, Madame is dead." Seven years later there is a great festival at Saint Cloud, October 10, 1677; the Great King is received by his brother with extraordinary solemnity, at the inauguration of the Gallery of Apollo, decorated by Mignard.

Towards the end of the next century Marie Antoinette visited Saint Cloud in the summer of 1790. It was a moment of rest before the last march to the grave, and then this charming woman bade farewell to the flowers, the country, the natural scenery which she loved so much. I recalled the sole interview between the Martyr Queen and Mirabeau; it took place July 3, 1790, in the park, at the circle in the top of the Queen's private garden. It was a memorable meeting between a man of such marvellous genius and eloquence and a woman of her station and beauty. I fancied that I heard him, as he left her presence, saying in an outburst of enthusiasm, "Madame, the monarchy is saved."

Then there was Saint Cloud on the 19th Brumaire, year **VIII.** The Council of the Ancients was sitting in the Gallery of Apollo, and the Five Hundred in the orange-house. I recalled Bonaparte saying to the Ancients: "Remember that I am supported by Fortune and the God of War." Then I saw him in the orange-house, threatened by daggers, pursued with imprecations. I saw the grenadiers invading the hall, and I heard the roar of the drum drowning the voices of the representatives of the people, as it drowned that of Louis XVI. Where now is the orange-house where took place the scene which settled the fate of France? The guard told me that it was situated where the flower-beds now are, on the right of the palace. But it was destroyed a few years ago, and not the least trace of it is left.

It was in the Gallery of Apollo that the First Empire was proclaimed in 1804, and in the same gallery the Second Empire was proclaimed forty-eight years later. After Waterloo, Blücher slept at Saint Cloud, in Napoleon's bedroom. He lay there, all dressed, amusing himself by dirtying with his boots the bedclothes and curtains of his old conqueror. It was in the red drawing-room that the surrender of Paris was signed in 1815; and in the same room, July 25, 1830, Charles X. and his unwise ministers signed the fatal orders. July 27 the old King was quietly playing whist in the drawing-room which looks out on the main courtyard, and from which Paris may be seen on the horizon. From one of the windows a servant saw a distant fire. It was the guardhouse of the Place de la Bourse that was burn-

ing. The servant called the attention of one of the
gentlemen in waiting to the smoke and flame. He
went up to the King; but since Charles X., although
he had been told of the troubles that had broken out,
went on quietly with his game, the gentleman did
not dare to break the rules of etiquette by addressing
him. That same evening, M. de Sémonville said to
the old King, " Sire, if your Majesty does not revoke
the orders, if there is no change of ministry, to-morrow perhaps there will be no king, or dauphin, or
Duke of Bordeaux." " I don't agree with you,"
answered Charles X. " My brother, Louis XVI.,
perished by weakness. At any rate, I am ready to
appear before my God." July 30 the legitimate
kingdom had ceased to exist. The Duke of Ragusa
arrived in consternation at Saint Cloud. " Sire," said
he, " the battle is lost. A ball intended for me killed
the horse of an officer at my side. I should prefer
death to the sad sight I have just witnessed." That
same evening the Duke of Angoulême, by advice
of the generals, who all declared that they could
not be responsible for the safety of the royal family,
had the King awakened from sound slumbers. The
brother of Louis XVI. got up, and sadly left Saint
Cloud with his unhappy family, to depart for his
last exile.

The palace knew brilliant days under the Second
Empire. There was a succession of royal guests and
of magnificent entertainments. The bed-chamber of
Marie Antoinette, of Josephine, of Marie Louise, of

the Duchess of Angoulême, became the ministers' council-hall. Louis Philippe's study became the chamber of the Empress Eugenie. The young Prince Imperial had the rooms on the ground floor which were formerly occupied by the King of Rome, by the Count of Artois, the Duchess of Berry, and by Madame Adelaide. From it the King of Rome used to start in his gilded carriage, drawn by two white sheep. Saint Cloud was the favorite resort of Napoleon III. Thither he returned July 16, 1859, after the Italian campaign, and thence he departed for the fatal war with Germany. It was from Saint Cloud that, on the 9th of May, 1812, Napoleon I., amid the great men of his court, like Darius among his satraps, started in great pomp for a no less unfortunate war — that with Russia. The departure of Napoleon III., July 28, 1870, was much more modest. His proclamations were stamped with melancholy, as if he wished to warn the nation by calming its frenzy rather than by adding to it. An ovation was promised him if he would go through Paris, but he refused. Even before the conflict began he was overwhelmed by a sort of prophetic depression. In 1859 he started solemnly for the war, amid the excited transports of the multitude, but then he had confidence in his star; in 1870 this trust had vanished. He went, pursued by presentiments which, however mournful they may have been, were outdone by the reality. In going by rail on the right bank from Paris to Versailles, there is to be seen on the left, in the park of Saint

Cloud, a little rustic rotunda close to the line. There it was that, July 28, 1870, at ten o'clock in the morning, the unfortunate Emperor and the Prince Imperial got into the train which took them straight to Metz. Would not one say that they were the victims of a real fate?

During the siege, the National Guards upon the ramparts saw on the horizon a large fire; it was the palace of Saint Cloud, burning like a woodpile. Some say it was ignited by shells from Mont Valérien, and others maintain that it was drenched with petroleum by the Germans and burned by them. This unfortunate palace could not be saved by the proud motto of the brother of Louis XIV., *Alter post fulmina terror*, or by the poetic reminiscences of Marie Antoinette, or by the legendary greatness of the Empire. Thus perished so much grandeur. It is written in letters of fire, like those of Belshazzar's feast. The Gallery of Apollo, all resplendent with gold, the mythological decorations, the frescoes of Mignard, — all these wonders perished in the fiery furnace. The sky was as red as blood. The whole hill which overhangs the left bank of the Seine, and is surmounted by the lofty trees of the park, from the palace to the rising ground of Sèvres, is lit by the flames, and this fire is but the forerunner of others still more lamentable, because they were lit, not by German, but by French hands.

All these various visions passed before my eyes like the scenes of a play, now bright, now gloomy, and I felt myself distressed by this multitude. Now

it may be worth while to see what it is under the
Consulate. The Saint Cloud we have to study is
the Saint Cloud of 1802, of 1803, of 1804, in all its
majesty, the abode of power and glory. Bonaparte
had just been elected Consul for life by 3,568,885
votes out of 3,577,259. The Senate had presented
him with its expression of "the confidence, the admiration, and the love of the French people." That
is the official language. A statue of Peace had been
erected, holding in one hand the laurel wreath of the
victor, and in the other the decree of the Senate,
bearing witness to posterity of the nation's gratitude.

Saint Cloud was the summer residence of the new
sovereign; for what other name can be given to a
ruler whose powers are for life, and who has the right
of appointing his successor to suit himself? The
former monarchs had no such power, for they had to
accept for heir the man born to the throne. Malmaison was a private castle; Saint Cloud a royal one, in
which all the pomp of a monarchy could be displayed.
The staircase was in the middle of the castle as one
enters from the central court; it was adorned with
marble columns, and built by Micque, Marie Antoinette's architect. Up one flight was the main hall
with its painted ceiling on which was History writing
the life of the brother of Louis XIV. A door to the
right led into the room of Mars, an anteroom of the
Gallery of Apollo. The roof, the covings, and the
space over the doors of the hall of Mars were decorated
by Mignard, as was also the Gallery of Apollo. Over

the entrance was the birth of Apollo and Diana; in the middle of the arch, Apollo, the god of day, driving his chariot; to the right and left were the four seasons; and at the end of the gallery, above the windows, was Parnassus. Gilding, pictures, flowers, allegorical figures, medallions in bronze and cameo, and other works of art completed the wonderful decoration of this beautiful gallery. At the end was the door into the room of Diana, where Mignard had painted his masterpieces. On the ceiling the goddess of night; in the covings the toilette, the hunt, the bath, and the sleep of the huntress Diana. Returning through the Gallery of Apollo and the room of Mars, we entered the room of Venus, where Lemoyne had painted on the ceiling Juno borrowing the cestus of the Queen of Love; beyond was the room of Truth, so called from a ceiling-picture of that goddess, painted by Antoine Coypel; further still were the rooms of Mercury and of Aurora, likewise adorned with allegorical paintings.

All these majestic halls, with their mythological names and decorations, appealed to Bonaparte's southern imagination and recalled the familiar reminiscences of pagan antiquity. He liked to go through the brilliant Gallery of Apollo, which had brought him good luck on the 19th Brumaire, and which was for Saint Cloud what the Gallery of Mirrors is for Versailles. It was thickly crowded every Sunday after mass — cardinals, bishops, senators, councillors of state, deputies, tribunes, generals, am-

bassadors, magistrates, Royalists, Republicans, all the
most distinguished French citizens, as well as foreigners were there together, and on an equal footing.
The First Consul spoke to almost every one, and
often their private affairs were discussed. The most
astute confined themselves to paying their court to
him. Then they went to Madame Bonaparte, who
had taken the apartment of Marie Antoinette in the
left wing. The most distinguished foreign ladies
were presented to her, among whom were the Zamo-
ïskas, the Potockas, the Castel-Fortes, the Dorsets,
the Gordons, the Newcastles, the Dolgoroukis, the
Galitzines. When Bonaparte permitted the members of the Diplomatic Body to pay their homage to
him, had he not the airs and language of a monarch? And did not Josephine receive like a queen
or empress?

From that time a rigid etiquette prevailed at Saint
Cloud. General Duroc, the governor of the palace,
maintained a table for the officers and ladies-in-waiting and for the aides. The First Consul dined alone
with his wife, but twice a week he invited officials to
his table. The military household consisted of four
generals in command of the Consular Guard,— Generals Lannes, Bessières, Davoust, and Soult; and
seven aides,— Colonels Lemarois, Caffarelli, Caulaincourt, Savary, Rapp, Fontanelli, and Captain Lebrun,
son of the Third Consul. There were four prefects of
the palace, — Messrs. de Luçay, de Rémusat, Didelot,
and de Cramayel; and four ladies of the palace, — Ma-

dame de Luçay, Madame de Talhouet, Madame de Rémusat, and Madame de Lauriston. The prefects of the palace had charge of the service, the etiquette, and the performances. The ladies had to be in waiting upon the wife of the First Consul and to make the presentations. There was so complete a return to the customs of the Court of Versailles that it was seriously proposed to require that powder should be worn by every one who came to the castle. But the First Consul could not bring himself to wearing it, and so every one was left free to do as he pleased about it. Every one was given to understand that the First Consul preferred to see powder and "bag-wig"; so most of the foreigners, and especially the English, who wore their hair short and without powder, used to attend his receptions with whitened hair and a bag fastened to their coat-collar.

The chapel at Saint Cloud was not unlike that at Versailles. Bonaparte required atheists to be present at mass on Sundays. I am reminded of what La Bruyère has said: "The great people of the nation meet at a certain hour in a temple which they call a church; at the end of the temple is an altar consecrated to their God. . . . The grandees form a large circle at the foot of this altar, and stand with their back to this altar, and the holy ministers with their faces turned towards their King, who is to be seen kneeling on a tribune, and to whom they seem to direct their attention and devotion. There is a sort of subjection in this custom, as if the people were adoring the King, and the King adoring God."

The appearance of the theatre which Bonaparte had built in 1803, beyond the orange-house, completes the resemblance to monarchical ways. No one can applaud or weep or laugh without the master's signal. The Diplomatic Body was formally invited to the representations. The First Consul sat in the front of a box on the right of the stage; behind him stood the aides and officers in waiting. Opposite was the box of Madame Bonaparte with her ladies. The other boxes in the first balcony were occupied by the members of his family, the ministers, the ambassadors, and their wives. Every one stood up when Bonaparte and Josephine came in and bowed to the audience. Sometimes the large door at the back, through which the scenery was brought in, would be thrown open, showing the brilliantly illuminated gardens.

The park of Saint Cloud, which is nearly a thousand acres in extent, is most beautiful with its venerable trees, its green turf, its picturesque eminences. The fountain rises eighty-eight feet; the arcades are of most graceful construction, and the celebrated cascades where the water falls down a series of high steps are most brilliant in the blazing sun or under the colored lights of an illumination. The lantern of Demosthenes, the little Greek building which used to stand on the highest point of the park, commanding a lovely view of the river below, was especially charming. It would have been hard to find a more beautiful view, a grander panorama. Obviously a place like this was full of attractions for the young enthusiastic officers in the suite of the First Consul, and everywhere he appeared as a sovereign who was also a general. All this display of grandeur had a military quality. He carried no sceptre, but something better, — his sword. The hero of the Pyramids is greater than the civil ruler; his glory outshines his rank.

Bonaparte's working-room at Saint Cloud was a large room, lined with books from floor to ceiling. There he used to sit on a small sofa covered with green watered-silk, near the fireplace, above which were placed two bronze busts of Scipio and Hannibal. Behind the sofa, in the corner, was the desk of Méne-val, his secretary, who had taken Bourrienne's place By the side of this room was a little drawing-room where the First Consul used to receive Talleyrand, his Minister of Foreign Affairs, and where he gave private audiences. In this drawing-room he had placed a portrait of Gustavus Adolphus, his favorite hero. The only ornament in his bedroom on the ground floor, commanding a view of the garden, was an antique bust of Cæsar.

Bonaparte understood how to satisfy his visitors with a word or a smile. In the Memoirs of General de Ségur is a good description of those glorious days at Saint Cloud. Ségur had at first been opposed to Bonaparte, from his feeling of caste and his devotion to the Republic. On the day of the *Te Deum* on account of the Concordat, he had been one of the band of discontented officers; but the hero of Marengo said a few kind words to him and he was at once overwhelmed with happiness and enthusiasm.

"Citizen Ségur," Bonaparte began, with a loud voice, in the Gallery of Apollo, among a number of senators, tribunes, legislators, and generals, "I have appointed you on my personal staff; your duty will be to command my body-guard. You see what confidence I place in you, you will deserve it; your ability and your worth promise swift promotion." Then he passed along the gallery, through the double line of courtiers, to the tribune in the chapel where he heard mass. Ségur was in an ecstasy. "Drunk with joy," he says, "and scarcely conscious of touching the earth, I hastened through the brilliant halls, and took possession of them. I returned and stopped at the place which I now see before me, where I had just heard those gratifying words; I paused and repeated them a hundred times. It seemed to me that they made me a partaker of .the glory of the conqueror of Italy, Egypt, and France. I do not know what was the real weather of that autumn day (October 27, 1802), but it remains in my memory as the brightest, most beautiful day of the year that I had yet seen."

All the contemporary writers describe this period as one of real enchantment. France is never so happy as when it is exultant with pride; no nation endures so ill misfortune or mediocrity. Nothing but the highest position will satisfy it. Bonaparte, who thoroughly understood the French character, ruled it through its vanity. He continually said, " You are the happiest, the best, the most famous, the greatest of nations !" And France believed him; for the country was like a beautiful woman gazing with rapture into a mirror. With this spirit in prosperity, there exists the impossibility of believing in the remotest chance of defeat; its self-confidence amounts to infatuation. What is true of the country is also true of Bonaparte after his election to the Consulate for life. He imagined himself faultless, infallible, invincible, and this confidence he communicated to others. Louis XIV. in all the brilliancy of his youth never received such adulation.

But twelve years later Saint Cloud presents a different spectacle. The Prussian horses are drinking in the waters of the park, which is converted into a camp, and invaded by a horde of foreigners. A pack of dogs which follows Blücher everywhere occupies and ruins the boudoir of the Empress Marie Louise. The books of the library are strewn helter-skelter over the floor. July 13, 1815, Prince Metternich wrote to his daughter: " I have dined with Blücher, who has his headquarters at Saint Cloud. He inhabits this castle as a general of hussars. He and his aides smoke where we have seen the court in its greatest splendor; I dined in the room where I have spent hours talking with Napoleon. The army-tailors are quartered where we used to see the plays, and the

musicians of a regiment of riflemen were catching the
goldfish in the large basin under the castle windows.
As I was going through the great gallery, the old
marshal said to me, ' What a fool the man must be to
go running off to Moscow when he had all these fine
things at home ! ' As I looked down from the balcony
at the great city, with all its domes shining at sunset,
I said to myself, ' This city and this sun will glow
like this when there is nothing remembered of Napoleon or of Blücher, and certainly nothing of me.'
The immutable laws of nature are always the same,
and we, poor creatures, who think so much of ourselves, live only to make a show by our perpetual
movement, by our dabbling in the mud or in the
quicksand."

Bossuet was right when he spoke of that "foolish
wisdom, ingenious in self-tormenting, skilful in self-
deceit, corrupt in the present, vain in the future,
which by much reasoning and vast efforts, only wastes
itself to no purpose, collecting things which the wind
scatters." When from the heights of Saint Cloud the
two Napoleons looked upon their fête-days at the
great capital all ablaze with illuminations, at the
Panthéon, Saint Sulpice, the Tuileries, the Louvre,
the bright dome of the Invalides, at the bursting fireworks, could they have anticipated the other flames
which a few years later were to destroy their two
palaces ? Nowhere is the emptiness of human glory
more strongly impressed upon the beholder than by
these ruins. Whenever the imagination is fascinated

by the splendor of imperial pomp, by the memory of so many victories, so many wonders, a hidden voice, like that of the slave in the ancient triumphs, seems to murmur those two names, Saint Cloud and the Tuileries.

II.

IN history, as in art, there is always infatuation
and fashion; and reputations, like the pictures
of the masters, rise or fall according to the time or
the circumstances. Glory is eclipsed, like the sun.
Napoleon who was perhaps more famous at the Restoration and during the reign of Louis Philippe than in
that of Napoleon III., now finds possibly more to condemn than to praise him. In the time of Louis XVIII.
and Charles X., the opposition, to whatever party
it belonged, made out of Napoleon's glory a weapon
against the Bourbons; and the most advanced liberals,
with an enthusiasm which was perhaps not quite sincere, chanted the praises of the new Cæsar. It was a
Republican poet, Béranger, who was the most popular
singer of an emperor, and in the days of July, it has
been said that there were as many Bonapartists as
Orleanists among the insurgents. Louis Philippe
felt bound to preserve the memories of the Empire
even in the palace of Louis XIV., and to place David's
picture of the coronation of Napoleon at the top of
the marble staircase. He sent his son, the Prince of

Joinville, to Saint Helena to bring back the ashes of the hero of Austerlitz. On the threshold of the Invalides, the Prince said to his father, " Sire, I present to you the body of Napoleon, which I have brought back to France in obedience to your orders." Louis Philippe answered, " I receive it in the name of France." Napoleon's sword was brought in on a cushion. The King took it from the hands of Marshal Soult and gave it to General Bertrand, the courtier of Saint Helena, saying, " General, I charge you with placing the glorious sword of the Emperor upon his coffin." It was then the fashion among liberals to hold to this conclusion of a history of Napoleon by Laurent de l'Ardèche, illustrated by Horace Vernet: " Yes, in spite of all the past, the people went back to him, and will always stay with him; yes, in spite of the attempted aristocratic reorganization, the crowned soldier will be to future generations what he was for contemporary monarchs, the terror of old Europe, the genius of the new France, the child of Democracy, the hero of the Revolution." Curiously enough, the four writers who have done the most for Napoleon's glory, did not belong to the party of the Empire, — Béranger, Victor Hugo, Thiers, and Chateaubriand.

To-day the dithyrambs are silent. The only man who in these later years has sung in epic form the giant of battles is Victor Hugo, and he did it in a book without mercy for the Emperor's successor, in the " Châtiments." But there was such secret affinity between the poet and the general, that in spite of himself he composed the most magnificent and most wonderful verse about Napoleon that was ever written.

Now, the critical, analytical spirit has succeeded to this lyrical fire. The popular songs are silent. No one sings in the streets the "Memories of the People," and the impartial judge tries to determine the truth between the dithyramb and the satire. Hence the moment is favorable for studying Napoleon's character, without fanaticism, without prejudice, calmly and loyally.

There are many ways of looking at a man; he changes with time; and the great fault of historians, when they have to judge a celebrated person, is, that they make but a single portrait, instead of a series, which to be true to the model ought to be unlike one another. The Count of Las Cases, in the "Memorial of Saint Helena," shows an exact image; but we cannot judge, from the Napoleon of 1816, of the Napoleons of earlier years. The Emperor, beaten, unhappy, a prisoner, became a great philosopher, under the lessons of an experience of human vicissitudes. He had no more exultations of pride, no more intoxication of power, no more clouds of incense. Purified, regenerated by misfortune, Napoleon improved morally, as he sank materially.

Nor must we confound the First Consul with the Emperor. The Empire is an exaggeration of the Consulate. It is as First Consul that we see Napoleon most truly himself, before he was caught in the tempest of war which ended by making him like a blind, unconscious force. Napoleon as Emperor assumes superhuman proportions, to say which, to my thinking, is far from praise. Amid the splendor of Imperialism he was so carried away and fascinated by his own glory, that he, so to speak, lost consciousness of his identity. Beneath the mantle of the sovereign one can scarcely hear the beating heart of the man. The hero's destiny is like a wonderful romance, which with its incidents plunges him into ecstatic surprise. He attains so lofty a height that we cannot understand why his head did not reel.

As Thiers has well said: "It is hard to detect kindness in a soldier forever occupied in strewing the world with corpses, friendship in a man who never had equals, honesty in a potentate who was master of the wealth of the world." We are about to study the Consul for life, and we shall consult the testimony of his contemporaries for answers to these questions: Was Napoleon a religious man? Had he a good heart? Had he intelligence? imagination? Was he a genius? We shall study the two sides of each question, summoning the witnesses for and against, who appear before the highest tribunal, the tribunal of history.

Was Napoleon a religious man? This is the testimony of Prince Metternich: "Napoleon was not irreligious in the ordinary sense of the word. He did not admit that there ever was a sincere atheist. As a Christian and a Catholic, it was to a genuine religion alone that he granted the right of governing human society. He looked upon Christianity as the basis of all real civilization, and on Catholicism as the most favorable, used for the maintenance of order and of the peace of the moral world. Protestantism he held to be a source of trouble and dissension. Indifferent himself to the rites of religion, he respected them too much to allow any ridicule of those who practised them. Possibly religion was with him less an affair of feeling than one of policy; but whatever may have been his secret thought, he never betrayed it."

For myself, I am inclined to believe that Napoleon's religion, however incomplete it may have been, was at least sincere. He had faith in God, and thought that Heaven had given him a mission to fulfil on earth. The Baron de Méneval says: "When he used to say that the bullet which was going to kill him had not yet been moulded, it was mere fatalism; he thought that his providential mission was not yet finished. When he wrote to the Directory that just when approaching Egypt he saw a ship which he thought belonged to the hostile fleet, and that he besought Fortune not to abandon him, but to grant him only five days, he mentally translated Fortune by an omnipotent Providence." He was not merely a deist and interested in spiritual things; he had Catholic feelings which were intimately connected with his infantile memories. Méneval says on this subject: "His habit of crossing himself mechanically

at the revelation of a great danger, on the discovery
of any important fact bearing on the interests of
France or his own plans, at the announcement of an
unexpected piece of news, good or bad, was not
merely a reminiscence of his early religious training,
but rather an expression of his feeling that to the
Author of all things he owed these favors or these
tidings. His expectation of aid from on high at the
decisive moment of a battle; his frequent allusions
in his talk, in his proclamations, in his bulletins, to
the sole Judge who holds in his hands the issues of
all events; the religious thoughts called up to his
mind at the sight of a church or at the sound of its
bell; his re-establishment of Catholicism in France;
his recourse to the consolations of religion in his last
moments, — all attest his faith in Providence."

Napoleon was not a devout Catholic. It cannot
be said that he was a believer, but still less that he
was an unbeliever; he doubted and hoped. Doubtless, if he had been a fervent Christian, he would
have hastened to have his marriage with Josephine
blessed by the Church, for during the Consulate it
was only a civil marriage; and he would have taken
communion, which he did not do. Yet, like many
men, he was at heart religious, although not practising the forms. The Voltairian spirit filled him with
repugnance, and he bowed before the cross with deep
respect. Under the Consulate political considerations
were superior to those of religion; but at Saint Helena,
face to face with death, the Christian reappeared,

and the conqueror of so many battles terminated his agitated career as a good Catholic. He piously received the consolations of religion, asking for all the usual Catholic rites at his funeral, and that he should lie in state in the dining-room in which he was accustomed to hear mass; and when Dr. Antomarchi smiled at hearing these instructions given to Abbé Vignale, Bonaparte said to him with some severity, "Young man, you are perhaps too intelligent to believe in God. I'm not like you. Not every one who wants to be is an atheist."

Was Napoleon kind? This is what Madame de Rémusat testifies as witness for the prosecution: "I ought now to speak of Napoleon's heart. If it is possible to believe that a being, in other respects like to ourselves, could yet be without this part of our organization which makes us require to love and to be loved, I should say that at his creation his heart was forgotten, or else that he succeeded in entirely silencing it. He always takes too much interest in himself to be controlled by any feeling of affection whatsoever. He almost ignores even the ties of blood, the rights of nature."

After Madame de Rémusat let us hear Prince Metternich, whose testimony inclines to neither side: "Napoleon had two forces. As a private citizen he was gentle and tractable, neither kind nor malicious. As a statesman, he was not moved by feeling; he decided without bias of love or hate. He crushed or removed his enemies, without consulting anything but necessity or interest. The end once attained, he forgot them."

So much for the testimony for the prosecution. Bourrienne who, perhaps in spite of himself, nourished a certain occult jealousy against his former college-comrade who had become the arbiter of Europe, does not hesitate to say: "Bonaparte was tender, kind, open to pity; he liked children very much, and wicked men seldom know that feeling. In his private life he was pleasant and indulgent to human weakness, which he knew and appreciated well. . . . Most men, he used to say, are weak, and deserve pity rather than hatred. They cannot be lifted up by overwhelming them with scorn; on the contrary, it is better to persuade them that they are better than they really are in order to get from them whatever they may be capable of."

After Bourrienne, let us call on his other secretary, Méneval: "Bonaparte seemed like a father in the midst of his family. His renunciation of greatness had an inexpressible charm. I could never get over my surprise at seeing the simple ways of a man who from afar appeared so imposing. I expected roughness and an uncertain temper; instead of that, I found Napoleon easy-going, not at all exacting, full of a sportive and sometimes boisterous gayety, and sometimes really delightful."

His aide, General Rapp, says: "No one was more constant in his affections than Napoleon. He loved his mother tenderly, he adored his wife, he was very fond of his brothers and sisters, and of all his relatives. All, except his mother, treated him most unkindly, but nevertheless he continually overwhelmed them with wealth and honors."

Napoleon's family feeling is undeniable.   Prince Metternich himself recognized it when he said: " A good son and a kind relative, with distinctions such as one often finds in middle-class Italian families, Napoleon endured the attacks of some of his family without exercising sufficient force of will to stop them, even when his interests required it.   His sisters, in particular, got from him whatever they wanted. Neither of his wives had occasion to complain of his treatment."   October 18, 1801, Josephine wrote to her mother in Martinique: " You ought to love Bona-parte.   He makes your daughter very happy.   He is a charming man."

Once, when a boy, he had just left his brother Joseph, to go to the school in Brienne, and in taking leave he had shed but one tear, which he had in vain tried to hide, while his brother was all in tears.   A priest, their teacher, who saw them, said to Joseph, " He has shed only one tear, but that shows his grief as much as all of yours."   King Joseph, who reports this anecdote in his Memoirs, adds that there was a great difference between his brother's real character and the artificial character which circumstances had compelled him to assume.   " Napoleon," he goes on, " had some rare qualities, which he later thought it necessary to hide under the artificial character which he tried to acquire when he came to power, on the pretext that men needed to be led by a man as strong and just as the law, and not by a ruler whose kindness would be interpreted as weakness when it did not rest on inflexible justice." Joseph concluded that his brother "was much more truly a just and good man than a great warrior or great administrator"; and Thiers is not far from this opinion when he says, " As soon as Napoleon ceased to rule, and had no need to restrain or arouse men, he became gentle, simple, just, with the justice of a great mind that knows humanity, understands its weaknesses, and pardons them because they are inevitable."

To those who maintain that Napoleon was kind, there has been objected his cold indifference on the battle-field, but for soldiers this indifference is a matter of professional duty. War is like hunting. A man who is prominent in the Society for the Prevention of Cruelty to Animals becomes absolutely cruel when he is hunting a hare or a partridge. For a general in the hour of action, the enemy is only human game; but after the battle, the soldier becomes once more generous and humane. A soldier who has returned home is as mild as a child, yet he was a terrible creature in a hot fight with his bayonet at the end of his gun. Was there ever a kinder father than Marshal Pélissier? yet, when he had to give the signal of the assault of Sebastopol, did he feel a moment's hesitation or pity?

Some may urge Napoleon's outbursts of anger;

but these did not arise from an evil disposition, they were rather put on for show, wilful outbreaks to produce some needed effect; the result of calculation, not of passion.

To this question we may add another: Did Napoleon like women? Again, Madame de Rémusat appears for the prosecution. According to her, Napoleon despised women, which, as she says, is not a way of loving them. " Their weakness," she adds, "seemed to him an uncontrovertible proof of their inferiority, and the power they have acquired in society appeared to him an unendurable usurpation, a consequence and an abuse of the progress of civilization, which, as M. de Talleyrand expressed it, was always somewhat his personal enemy. Consequently, Bonaparte was never quite at his ease with women; and since this lack of ease put him somewhat out of temper, he always approached awkwardly, not knowing how to talk with them. . . . I should be inclined to believe that Bonaparte, who was almost always busy with political questions, was scarcely ever moved by love except through his vanity. He cared for a woman only if she was handsome, or at least young. He may perhaps have thought that in a well-organized society we should be put to death, as certain insects die naturally, the work of maturity once accomplished." This is damaging testimony; and were it not for Madame de Rémusat's unimpeachable reputation, I should be tempted to detect something like spitefulness in her language.

Yet Prince Metternich is scarcely more favorable in his judgment. " Never," he says, " did he address a gracious or even a polite phrase to a woman, although one could perceive by his expression, or the sound of his voice, that he tried to do so. He spoke to women only about their dress, of which he boasted that he was a particular and severe judge; or else about the number of their children, and one of his favorite questions was whether they nursed them themselves, — a question which he often asked in language unusual in good society. Sometimes he made a number of inquiries about the secret relations of society, which, so far as the choice of place and methods was concerned, gave to his conversations an air of misplaced admonitions rather than the character of drawing-room talk."

Certainly the man of the camp was never a man of society. The trivialities of gallantry seemed to him absurd, and his voice, accustomed to commanding, could not adopt soft modulations. Like most of the men of his generation, he paid his tribute to the school of Jean Jacques Rousseau, and his letters to Josephine during the first Italian campaign were written in the style of the "Nouvelle Héloise"; but he soon abandoned a method which only suited the honeymoon, and would sound very odd after a few years of matrimony. Without doubt he lacked the exaggerated sensibility which Berquin and Florian had introduced; he looked upon it as an affectation as it existed at the end of the eighteenth century, when the word, if not the thing itself, had become ridiculous in his eyes. Since in his heart he remained a military man, he detested sentimentalism. Whenever he fell in love, it was with a sort of wild fury. He conquered a woman like a province; he never wooed, he subjugated; to humiliate himself before a woman would have seemed like a sort of abdication. His imperious and masterful character appeared in his amours; he reproached the old kings for their gallantry as a form of weakness, and never let himself be enslaved by love. He made it a point of honor to seem invulnerable and proof against the shafts of love; hence in his relations with women of renowned beauty or intelligence he assumed rough ways, though he could be, when he wished, very charming. The women who wanted to rule him but failed all owed him a grudge, as we see from their words or their writings. They accused the man who resisted them of being insensible, brutal, ill-mannered, heartless. But there is evident exaggeration in these readily explicable accusations.

Napoleon did not, as has been unjustly said, despise women; he esteemed virtuous women and set great store by domestic life and Christian marriage. He adored and revered his mother, and many of the most odious accusations brought against him fall to the ground from lack of proof and do not demand discussion.

Another question arises: Was Napoleon a man of intelligence? The affirmative answer seems certain.

Even Madame de Rémusat acknowledges the extreme pleasure she took in his conversation. "With him, one idea called forth a thousand others, and the slightest word raised his conversation to the loftiest heights, in which perhaps sound logic falls away, but his intelligence is no less remarkable. . . . His language is generally animated and brilliant, his errors in grammar often give it an unexpected strength, which is well supported by the originality of his ideas. He grows interested in his conversation without plying. From the moment he takes up a subject, he is off far away, but careful to notice if he is followed, and grateful to those who understand and applaud him. . . . Like an orator who gathers strength from the effect he produces, Bonaparte enjoys the approval which he sought for in the eyes of his audience."

Prince Metternich pays like homage to Napoleon's intelligence. "Talking with him has always had a charm for me that I find hard to define. He would seize the essential point, strip it of all useless accessories, develop his thought, and go on elaborating it until it was perfectly clear and conclusive, always finding the right word, or inventing it if it did not exist, so that his conversation was always full of interest." In the whole history of humanity there has perhaps never been a keener, more profound, more original, more brilliant intelligence.

Was Napoleon a man of imagination? On this matter, doubt is impossible. All his life Napoleon was a man of action and a dreamer. When tired with his grandiose plans, his mind would rest by recalling the happy days of his youth. He liked to calk about Corsica, his infancy, and his old father, who had said to him, " You, Napoleon, you will be a great man ! " His life was full of poetry from his cradle to the tomb. The instincts of an artist lay at the bottom of this conqueror's heart. " When I first knew him," says Madame de Rémusat, " he liked everything which tended to revery, — Ossian, twilight, melancholy music. I have seen him listen with rapture to the murmur of the wind, and speak with delight of the roar of the sea ; and I have known him to be tempted to believing in the possibility of midnight apparitions ; in a word, to incline towards certain superstitions. When in the evening he had left his working-room for Madame Bonaparte's drawing-room, he would sometimes have the lights covered by a white veil ; and then, after commanding strict silence, he took pleasure in telling and hearing ghost stories, or else he would listen to low, soft songs from Italian singers, with a very gentle accompaniment. Then he would fall into a revery, which every one was afraid to disturb by moving or changing place. When aroused, he seemed rested, and became calmer and more communicative."

More of a poet in action than any other great man, more than Alexander, more than Cæsar, and more than Charlemagne, Napoleon, in prosperity and in adversity, was like a great actor, playing, not merely for his contemporaries, but still more for posterity. Had he been a mere tactician and administrator, he would not have roused the masses. Lamartine is wrong in saying that during the Napoleonic period there were only two things, — the budget and the sword; there was an ideal, glory. Great things are never accomplished without immaterial elements; and as Napoleon himself said, it is imagination that rules the world.

The man who inspired Chateaubriand with the finest passages of his "Mémoires d'Outretombe," Thiers with his "History of the Consulate and of the Empire," Lamartine with his "Ode to Bonaparte," Béranger with his "Memoirs of the People," Heine with his "Two Grenadiers," and Victor Hugo with the most magnificent words that have ever sounded on the lyre, — that man, if he possessed no other merit, would deserve to be called a man of genius. Prince Metternich is in error when he says, "The opinion of the world is, and always will be, divided on the question whether Napoleon is entitled to be called a great man." Doubt on that subject is impossible. Napoleon is great by his successes, his faults, and his misfortunes. Everything about him was colossal, immeasurable, — the evil as well as the good. His was a prodigious character that cannot be judged by ordinary standards. Pigmies are too short and their eyes are too dim to be able to look at the giant. Great men are like wide views — they

are best seen from a height; they require to be looked
at from a distance and from a lofty position, with
due regard to optical effects; otherwise it is impossible to take account of the changes of opinion,
and history becomes inexplicable.   One does not
look at the sun through a magnifying-glass.   It is
impossible to understand Napoleon without understanding the French Revolution, which produced him.
There was in him something novel, violent, and
strange, as in the events in which he grew up.   He
was the principal figure in a period which is one
long series of unprecedented phenomena.

Doubtless it may be maintained that his genius was
an evil for humanity, that he brought on France a
real avalanche of woe, that the results obtained were
singularly disproportionate to the loss of life; but
however Napoleon may be denounced, it is impossible
to deny his greatness.   His bitterest enemies have
cursed him, but without questioning his glory; and
even Chateaubriand himself, the author of the famous
pamphlet, " Bonaparte and the Bourbons," which was
of more service than an army to Louis XVIII., said
after Napoleon's death, " I could not measure the
giant's greatness until he had fallen."   No man can
so take possession of his time and of history, unless
he is really extraordinary.   What country has not
echoed with the magic name of Napoleon?   When a
few years ago the Shah of Persia came to Paris, his
first visit was to the Emperor's tomb, and before

going down into the crypt, he respectfully removed his sword, as if he did not dare to appear armed before the shade of the great man. In the eyes of posterity Napoleon will diminish as a politician, but he will always grow as a poetical figure.

III.

JOSEPHINE IN 1803.

IN 1803 Josephine was forty years old. Her beauty was a little faded, but she treated her face so skilfully, and dressed with such taste, her expression was so charming, her smile so sweet, her bearing so graceful, her manners so fine, that she was still very attractive, and might almost pass for a pretty woman. She was treated like a queen, and yet unexpected and moral greatness sat easily upon her. She received so well, had such command of the art of saying a kind word to every one, her memory was so good, her tact and readiness so conspicuous, that she seemed born on the steps of the throne. No party was hostile to her. The Republicans were grateful for her friendship with Fouché, who represented the revolutionary element in Bonaparte's surroundings; those who belonged to the old régime regarded her, and with reason, as their ally, and as a real Royalist. Since she had been kind to every one without exception, she aroused neither hate nor anger; those who judged that her morals were not all that could be desired, never reproached her, and the bitterest enemies of her husband spared her. By her kindness she found favor among men of all parties.

In the beginning of 1803 a member of the Institute, M. Ventenat, in dedicating to her a book entitled "The Garden of Malmaison," wrote this letter in a style as flowery as the subject: "Madame, you have thought that the taste for flowers should not be a sterile study. You have brought together the rarest French plants, and many which had never left the deserts of Arabia and the burning sands of Egypt have been naturalized by your orders, and now, carefully classified, they present to our eyes, in the garden of Malmaison, the most charming memory of the conquests of your illustrious husband, and a most attentive token of your studious leisure. You have been kind enough to choose me to describe these different plants, and to inform the public of the wealth of a garden which already equals the best that England, Germany, and Spain can boast of. Deign to accept the homage of a task undertaken by your command." The gallant botanist ended his letter with a compliment turned after the fashion of his day: "If in the course of this work I have described any one of the modest and beneficent plants that seem to exist only to spread around them an influence as sweet as it is salutary, I shall have, Madame, great difficulty to avoid making a comparison which, doubtless, will not escape my readers."

Josephine was popular, and she deserved her popularity. All classes of society united in paying her homage. This is the way in which her portrait is drawn by some of her contemporaries. Madame de Rémusat readily acknowledges the charm of the First Consul's wife. "Without being exactly pretty," she says, "her whole appearance had a peculiar charm. Her features were delicate and harmonious; her expression was gentle; her mouth, which was very small, did not disclose her teeth, which were not good; she disguised the brownness of her complexion with the aid of rouge and powder; her figure was perfect, her limbs were delicate and graceful; every movement was graceful, and of no one could it be said more truthfully than of her, that her grace was more beautiful than beauty. She dressed with great taste, and graced what she wore; and thanks to these advantages and her constant attention to dress, she escaped being effaced by the beauty and youth of the many women who surrounded her."

Napoleon's first valet, Constant, describes Josephine as follows: "She was of medium height and very well made. All her movements were light and graceful, so that her walk was almost flitting, yet without losing the majesty expected of a queen. Her expressive countenance varied with her emotions, and yet it always retained the charming sweetness which was its main characteristic. Happy or unhappy, she was a beautiful object. No woman ever more thoroughly proved the truth of the statement that the eyes are the mirror of the soul. Her own were dark blue and almost always half hidden by her long lids, which were slightly arched and bordered by the most beautiful lashes in the world, so that they had an irresistible charm. Her hair was beautifully long and silky. In the morning she liked to wear a red turban, which gave her a most piquant creole air." One of Josephine's great charms was her soft, insinuating, musical voice. "How often it happened," says Constant, "that I, like a good many others, would stop on hearing this voice, simply for the pleasure of listening to it!" She read aloud very well, and liked to do it. Napoleon preferred her to all his readers.

The most marked quality of her nature was kindness. Being truly kind, she would have acquired the quality of set purpose if she had not already been born with it. She had all that goes to make up this disposition: gentleness, modesty, simplicity, compassion for the unhappy, the desire to be useful and agreeable, generosity, charity, and love of her neighbor. Here is what Mademoiselle Avrillon says on the subject: "There was only one opinion about the exquisite kindness of Madame Bonaparte; instances were abundant, and there was no limit to the eulogies of her many admirable qualities. She was extremely affable with all who were about her; I do not believe that there ever was a woman who made her high station less perceptible." On this point Madame de Rémusat offers corroboratory testimony for she says, speaking of Josephine: "With all her advantages she united extreme kindness. Moreover, she was remarkably even-tempered; she was very well disposed and always ready to forget any evil done to her." Constant speaks in the same way: "Kindness was as much part of her character as grace of her person. Being extremely kind, tender almost to excess, generous to profusion, she made all who were near her happy, so no woman was ever better loved or more deserved to be loved. . . . Having known unhappiness, she had sympathy for others ; being always good-tempered and cheerful, as obliging to her enemies as to her friends, she made peace where formerly there had existed quarrel and dissension."

Was Josephine clever? Yes, but she did not possess that cleverness which manifests itself in ingenious thoughts or paradoxes, which is inspired by malice, which finds utterance in witticisms and bits of sarcasm, and delights in gossip and scandal, but rather a quiet, amiable cleverness, consisting mainly of tact, of a comprehension of the most delicate and subtle distinctions, which readily finds the exact word; in short, the best cleverness that there is, because it comes from the heart. She had that rare and charming gift of listening well. Her good memory made her many friends. If she happened to meet any one whom she had not seen for a long time, she recalled the minutest circumstances of the past, and entered into the minutest details about things which even the persons concerned had sometimes forgotten.

In justice it must be said that, of course, Josephine had the faults of her qualities. Generally, generosity easily becomes extravagance, amiability often degenerates into silliness, and gentleness into weakness.

Josephine was charitable, but she used to get into debt. "People bring me beautiful things," she said one day to Bourrienne; "they show me how precious they are and I buy them. They don't ask me to pay them at the time, but send me the bill when I have no money. Then that gets to Bonaparte's ears, and he is angry. When I have any money, you know what I do with it; I give most of it to suffering people who come to beg, to penniless émigrés. Josephine was kind and benevolent, but she received with equal warmth honorable persons and those of a tarnished reputation. She was gentle, but her character lacked seriousness; she displayed excessive indulgence to women of a blemished reputation; all her tastes were frivolous, her conversation was empty and she had no influence over her husband in important matters. It would not have been easy for any woman to give political advice to a man who stoutly upheld the privileges of his sex. Prince Metternich said of Josephine: "Her mind was not a powerful one, but it was of an excellent sort as far as it went. It would be unjust to hold her responsible for the excesses of Napoleon's ambition. Had she been able she would doubtless have put a drag on the chariot in which, at the beginning of his career, she helped to place him."

In 1803 the First Consul and his wife were still living harmoniously, although Bonaparte, in Paris if not at Saint Cloud, was at times unfaithful. At Saint Cloud peace prevailed, and no eye could have detected any scandal. At eight in the morning the First Consul would get up and betake himself to his study; he lunched there alone, and while at table, he received artists and actors, — he was very fond of their society, — and then he went back to his work till six in the evening; then he drove in a barouche with his wife. On their return they dined, and then he would talk more or less, according to his feelings, and then he would go back to his work. Josephine spent the evening playing cards; between ten and eleven a servant would come in and say, " Madame, the First Consul has gone to bed," then she dismissed her company and went to her room. Everything was smooth at Saint Cloud, but at the Tuileries, in the same year, there were stormy scenes, one of which is told by Madame de Rémusat in her Memoirs.

In 1796 it was Bonaparte who complained of Josephine's indifference; in 1803, after seven years of marriage, it was Josephine who had learned to know all the uneasiness, suspicion, and mental anguish of a woman who sees her husband growing calm and cold. It must be remembered, however, that the First Consul was six years younger than his wife; and while her beauty was fading, — he was thirty-four when she was forty, — he was gaining not merely fame, wealth, and power, but also health and beauty.

The First Consul of 1803 was very unlike the general of the early months of 1796. When he married, Bonaparte was puny, delicate, ailing, penniless, with no other reputation than that of the 13th

Vendémiaire; and Josephine's friends thought that she had made a very poor match. But in 1803 things had changed very much. Bonaparte had acquired all the ascendancy that can be given by the sovereign power in the hands of a man of genius. All the fashionable beauties regarded him with enthusiasm, and thus destroyed poor Josephine's peace of mind, while she was unable to arouse any spark of jealousy in him. Even if she had wished (and she certainly never did) to make him jealous, she could not commit the slightest imprudence. Since she was under continual observation at the Tuileries and at Saint Cloud, she could not repeat her foolish actions of the time of the Directory; the slightest coquetry, even in words, was forbidden; and when Bonaparte's brothers were trying to persuade him to take steps towards divorce, she could not, by word or deed, give them the least ground for criticism and condemnation. Men, in their egotism and vanity, — and even the best of them have selfish and vain points, — become indifferent to women when they are absolutely secure from rivals; and as Josephine's love for Napoleon grew, his for her cooled. And yet this woman, humble, submissive, and complaisant, coquettish only with her husband, deserved blame for only one thing; namely, her extravagance, which is certainly a pardonable fault; for by spending largely did she not encourage industry and trade?

At heart Napoleon did Josephine justice. He knew that she was useful to him and brought him

THE WIFE OF THE FIRST CONSUL.

happiness, and this fact served to defend her against the incessant attack and intrigues of her enemies. When he was kind and repentant of his faults, she was happy in the enjoyment of the prosperity of France and of her husband's greatness.

To sum up, Madame Bonaparte was not lacking in skill. She had to contend against women younger and prettier than herself for the possession of Napoleon's heart; against the whole Bonaparte family, who were jealous of her influence; against a multitude of people, who made much of her childlessness, continually saying that if Napoleon had no children, there was no hope for the future security of France. Josephine needed much skill and prudence to withstand for long so many enemies. She was successful in 1804, when she was crowned Empress by her husband's hand, and unsuccessful in 1809; but even after divorce she preserved her rank and title, and seldom has a repudiated queen been treated with so much respect.

On the rock of Saint Helena Napoleon often recalled the memory of this companion of his happy years, who had charmed and fascinated his youth. He spoke in praise of her qualities, her attractions, her grace. He said that her unvarying submission, devotion, and absolute complaisance amounted to virtues and attested the political skill of her sex. He added that her kindness was a weapon against her enemies, a charm for her friends, and the source of her power over her husband; that theirs had been a very happy

Darby and Joan marriage; that she had a thorough knowledge of his character; that she was always eager to please him, and he was sure that she would at any time have left a rendezvous with a lover to come to him. This last reflection, with its malice beneath a cloak of friendliness, was the last lingering trace of his old jealousy, and made even him smile. "It was necessary for me," he said again at Saint Helena, "and would have made me happy, not merely from the point of view of politics, but in my domestic life, to have had a son by Josephine. The political result would have been that I should still be on the throne; for the French would have been as devoted to it as they were to the King of Rome, and I should not have set foot in the flowery abyss which was my ruin. Then think of the wisdom of human plans, and dare to call a man happy or unhappy before his death!" In the remarks of the great captive there is more than sympathy, more than admiration, more than gratitude for the woman of whom he said: "I gained battles; Josephine gained me hearts. . . . She was the most loving and best of women." There is feeling and tenderness in this language; it is the radiant vision of youth and love that arose before him. The evening twilight recalls the dawn.

IV.

MADAME DE RÉMUSAT.

WE have often quoted Madame de Rémusat's judgments of Napoleon and Josephine, and it may be a good moment to bring her before us to judge her in her turn, with all the respect that is due to her memory. Clara Elisabeth Jane Gravier de Vergennes, Countess of Rémusat, was born January 5, 1780; her parents were Charles Gravier de Vergennes, a councillor in the Parliament of Burgundy, and Adelaide Frances de Bastard. She was the grand-niece of the Count of Vergennes, who was Minister of Foreign Affairs under Louis XVI. Her childhood was embittered by the most tragic incidents. When she was fourteen, her father and her grandfather were guillotined, three days before the fall of Robespierre. As the property of those who were executed was confiscated, Clara de Vergennes was reduced to want; but she found a protector in a Provençal nobleman, Augustine Laurent de Rémusat, a magistrate at Aix before the Revolution, whom she married early in 1796, when barely sixteen. Her mother had been intimate with the Viscountess of

Beauharnais, then Madame Bonaparte; and when the
question of a court came up, the First Consul and
his wife thought of M. and Mme. de Rémusat, who
became prefect of the palace, and the first lady-in-
waiting, respectively, at the beginning of the Consulate for life.

Were they Bonapartists? without any doubt. The
husband would no more have been false to Napoleon
than would his wife to Josephine. They both discharged their duties with zeal, loyalty, and pleasure.
Their position, too, was a very agreeable one: nearly
every minute they saw the most famous man of his
day, and beheld, as it were from an opera-box, a sight
which interested the whole world. Madame de Rémusat occupied a brilliant position which must have been
very attractive, especially after the poverty and unhappiness of the Terror; and when she recalled those
days of misery she must have thanked Providence
for so comfortable a harbor after such terrible storms.
At Saint Cloud and at the Tuileries she found everything that could gratify a woman's vanity. She had
much influence over Josephine, and through her over
Napoleon, and thus she could be of service to a great
many émigrés. She was almost the only woman with
whom the First Consul liked to talk. He was most
kind to her and discussed with her politics, history,
literature, giving evidence of his sympathy and esteem
which really touched her. She was lively and intelligent, and found amusement in everything she saw.
Her life was filled with most exalted entertainment.

No bright, imaginative woman could fail to enjoy the charm of this varied, busy existence, and she was perfectly happy in it. Her son, a minister under Louis Philippe and Thiers, wrote to Sainte-Beuve: "It was not as a last resource, by necessity, weakness, temptation, or as a mere temporary expedient, that my parents gave their adherence to the new régime. They joined their fortunes with it freely and with perfect confidence." In her Memoirs, Madame de Rémusat said of the man whom she really worshipped, "We loved and admired him: this confession I am ready to make."

When, in 1802, she assumed her position in the palace, Madame de Rémusat was twenty-two years old. Without being really a beauty, she was .very attractive. She had charm, distinction, breeding. Her eyes, black, like her hair, were fine and expressive; her features were regular, though perhaps a little large; her expression benevolent and worthy; in short, she had all the air of a great lady. Her friend, Talleyrand, has thus described her: "Clari [for that is what he used to call her] is not what would be called a beauty, yet every one says that she is agreeable. . . . Her complexion is not brilliant, but it has this merit, that it looks whiter the higher the light in which it is seen. Is not that like her whole nature, which appears better and more lovable the more it is known? She has large black eyes; long lashes lend her face an expression of mingled tenderness and vivacity which is perceptible

even when she is calm and wishes to express nothing;
but these moments are rare. . . . Her hair generally
hides a large part of her forehead, which is a pity.
Two dimples, which come when she smiles, give a
piquancy to her sweet appearance. She is often
careless in her dress, but she always shows good
taste and is very neat. This neatness is part of the
system of order and decency from which Clari never
varies."

In the moral sphere Madame de Rémusat was cor-
rectness itself. Her manners were faultless. She
was tactful, decorous, discreet, and thoroughly well-
bred; moreover, she was much better educated than
most of the women of the Consular Court. As Talleyrand said, " Clari's intelligence is broad and well
cultivated; I know no one who talks better; when
she wishes to appear instructed she gives a mark of
confidence and friendship. Clari's husband knows
that he has a treasure in her, and he has the good
sense to enjoy it."

Madame de Rémusat was a devoted and faithful
wife, and her husband did not need to be jealous of
her feeling for the First Consul; it was not love, but
rather warmly enthusiastic admiration. On his side
Napoleon was flattered at being appreciated by a
woman whose intelligence he so admired. " I remember," she says, "that because he interested me very
much when he spoke, and I listened with pleasure,
he said that I was an intelligent woman when I had
scarcely spoken two consecutive words."

It was only by talking with her that the First Consul gave evidence of his preference for Madame de Rémusat; and yet these conversations aroused a certain jealousy, and her reputation once came very near being compromised in spite of her correct conduct and blameless morals. November 3, 1803, Napoleon, accompanied by the generals of his guard, his aides, and M. de Rémusat, had gone to the camp of Boulogne, making his headquarters at Pont-de-Briques, a little village distant about a league from that town. M. de Rémusat was taken seriously ill almost at the moment of his arrival, and as soon as his wife heard of it, she went to take care of him. She arrived, unsummoned, in the middle of the night, very anxious as to what the First Consul might think of what she had done. Her own words will describe what took place the next day: " When the Consul was up, he sent word for me to come to him; I was agitated and somewhat flustered, as he saw the moment I entered the room. He kissed me at once, and making me sit down, calmed me by his first words: 'I was expecting you. Your presence will cure your husband.' At these words I burst into tears; he seemed touched, and did his best to soothe me. Then he told me that I must lunch and dine with him every day, adding with a laugh, 'I must take great care of a woman of your age, thrown among so many soldiers.'" Madame de Rémusat obeyed, and during Napoleon's stay at Pont-de-Briques she had the much-sought-for honor of dining *tête-à-tête* with him, and of hearing him discuss many interesting questions of politics and literature.

On the whole, the First Consul shines in his relations with her; he appears to have been kind to her, affectionate, I might almost say paternal, if he had not been so young, for Bonaparte was but thirty-four when she was twenty-three : he could scarcely be her father. There are, of course, sceptics who smile at the story of a pretty woman who arrives at a camp in the dead of night, and dines every day alone with a man who, besides great natural charm, has all the attraction of glory and power, and the incident is not a common one; but for ourselves we do not share their incredulity : her account bears all the stamp of accuracy. Madame de Rémusat was doubtless extremely annoyed by the suspicions of which, to her great surprise, she was the object. "It was the first time," she says, "that I saw myself judged in a way that I did not deserve; my youth and all my feelings were shocked by such accusations; one needs a long and bitter experience to be able to endure the world's injustice, and perhaps one ought to regret the time when they strike so hard and painfully."

Josephine was for a moment jealous of her, and treated her with less kindness than usual. "I could not keep myself," adds Madame de Rémusat, "from asking her, with tears in my eyes, 'What, Madame! is it I whom you suspect?' As she was kind and open to every passing emotion, she kissed me and was as open with me as in the past. Yet she did not wholly understand me. She was not able to comprehend my righteous wrath, and without troubling herself about the relations of her husband to myself at Boulogne, she was satisfied with knowing that at any rate they could have been of but brief duration."

Madame de Rémusat experienced much annoyance from this trip to the camp; but even the best of women are not without a tincture of coquetry; and judging from her frequent reference to this incident, one is inclined to think that it was not wholly unpleasant to her. The idea that it could have been thought possible that Napoleon had really distinguished her, was not entirely odious to her, and those who read her account will readily understand the feeling which made her say to the Emperor, as M. Charles de Rémusat takes pains to tell us:

" Va, je t'ai trop aimé pour ne point te haïr."

This trip to the camp at Boulogne marks the moment of Madame de Rémusat's warmest enthusiasm for Napoleon. She came back to Paris literally enchanted with the great man. "He had greeted me so warmly," she herself says, "he had shown so much interest in my husband's recovery; in a word, his consideration touched me in my anxiety and trouble, and then the amusements he had devised for me in that dull place, and the petty satisfaction which my vanity drew from his apparent pleasure in my society, — all these things affected me, and in the first few days after my return I was telling every one, with all the gratitude one feels at twenty, that his kindness to me had been extreme."

Gradually this enthusiasm lessened, and criticism succeeded to admiration. Under the influence of Josephine's sorrows, — for Madame de Rémusat remained a lady-in-waiting to her after the divorce, — she lived remote from the splendors of the Empire, in a retreat which was not wholly unlike disgrace. Gradually the great disasters dispelled her illusions, and when the final blow came, she forgot the tricolor in her love for the white flag. Even when the Consulate and the Empire were most flourishing, there yet lingered in the depths of her soul certain dim memories of Royalism, due to her birth and the first impressions of her childhood. On his return from Elba, Napoleon said to Benjamin Constant: "The nobles served me; they crowded my anterooms; there were no places which they did not accept, ask for, solicit. I have had Montmorencys, Noailles, Rohans, Beauvans, Mortemarts. But that is as far as it went. The horse curveted, and was well groomed, but I could feel him trembling." During the Hundred Days, Madame de Rémusat sided with the Bourbons, and her fear of Napoleon's resentment was so great that she lost her head, and threw into the fire the manuscript diary which she had kept faithfully while she was attached to the consular and the imperial court. Those Memoirs would have been the real expression of her thought. What a pity it is that she had not sufficient presence of mind to save them, — a thing she could easily have done !

Under the second Restoration, the former Prefect of the Imperial Palace became the Royalist Prefect of the Haute Garonne, and subsequently of the Nord; and his wife devoted the leisure of life in the provinces to literature. At Lille, in 1818, she began to write a novel, called " The Spanish Letters, or the Man of Ambition "; but there appeared a posthumous book of Madame de Staël's, " Thoughts on the French Revolution," which made so deep an impression on her that she wrote, May 27, to the son: " A new whim has seized me. You know that I wake up every morning at six, and write until half-past nine. Well, I was at work, with all the manuscript of my novel about me, but some of Madame de Staël's chapters kept running through my head. Suddenly, I threw my story away, took some clean paper, bitten by the necessity of writing something about Bonaparte. . . . Facts and words thronged upon me, and to-day and yesterday I have written twenty pages; it has moved me very much."

It is the Memoirs, written thus, in 1818, by Madame de Rémusat, that have been published, with an interesting preface by her grandson. In giving the book to the world, M. Paul de Rémusat has not merely complied with his father's wishes; he has done good service to letters and to history. The work has called forth numerous discussions; but discussion only helps a book and insures its success. Every original book needs to be subjected to criticism.

To judge Madame de Rémusat's Memoirs impartially, account must be taken of the successive influences to which she was exposed, and it must be borne in mind that her changes of opinion were those of the society and the time in which she lived. France, with its enthusiasms and its disenchantments, is like a woman. At first the country adored Napoleon most ecstatically; then, that feeling passing away, she hated him, though for but a moment, and after the first effervescence was over, the nation tenderly returned to him who had been its idol. Written earlier, or written later, Madame de Rémusat's Memoirs would not have been what they now are. Written earlier, they would have borne marks of the Imperial period; and later, they would probably show traces of the influence of the Liberals at the time of the Restoration, when they were all full of Napoleon's glory; and possibly Madame de Rémusat would have spoken of the Emperor as did her son, Louis Philippe's eminent minister. For we must not forget that it was Charles de Rémusat who uttered these words from the tribune of the Chamber of Deputies: "He was our Emperor and King, and thus is entitled to be buried at Saint Denis; but Napoleon does not require the ordinary burial of kings; he should still reign and command in the enclosure where shall rest the country's soldiers, and whence those who are called on to defend it shall draw fresh inspiration. His sword shall be laid upon his tomb. Art shall construct beneath the dome in the middle of the temple, consecrated by religion to the God of armies, a tomb worthy, if possible, of the name which is to be placed there. This monument ought to have a simple beauty, grandiose form, and that aspect of absolute solidity which seems to defy the effect of time. Napoleon needs a monument as lasting as his fame." In these words M. Charles de Rémusat did not think that he was unfaithful to his Liberalism, and the Minister of the government of July ended his discourse with these words: "It belonged to the Monarchy of 1830, which was the first to rally all the forces and to conciliate all the wishes of the French Revolution, to build and to honor the statue and the tomb of a popular hero; for there is one thing, and one thing only, which need dread no comparison with glory, and that is liberty."

Madame de Rémusat's life was too short; she died suddenly, aged forty-one, in the night of December 10, 1821, the year of Napoleon's death. The misfortunes which had swept over France were too recent. Her patriotic spirit had been sorely distressed by the invasion, and it was with a feeling of bitterness which we can readily understand that like many of her contemporaries she asked herself what was the final result of so many efforts, so much heroism, so many sacrifices, and so much bloodshed. Let us add, that she was sincere. If she had published her Memoirs during her lifetime to flatter the Restoration and to secure her husband's advancement, she would have done a disgraceful thing, something of which she was incapable. Like Saint-Simon, she wrote for no personal interest, but to make up for long restraint, and to say freely what she believed to be the truth. When her Memoirs appeared, all the persons were dead; the passions of the time had disappeared to give place to the impartial judgment of history, and although Madame de Rémusat had been in attendance on Napoleon and Josephine, her testimony will be listened to, if not accepted.

While there may be room for reserve as to the historical value of the book, its literary value is incontestable. It is a living work, one that has been lived, as people say nowadays. Madame de Rémusat always expresses herself like a woman of intelligence and like a lady. Her style is sober and incisive; she had a keen observation, and in a few strokes she made admirable sketches. Those who blame her harsh judgment of Napoleon should remember that towards the end of her life she took a gentler view of the great man, and that in 1821 she held very different views from those she had held in 1815 and 1818. As her son says: "Her letters will show how important a place Napoleon had kept in her thoughts, how much his memory moved her, and what pain and grief she felt in hearing of his unhappy exile to Saint Helena. When, in the summer of 1821, she heard of his death, I saw her burst into tears, and she never named him without evident sadness."

Already she was indignant with certain instances

of apostasy, and angry at the attitude of those who scornfully called the great Emperor Bonaparte, after they had been his flatterers and courtiers. One evening there was given at the Théâtre Français an adaptation of Schiller's " Mary Stuart," and there took place an incident thus described by M. Charles de Rémusat: " In one scene Leicester refuses to listen to a young man who, counting on his secret feelings, proposes to him a. way of saving the Queen of Scotland, and pretends not to know him. Talma gave admirably the haughty cowardice of the courtier, who disavows his own love from fear of being compromised, and refuses to listen to the young man with overwhelming insolence: ' What do you want of me? I know you not.' The act came to an end, and every one in our box was full of admiration for the scene, and my mother, who was much moved, had just said, in words to this effect, ' That's the way it was; I have seen it,' when there suddenly appeared at the door of the box M. de B., to whom certainly no particular application could be made, but who had been a chamberlain of the Emperor. My mother could not restrain herself. She said to Madame de Catellan, ' If you knew ' — and burst into tears." Noble and generous tears, which efface a great deal.

Doubtless Madame de Rémusat, when she was writing her Memoirs, had no idea of the noise they would make. Politics had some share in their success, and the fame of the book has grown from the discussion of which it was the cause or the pretext.

Certain critics have taken advantage of it to utter against Napoleon the usual denunciations; as, for example, M. John Lemoinne, speaking for humanity, has thundered against war and against the mighty victor. Speaking of Napoleon, and the great conquerors who resemble him, he says eloquently: "The most humiliating, the most revolting, the most hopeless thing, is not seeing them, like the Indian chariot, impassively crushing the wretches who, in their idolatry, fling themselves beneath the wheels, destroying bodies and soul, mind and matter, grain, trees, fruit, the product of toil, the bodies of children, mothers' hearts, every law, every liberty, everything which lived and only asked to live; no, it is seeing the ·moral degradation, the dishonoring need of servitude, which urge the human horde to worship the crimes of which it is the victim, to adore the hands which smite it, to kiss the feet which crush it."

On the other hand, another critic whose original talent, lively spirit, and sparkling style continually grew younger, Count Armand de Pontmartin, although a Legitimist, has undertaken the defence of Napoleon against Madame de Rémusat, as follows: " Can it be said that Madame de Rémusat's Memoirs is a prose version of the 'Châtiments'? Frankly, I think not. The success of the book is great, but it is due to curiosity, not to love of scandal; it comes from interest in Bonaparte, who is prominent throughout; although reduced in size, he overruns the canvas." And that is true; the excitement which the book produced in

Europe, and possibly still more in America, proves the ardent interest in everything relating to the strange and colossal figure of Napoleon. And was Madame de Rémusat justified in speaking ill of the Emperor who had been so kind and affectionate to her, to whom also she owed her fame with posterity? for had it not been for him, who would now remember her? Is she not like an immortal flower growing in the shade of a great oak?

But let us listen to M. de Pontmartin: "Madame de Rémusat wished to take from this man, on whom have been wasted so many verses, so many phrases, his state mantle, his legendary halo, his epical and magic fame. . . . But he remains still Napoleon Bonaparte; that is to say, a man so above and beyond human proportions that if his prodigious ability is denied, he can be explained only as the product of magic or of a supernatural intervention." And the Legitimist critic, doubtless annoyed at some sentences of M. Paul de Rémusat unfavorable to the Restoration, concludes thus: "There is only one way of looking at Napoleon, from which it is possible to disparage him, and that is from the position of the Royalists. If you do not grant me that, I shall for a moment forget my cockade and my flag to say: The lowering of great men and the exaltation of small ones are what is done by perishing nations, which do not know how to perish properly."

But we must not speak of France as perishing, for it is still full of life. The country has not yet come to an end of its strength or its wealth, of its liberty or its glory. But may it be wise enough to abstain from disparaging the great men and the great events to which it owes its fame! Let it never condemn its own history more harshly than do foreigners! May it be saved from the folly and madness of destroying its idols! Let it never on any account disavow its three imperishable legends, those of Royalty, Imperialism, and Republicanism. No, a woman's pretty claws cannot, with all her wit, even scratch the bronze of the Column Vendome. Carthage condemned itself the day it disowned Hannibal. Zama ought not to make us forget Cannæ. Waterloo does not destroy Austerlitz.

Certainly there would be justification if Napoleon were complained of by those who with such unwearying persistence had suffered so much, had fought so bravely for him, and without hope of gain, without a murmur, in the sands of Egypt or in the snows of Russia; had followed him tirelessly through all his battles, from Arcola and the Pyramids to Moscow, Leipsic, and Waterloo, and who, poor, crippled, scarred, found refuge, after so many combats, only under a cottage roof! Well, those men, far from cursing their leader, always worshipped him, victorious or beaten, and always were faithful to him with the fervor of Béranger's two grenadiers. If one wished to denounce the general, it would be the ice-cold hand of the veterans, of the dead, that would close the insulter's mouth. Let us not revile mili-

tary glory, for that would be a symptom of hopeless
decadence; and let us remember that the more gold
a nation possesses, the greater is its need of arms to
guard its wealth.   Our country's greatness cost it
too many efforts, too many sacrifices, too much blood,
for it to be willing to renounce its heroic inheritance.
Let us, who are the sons of soldiers, not forget our
fathers, or fold our glorious banners!

V.

GOING back to 1803, we find France triumphant. Piedmont had just been annexed to its territory, which extends from the ocean to the Rhine, from the Gulf of Genoa to the mouth of the Scheldt. Italy, Switzerland, Holland, seem to be only a line of sentinels, ready to second the power of the Consular Republic. The English, who find it perfectly natural to have taken nearly all the French colonies, and to rule over every sea, are unwilling to admit that France can have a preponderating influence upon the continent. They looked with alarm on Napoleon's glory and the prosperity of the country. Sheridan said in the House of Commons: "Look at the map of Europe now, and see nothing but France. . . . Russia, if not in Napoleon's power, is, at least, in his influence; Prussia is at his beck; Italy is his vassal; Holland, in his grasp; Spain, at his nod; Turkey, in his toils; Portugal, at his feet. What is there left for Bonaparte to conquer, except England? But a country as great as England cannot submit to defeat." In fact, the treaty of Amiens produced only a truce, an experimental peace, as it was called in England. The English, who were always hostile and always jealous, remembered Pitt's words: "No regular government must be established in France. We must fight with France to the end." Hence, in spite of the formal stipulations of the treaty, they refused to evacuate Malta. The First Consul said to the English ambassador, Lord Whitworth: "I shall never yield on this point. I had rather see you in possession of the Faubourg Saint Antoine than of Malta. . . . Every day my irritation with England increases, because every puff of wind that comes from there carries only animosity and hate towards me. . . . I am stronger than you on land; rule the seas. If we can come to an understanding, we shall rule the world." England remained obstinate. Napoleon did the same. A renewal of the conflict became inevitable.

March 14, 1803, a few days before the peace was terminated, the Diplomatic Body met as usual at the Tuileries, and was awaiting in Madame Bonaparte's drawing-room the arrival of the First Consul and his wife. Meanwhile Josephine was finishing her dressing in her own room, and Napoleon was sitting on the floor by her side, playing with the son of Louis Bonaparte and Hortense, a baby five months old. The First Consul seemed in the best humor. Madame de Rémusat spoke to him about it, adding that probably the despatches to be forwarded after the audience would breathe nothing but peace and concord. Soon word is brought that the Diplomatic Body is assembled. Then Napoleon's face changed. " Come, ladies ! " and pale, his face drawn with the anger which is soon to break forth like a terrible thunder-storm, he hastily entered the drawing-room, and, without saluting any one, walked straight up to the English ambassador. His lips were trembling, his eyes flashing. " So you have determined on war ? " he said to Lord Whitworth. " We have already had ten years of it ; you want ten years more of it, and you force me to it." Then turning to the ambassadors of Spain and of Russia, " If they are the first to draw the sword, I shall be the last to sheathe it ; they have no respect for treaties ; henceforward we must cover them with black crape." The First Consul then left the English ambassador, but, growing a little calmer, he returned to him after a few seconds, and spoke to him politely on purely personal matters. But his wrath, which was allayed only for a moment, broke out again with more violence. " What is the meaning of those armaments ? Against whom are these precautionary measures ? I have not a single armed ship of the line in the ports of France. But if you arm, I shall arm, too. You may, perhaps, destroy France ; but as to intimidating it, never ! " At that moment Napoleon seemed overwhelmed with anger. His face was ablaze. Josephine and Madame de Rémusat looked at one another without a word.

The die was cast. The English ambassador demanded his passports and left Paris the night of May

12. It became necessary for the First Consul to prepare for the great struggle. To strike the imagination of the people, it was thought desirable that he
should make a triumphal appearance in Belgium,
which was the object of much jealous yearning, and
in Antwerp, which was like a loaded pistol aimed at
the heart of England. To arouse popular enthusiasm
and to strengthen public confidence, Bonaparte began
by asking officially the prayers of the archbishops and
bishops. Had he not said to Bourrienne at the time
of the Concordat, " You will see how much good I
shall get from the priests " ? The prelates in their
charges to the faithful, rivalled one another in patriotism and in devotion to the Ruler of the State. " Be
of good heart, my very dear brother," wrote the Archbishop of Paris, " the Giver of victory always guides
our armies; they have scarcely broken camp, and
already we are masters of the continental possessions
of our rival. But the conqueror of Europe knows
well that fortune of arms is fickle, and that our only
confidence is in conciliating the God of battles. He
wishes us to ask for prayers to secure the blessing of
Heaven upon our just undertakings. The love that
you have, my very dear brothers, for your country,
the gratitude that you owe to a gentle, beneficent,
and paternal government, are a sure guarantee of the
zeal with which you will second our religious sentiments." Among other charges we will quote from
that of the Archbishop of Rouen: " Let us pray
God, that this man of his right hand, this man who

by his command has done so much for the restoration
of his worship, and who proposes to do still more,
shall continue to be like Cyrus, the Christ of Providence, that it may watch over his life and cover him
with its wings; that it may protect his person from
the dangers to which the bold are exposed in battle,
and from the envy and calumny which pursue the
deserving."

The clergy kindled enthusiasm. The First Consul
started for Belgium with all the glory of a favorite
son of the Church. In this journey, which was a
long triumphal march, all the monarchical ceremonies
reappeared: the mayors brought to him the keys of
the cities; the priests sang the *Te Deum ;* young
girls, clad in white, presented him with bouquets;
rich young men formed guards of honor and brilliant
cavalry escorts; there was an abundance of military
music; church-bells were rung at full peal, drums
were beaten; everywhere he was warmly greeted;
and the people were drawn by curiosity, as much as
by admiration and gratitude, to crowd about the hero
of the Pyramids and of Marengo. Everywhere there
were triumphal arches and illuminations; and Bonaparte, who was generally very impatient, did not tire
of this ceremonial. There is one fragrance that the
rulers of empires, kingdoms, and republics always
breathe without fatigue: it is that of incense. Josephine accompanied him, with a suite of ladies, like a
queen; she followed her husband from town to town.
He was anxious to have his gracious and sympathetic

wife with him to complete his list of fascinations. He withdrew the crown-diamonds from the place where they were stored, and insisted on her wearing these precious jewels which formerly belonged to the Queens.

They left Saint Cloud June 24, 1803; a stop was made at Compiègne; and on the 26th they reached Amiens, where Napoleon was welcomed by a crowd of more than thirty thousand persons. The most ardent wanted to unharness the horses and drag his carriage. The ovation was most enthusiastic. Josephine wept for joy, and even Bonaparte's eyes moistened. The priest of a parish of Abbeville said to him, "Religion, as well as France, owes everything to you; we owe everything that we are to you; I owe to you all that I am." There was an old custom that whenever a King of France lodged at Amiens, the city should present him with four swans, and this custom was revived in honor of the First Consul, who ordered the swans sent to Paris to be placed in one of the basins of the Tuileries gardens, in order to show that he was regarded as a sovereign.

In leaving Amiens by the Calais gate, Bonaparte read the inscription, "Road to England." From there he went to Boulogne, to Dunkirk, and thence to Lille, where he arrived July 6. The greater part of the inhabitants of Douai, Valenciennes, Cambrai, and all the adjacent villages, had assembled on foot, on horseback, in carriages and chariots. The mayor of Lille, in presenting the First Consul with the keys of the city, said, "If the inhabitants were fortunate enough to preserve them from every attack of a hostile army, they are proud to offer them without a stain to you to-day." The municipality gave him a grand banquet in the theatre, and when he entered he was greeted with the popular song, —

"Where is one happier than in the bosom of one's family?"

Josephine wrote, July 9, to her daughter Hortense: "I have been busy receiving compliments ever since I left Paris. You know me, and you may judge for yourself whether I should not prefer a quieter life. Fortunately the society of my ladies consoles me for the noisy life I lead. I receive every morning, and often every evening, and then I have to go to a ball. This I should enjoy if you could be with me, or I could see you amusing yourself. What I miss more than anything is my dear Hortense and my little grandson, whom I love almost as much as I do his mother."

From Lille they went to Belgium, the country to which, and with reason, Napoleon attached so much importance. At the signing of the treaty of Amiens, he had said to a Belgian delegation: " The treaty of Campo-Formio had already defined Belgium's position. Since then our armies have known reverses. It was thought that the Republic might grow weak and yield in consequence of its misfortunes, but this was a great error. Belgium makes part of France, like its oldest province, like all the territories ac-

quired by formal treaty, like Brittany and Burgundy.
. . . Were the enemy in the Faubourg Saint
Antoine, the French government ought never to
abandon its rights."

On his arrival at Ostend, in the evening of July 9,
the First Consul found the streets illuminated and
decked with flags. On the 13th he was at Bruges.
On the bridge of Molin there was an imitation of the
bridge of Arcola. Bonaparte was represented in a
general's uniform, with a flag in his hand, among
life-size figures of French and Austrian soldiers. It
was all somewhat grotesque, although a tolerably
accurate reproduction of the celebrated battle, and it
did not fail to amuse the First Consul; but he saw
the kind intentions of the citizens of Bruges, and
thanked them for recalling memories which were
dear to him.

At Ghent, where he arrived July 14, the prefect
of the Department said to Josephine: "You, whose
tender affection is for the First Consul's happiness
what the admiration of his century is for his glory,
you we beg to accept our respects. We know, madame, how you rule every heart by your kindness.
Since this quality is adorned by every grace of mind
and talent, it is all-powerful; deign then to believe,
madame, that here all are submissive to your laws."
Nevertheless, the reception on the part of the populace was a little less enthusiastic than that of other
places. Bonaparte noticed this, and that evening he
said to Josephine, "The people here are devout, and

under the influence of the priests; to-morrow we must make a long visit to the church, win the clergy by some device, and so we shall regain ground." In fact, he heard mass with all the air of profound devotion, addressed some particularly amiable words to the bishop, and from that moment enthusiasm was at its height, and the First Consul and his wife were cheered at a ball given them by the city. The next day there was a grand entertainment on the parade, where a sort of a play was acted, consisting of many allegories. The rivers of Belgium were represented as making an alliance with the Seine and, under the protection of the god of Commerce, crushing the pride of the Thames.

July 18, they arrived at Antwerp, whence Davoust wrote to his wife: "We are here in a very pretty city which needs only a few years of peace to become one of the first of Europe. The inhabitants received the First Consul as if they had been French for a century. This is more surprising because they have never given a reception to any of their sovereigns. When Joseph II. came to see them, the windows were kept closed, and there was no one in the streets." On this occasion, however, the population of Antwerp was wild with enthusiasm. There was a curious procession in which a huge giant was carried through the streets, a ceremony only known on very great occasions, and one which had not been repeated since 1767. The mayor offered the First Consul, in the name of the city, six magnificent bay horses. Bon-

aparte, in return, presented this official with a scarf
of honor, a distinction previously accorded to but
two mayors, those of Lyons and of Rouen. Bonaparte was incessantly thinking of Antwerp as the
city where he hoped to build a navy that should
always rule between the Scheldt and the Thames.

Napoleon and Josephine stopped for a few hours
at Mechlin, on their way from Antwerp to Brussels.
They met there the Archbishop, Monsignor de Roque-
laure, a dignitary of the old régime, formerly Bishop
of Senlis, under Louis XVI. The kindly and witty
prelate said to Josephine: "Madame, after being
united to the First Consul by the sacred bonds of
a holy alliance, you now find yourself surrounded by
his glory. This situation adds to the charms of your
intelligence, to the sweetness of your character, and
the fascinations of your company. Continue, madame,
to exercise those amiable qualities which you have
received from the Author of every perfect gift; they
will be for your husband an agreeable relaxation from
the immense and painful tasks to which he devotes
himself every day out of love for his country. If our
prayers and our vows determine our mutual destinies,
you will both be happy, and your happiness will secure
ours." Bourrienne noticed the combination of religion
and gallantry in this short address. "Was there not,"
he adds, "a slight deviation from ecclesiastic propri-
ety in speaking as he did of sacred bonds and a holy
alliance, when it was a matter of common notoriety
that these bonds and this alliance existed only on

the municipal records? Or did the Archbishop have recourse to one of those formulas which casuists call, I believe, pious frauds, in order to induce the pair to do what he congratulated them on having done?"

Josephine played admirably her part as sovereign, for she deserved no other name when she was wearing the crown-jewels. She was happy, and thoroughly enjoyed her undeniable success. The people who showed her so much sympathy were sincere; then there was no artificiality in the sentiments she inspired; they were the reward of her charm, her grace, her sweetness, her kindness, her amiability, and her bounty. Her face, her smile, her voice, attracted every one. Her bearing and words were modest and amiable, with no trace of haughtiness. Rich and poor, nobles and plebeians, paid equal homage to the woman who possessed so much tact and heart, whom every one knew to be generous, obliging, charitable, and who excited no envy by her unexpected good fortune. It seemed as if she had been born to the purple. She might have served as a model to more than one princess whose ancestors for many years had been crowned heads.

The stay at Brussels was the culmination of the success of this journey. When they reached the boundaries of the department of the Dyle, in which the capital of Belgium is situated, Napoleon and Josephine saw an image symbolizing the river, in the form of a colossal statue seated by an urn. On the pedestal were these words: " I give my name to

the department; you, yours to your century." At a
distance of two leagues from Brussels, the First Consul was met by an army corps of twelve thousand
men from the Belgian fortresses, and a guard of
honor, consisting of five hundred mounted men, in a
red uniform, the flower of the young men of Brussels,
under the command of the son of the Prince of Ligne.
As soon as Bonaparte saw the troops, he descended
from his carriage, got on horseback, and placed himself at their head. It was as a general, rather than as
a civil ruler, that he wanted to enter Brussels. At
the end of the Allée Verte a triumphal arch had
been erected in his honor, after the model of the
arch of Titus in Rome. On each side was an amphitheatre, covered with carpets, where were seated
a number of women richly dressed. Cries of " Long
live Bonaparte! Long live the great man!" resounded from all quarters. Cannons were fired as
the First Consul passed under the triumphal arch.
Before the cathedral of Saint Gudule he was greeted
by the clergy, who, in their robes, with a cross in
front of them, were awaiting him on the steps at the
entrance. All the bells and chimes were rung. Josephine made her way, in a carriage presented by the
city, through a rain of flowers. The weather was
perfect, and every face was radiant with joy. Besides
the people of Brussels there were more than thirty
thousand strangers who had come from the Rhenish
Provinces and Holland to see the great man and his
charming wife. Their stay at Brussels was one long

series of ovations. Every evening the crowded streets were illuminated.

Announcement was made that Bonaparte and Josephine were to be present on Sunday at Saint Gudule to hear mass, with music, which was celebrated with extraordinary pomp. It was decided that the First Consul should be met at the entrance by the clergy with the cross, and that he should be led in a procession beneath the canopy, to the high altar. He was unwilling that Josephine should share this honor, and ordered her to take a place in a tribune with the Second Consul.

Mass was to be said at noon. The clergy had assembled at the entrance, awaiting Bonaparte's arrival, and contrary to his usual habit he was a few minutes late. They began to be uneasy, when suddenly he was seen entering by a side door; he came in alone, and took his place on the throne prepared for him near the high altar. The astonished priests hastened back to the choir, and the service began. Why had Napoleon thus surprised them? Because he had heard that on a similar occasion Charles V. had entered the cathedral by that little door which had since been called the door of Charles V. He wanted to do what the great Emperor had done.

There was great enthusiasm among the populace when the hero of so many battles reviewed the troops and spoke with his old comrades of Egypt and Italy. At Brussels he held his court like a king. He received Cardinal Caprara, whose presence made a most favorable impression on the Belgians, who are devout Catholics. He was surrounded by ministers, members of the Diplomatic Body, and a number of generals. No Emperor of Germany ever displayed greater magnificence.

Napoleon and Josephine visited Liège and Maëstricht after leaving Brussels, then they returned to the old limits of France by Mézières and Sedan, and reached Saint Cloud again August 12, after an absence of forty-eight days, during which time they had visited seventeen departments and eighty towns. General de Ségur speaks thus in his Memoirs of this triumphal journey: "How often have we seen Napoleon's interlocutors surprised by his perspicacity, which was so keen and penetrating that it seemed almost superhuman! And how proud we were at having been picked out by him, to seem to be in his confidence, to be at times his spokesmen, to be in the service of a man of such great and universal genius! Those who left him, to give way to others, were loud in their admiration and warm in their gratitude, as we often saw when, after his departure, his orders showed that everything was to be embellished, improved, perfected!" The First Consul's return to Saint Cloud was the signal for fresh congratulations, new addresses, which proved that the art of flattery was making progress from day to day. Louis XIV. himself never received more adulation; whatever the form of government, even under a Republic, France is a country that needs idols.

But consider the nothingness of human glory ! On his triumphal march to Brussels, Napoleon did not dream that near the great Belgian capital there was a little obscure village called Waterloo ; on his way back through Sedan, he little suspected what was to take place within the walls of that town sixty-seven years later. If it were granted to us to know the future, what man could have a moment of pride or even of vanity, even if he called himself Alexander, Cæsar, Charlemagne, or Napoleon? Power, wealth, glory, all are but trinkets. They are but the rattles with which fickle Fortune plays for a moment and then breaks in wantonness.

VI.

AFTER the First Consul's journey through Belgium, Saint Cloud acquired all the air of an
imperial or royal residence. There was a renewal
of the etiquette and the usages of the old régime.
When Madame Bonaparte received an official deputation, she arose and listened, standing, to the President's remarks, thanked him for the sentiments he
had expressed, then sat down without inviting her
visitors to do the same, and after a few minutes of
unimportant conversation stood up again, and dismissed her courtiers. Boots, trousers, sabres, disappeared, and silk stockings, buckled shoes, dress-
swords, hats carried under the arm, and lace ruffles,
took their place. In respect to headdress there was
a question whether the fashion of Louis XV. or that
of Louis XVI. should be revived; the old wig-makers
were at swords' points with the new. Every morning
Bonaparte's head was an object of great interest; if
he was powdered, every one had to imitate him.

In this monarchical, rather than Republican, circle,
the official presentation of Pauline Bonaparte, with

276

her new title of the Princess Borghese, produced a
sensation that was the delight of every Dangeau of
the time. Napoleon's sisters were treated like princesses of the blood. Caroline, whose husband, General Murat, held the important post of governor of
Paris, already displayed a boundless ambition and
great family pride. Elisa Bacciochi, who was always
surrounded by a little court of men of letters, of
whom Fontanes was the most devoted, desired a reputation as a wit, as a female Mæcenas, and played in
tragedy with her brother Lucien, who fancied himself
a second Talma. As for Pauline, she wished to wield
only one sceptre, and that sceptre no one could deny
her; it was that of beauty.

Pauline Bonaparte was born at Ajaccio, October 20,
1780. During the first Italian campaign she had
married one of the bravest and most brilliant of her
brother's comrades in arms, General Leclerc, who,
although born in 1772, had succeeded in acquiring a
reputation, in spite of his youth. Leclerc received a
command in the expeditionary corps which made the
perilous campaign of Saint Domingo, and the First
Consul, being unwilling that so pretty a woman as
Pauline should stay in Paris alone, ordered her to
follow her husband. If we may believe Madame
Junot (the Duchess of Abrantès), the beautiful
Madame Leclerc was in despair at the thought of
leaving France. "O Laurette," she said, throwing
herself into her friend's arms, "how fortunate you
are! You are going to stay in Paris, and heavens,

what a tedious life I shall have! How could my
brother be so hard and cruel as to exile me to the
society of savages and serpents? And then, I am ill;
I shall die before I get there!" Madame Junot, seeing her in tears, and fearful of the result, consoled
her with toys and finery, like a child. "Pauline,
you will be a queen there; Pauline, you will go
everywhere in a palanquin; you will always have a
black woman to wait on you, and you will walk
under orange-trees in blossom. How pretty you will
look in a creole dress!" As Madame Junot went
on, Pauline's sobbing lessened. "And so you think,
Laurette, that I shall look pretty, look prettier than I
do now, with a turban like a creole, a short waist,
and a skirt of striped muslin?" Madame Leclerc
rang for her maid, and had a fine collection of turbans
brought, which had just come from India. Madame
Junot picked out the most brilliant, and placed it
becomingly on Pauline's graceful head. "Laurette,
you know how much I love you, but you preferred
Caroline to me; well, we shall see if you don't repent
your choice. Now, I am going to give you a proof
of how much I love you. You must come to Saint
Domingo; you shall be the first after me. I shall be
queen, as you said just now, and you shall be vice-
queen. I am going to speak to my brother about it.
. . . We will give balls, and we will have picnics
among those beautiful mountains. Junot shall be
commander of the capital, — what is its name? I
shall tell Leclerc that he must give a party every

day." And while talking, Pauline pulled Madame
Junot's ear, in imitation of the First Consul's favorite
gesture.

Madame Leclerc departed without Madame Junot.
The fleet set sail for Saint Domingo in the month of
December, 1801. Every luxury and elegance had
been provided for the ship in which the sister of
the First Consul was to make the journey. The
beautiful Pauline resembled Cleopatra in her barge.
The voyage begun thus sumptuously had a sad issue.
The expedition was a complete failure; and in this
first check France had a warning of future disasters.
During this unsuccessful campaign, Pauline comported
herself nobly, displaying an energy worthy of her
blood. She had taken with her her little boy named
Dermide, a curious name given him by his godfather,
Napoleon, who at that time was passionately fond of
Ossian. At Saint Domingo she was a fond mother,
a devoted wife; she showed no fear of the epidemics
which were raging on the island, nor of the insurrec-
tion which broke out. Her husband ordered her to
sail back for home with the boy; but she refused,
saying that a Bonaparte could not run from danger.
When Leclerc was attacked by the illness which
carried him off in a few days, she nursed him with
incessant care, regardless of the danger of contagion
from the yellow fever, and piously carried back to
France the remains of the husband whom she mourned
sincerely. All these emotions and perils had affected
her health. That of her son, too, was destroyed by

the deadly climate, and the boy had but a few months to live.

Early in 1803, the news of General Leclerc's death reached Paris. The First Consul was deeply grieved, for he esteemed and liked his brother-in-law. The next day letters from Toulon announced the arrival at that port of the ship that brought Madame Leclerc and her son, together with the remains of the lamented general. " In January, 1803," says Madame de Rémusat, " the young and pretty widow returned to France. She was at the time the victim of an illness from which she always afterwards suffered; but though weak and ailing, and dressed in mourning, she seemed to me the most charming person I had ever seen."

General Leclerc's death gave rise to a little diplomatic incident, and the way this was settled shows once more how much the Republic under a Consul resembled a monarchy. It is thus told by Madame de Rémusat: " Bonaparte went into mourning as well as Madame Bonaparte, and we who were attached to the household received orders to do the same thing. That in itself was somewhat striking, but the question came up about the visit to be made to the Tuileries by the ambassadors, in order to condole with the Consul and his wife in their loss. It was conveyed to them that politeness required that they too should wear mourning when they called. They met to deliberate, and not having time to receive instructions from their various courts, they decided to make the visit and to observe the formalities usual in such cases."

At first Pauline seemed an inconsolable widow, a real Artemisia. She had her hair cut off in order to place it, in token of her grief, within her husband's coffin. "Oh!" said the First Consul, "she knows it will come out much handsomer for having been cut."

A lady equally conspicuous for intelligence, kindliness, and talents, the Marchioness of Blocqueville, the worthy daughter of the famous Marshal Davoust, has published a remarkable book, called "Marshal Davoust, Prince of Eckmühl, described by his family and by himself." In this volume, which is full of interesting details, is to be found a curious note on the subject of Pauline's grief. Davoust, it should be said, had married Mademoiselle Aimée Leclerc, sister of General Leclerc, and hence sister-in-law of Pauline Bonaparte. "The body of General Leclerc was brought back from Saint Domingo, and laid in the park of Montgobert. His heart was enclosed in a gold urn. The Princess Pauline Bonaparte, his wife, who had been anxious to accompany him on that fatal expedition, after covering his face with her beautiful hair, like another Agrippina, but more beautiful, tenderer, less ambitious, as well as less severe than the first, brought back the heart of her husband, after having engraved on the vase which held it a few words of love. Doubtless it would be possible to inscribe beneath this utterance of ostentatious grief the famous lines scratched, according to tradition, by Francis I. on a

window of Chambord. Nevertheless, my mother has
often told me that her sister-in-law had assured her
that she had never loved any one so much as Leclerc.
It is possible. A witty critic has maintained that all
princesses imagine themselves to be almost demi-
gods; in that case, they feel authorized to practise
the religion of memorials like ordinary mortals."

What is certain is that in 1803, Pauline Bonaparte,
more beautiful than ever, seemed almost consoled.
She had made the conquest of a great Italian nobleman, Prince Camille Borghese, born in Rome, in
1775, who asked to marry her. The First Consul did
not give his assent at once. He did not wish by any
undue haste to seem to be over-gratified by an aristocratic alliance with which, in fact, he was very well
pleased. At Saint Helena he said on the subject of
this marriage: "My foreign birth, which was sometimes brought up against me in France, was of great
value to me. One result was that all the Italians
looked on me as a fellow-countryman. . . . When the
question came up of the marriage of my sister Pauline
and Prince Borghese, there was only one feeling in
Rome and in Tuscany, in this family and all its
branches. 'There is no objection,' they all said; 'it's
between ourselves; they are one of our families.'"

The wedding of Pauline and Prince Borghese took
place November 6, 1803, in Joseph Bonaparte's castle
at Mortefontaine. A few days later the new princess and her husband were formally presented at
Saint Cloud, and the ceremony is thus described by

the Duchess of Abrantès. It was evening, and the wife of the First Consul was awaiting the arrival of her sister-in-law. She, too, was anxious to appear well. Although it was winter, she wore a thin dress of India muslin. At the lower edge there was a little border, as wide as a finger, of gold foil. The waist, which was draped in thick folds in front, was caught at each shoulder by a lion's head in black enamel; an embroidered girdle was fastened by a clasp like the lions' heads on her shoulders. With her short sleeves, bare arms, and her hair enclosed in a gilt net, the meshes of which met on her forehead, she looked like a beautiful Greek statue. The First Consul led her to the mirror over the mantelpiece that he might see her on all sides at once, and, kissing her shoulder, said: "Ah! Josephine, I shall be jealous; you have some plan in your head. Why are you so beautiful to-day?" "I know that you like to see me in white, and so I put on a white dress; that is all." "Well, if you did it to please me, you have succeeded," and he kissed her again. But the princess was a little late, and Bonaparte went back to his study a little annoyed. Suddenly a carriage was heard in the courtyard; it was a magnificent barouche, adorned with a coat-of-arms, and it was drawn by six fine horses. The outrider and the footman carried lighted torches. Then the newly married pair, who had come to make their wedding call, alighted, and reached the door of the great drawing-room. An usher flung open the door and in a loud voice announced: "Prince and Princess Borghese." The princess was in great splendor, in a dress of green velvet covered with diamonds. On one side she carried a cluster of precious stones, emeralds, and pearls of incalculable value, and on her head she wore a diadem of emeralds and diamonds. Josephine assumed all the airs of a queen, and let her sister-in-law come up to her along nearly the whole length of the drawing-room. A few minutes later Pauline said to Madame Junot, "My sister-in-law thought she would put me out by making me walk through the drawing-room, but instead I was delighted." "Why so?" "Because my train would not have shown if she had met me at the door, where as it was, my train was very much admired."

Suddenly, however, the charming princess discovered something which marred her triumph. She had forgotten — and she could not forgive herself — that the furniture of the room was covered with blue, an admirable background for Josephine's white muslin; but she had on a green dress which quarrelled frightfully with that color. "Oh, heavens!" she whispered in despair to Madame Junot, "I put on a green dress to sit on a blue chair." In a few minutes the Princess walked straight to Josephine to take her leave, and the two sisters-in-law parted.

If Pauline Bonaparte had belonged to an utterly obscure family, she would still have been famous for her beauty; but when we remember that to the beauty of a Venus, worthy to inspire a genius like Canova,

she had the advantage of being Napoleon's sister and
the wife of one of the great Roman nobles, it is easy
to understand that her success was without precedent.
Whenever she went to the theatre, every opera-glass
was turned towards her. Her entrance into a ball-
room was greeted by a long murmur of admiration.
Her attire was always carefully studied, and very
beautiful; her jewelry was of enormous value. She
inspired the wildest enthusiasm. In fact, these exceptional women, these "professional beauties," as the
English call them, are seldom happy. Living always
for show, they have no leisure for domestic joy or for
genuine emotion. In their artificial existence there
is a perpetual fever, as if they were actresses. They
are admired, to be sure, but this admiration arouses
jealousy; and the men on whom they do not smile
become as hostile as the women whom they eclipse.
They are the prey of gossip and scandal; their most
innocent actions are misinterpreted. In spite of the
incense burned before them, of the splendid luxury
which surrounds them, as if they were living idols,
of their pride gratified by a multitude of worshippers,
they feel that they live in an atmosphere of disappro-
bation, even of hate. The first sign of age, the first
wrinkle, the first deception, comes to them as a
calamity. Every new beauty who appears in the
drawing-room seems to them an insolent rival. They
wish to reign without dispute. Any one who does
not loudly praise them they regard as a foe; criticism
seems to them like rebellion. In a word, they seek

amusement so eagerly that they tire themselves; and
if any trace of moral dignity, of a moral ideal, is left
in them, they are sure to detect the bitter dregs in
the cup from which they thought to drink only nec-
tar and ambrosia.   In the early years of the century
the Princess Borghese was a model of flawless beauty.
Were such a woman living now, everything she did
would be published in the papers, especially in the
" society papers," as they are called.

VII.

MADAME MOREAU.

IS not history a tragi-comedy, in which Shakespea-
rian contrasts follow one another? After the
scene of the players comes the scene of the grave-
diggers; after the splendors of Saint Cloud, the moat
of Vincennes. We have just been speaking of a pretty
woman, a queen of beauty, of her jewels, her dresses,
her finery; now we have to turn to the gloomiest
subjects, — plots, treachery, death sentences, and a
murder. We have just seen Bonaparte happy and
triumphant, intoxicated with success, living in the
royal palaces with all the splendor of a new Louis
XIV.; now we shall see him uneasy, anxious, fearful
of ambushes at every turn, and finally losing his head
to the point of committing a crime, which shall haunt
his memory even at Saint Helena.

"Where is the woman?" used always to ask a
judge who well knew human nature. The woman
in the case of Cadoudal, Moreau, and Pichegru —
one of the consequences of which was the death of
the Duke of Enghien — was Madame Moreau. Had
it not been for her jealousy, vanity, and feminine

spite, her husband, instead of being the unrelenting enemy of Napoleon, would have become Marshal of France, duke, prince, like Davoust, like Ney, like Masséna. This thought suggested itself to me when I was looking at the little monument raised to him near Dresden, on the spot where the hero of Hohenlinden fell by the side of the Emperor of Russia. The ball, it will be remembered, took off both his legs.

What was the origin of Moreau's hatred for Napoleon, who had made him many advances? It was the petty jealousy of Madame Moreau, who was unwilling to acknowledge her inferiority to any woman. She said to herself: "I am younger, prettier, better educated than Madame Bonaparte. I was not mixed up in the society of Tallien and Barras, as she was. I don't mean to be her lady of honor, her servant. After all, we are living in a republic, and we have nothing to do with a sovereign. This parody of the old courts is a contemptible farce. If Bonaparte has won victories, my husband has also won them, and both are generals of the Republic, and my husband is the elder; he has commanded larger armies, and has served his country with equal glory. I have a right to be treated with respect; I should not be obliged to wait in anterooms. If there are people low enough to forget their dignity to that extent, I am not one of them."

Those who were interested in making a definite breach between the First Consul and General Moreau — and there were many, in the Republican as well as in the Bourbon camp—poured oil on the fire to the best of their ability. Those Royalists who had not yet given their allegiance to the Consular Court paid all sorts of attentions to Madame Moreau, and the leaders of the aristocracy made a point of frequenting her house in the rue d'Anjou Saint Honoré, where she used to give large balls. The First Consul detested pin-pricks as much as dagger-strokes, and feared much more the opposition of the drawing-rooms than that of public places, because it is subtler, more impalpable than the other; and he was extremely annoyed by this petty warfare, by these feminine skirmishings, in which, with all his power, he could never get the upper hand. The idlers, who always abound in Paris, the Republicans, wroth with the elevation of the Corsican Cæsar, the returned émigrés, who were enraged at not once more getting possession of their estates, were forever talking about these dissensions, which set the two greatest Republican generals at loggerheads.

Josephine, however, who was always courteous and kindly, tried her best to pacify the wife of the conqueror of Hohenlinden. Madame Moreau had been one of her schoolmates at Madame Campan's at Saint Germain, where she had acquired those accomplishments which, in conjunction with her beauty, had filled her with a pride which her marriage with Moreau had only augmented. Josephine had done much to further this match, which she regarded as favorable to the First Consul's interests.

At that time Bonaparte and Moreau were on good terms. In the morning of the 18th Brumaire, when the First Consul had gone on horseback from his house in the rue Chantereine to the Tuileries, Moreau was one of the generals who escorted him. Bonaparte took a malign pleasure in compromising him by bidding him to keep his eye on the Directors at the Luxembourg, thus making him the jailer of the representatives of legality, while the *coup d'état* was taking place in the orange-house at Saint Cloud. On his return from Marengo, the First Consul had wished to make Moreau a present, and he had made for him a pair of valuable pistols on which were engraved the names of the principal battles in which the general had distinguished himself. " You must excuse me," Bonaparte said when he gave him the pistols, " if they are not more ornamented; the names of your victories took all the place."

Moreau married Mademoiselle Hulot the 18th Brumaire, year IX. (November 9, 1800), exactly one year before the day when Bonaparte seized the highest power. In ten days the bridegroom went to take command of the Army of Germany, and December 3, 1800, he won the brilliant victory of Hohenlinden. On hearing of this battle, Madame Moreau hastened to the Tuileries to see the First Consul and Madame Bonaparte, but she called several times without getting in. The last time she went she was accompanied by her mother, Madame Hulot, a rich creole from the Isle of France, an ambitious woman, quick to take

offence and slow to forgive. Mother and daughter
waited for a long time, but in vain. As they were
going away, Madame Hulot was very angry, and said
in a loud voice that her daughter was not to be kept
waiting in that way.

Soon after, Madame Moreau joined her husband in
Germany, and her pride increased when she saw for
herself what fame and glory surrounded him. Madame
Hulot, who had stayed in France, went one day to
Malmaison to solicit the promotion of her eldest son, a
naval officer; Josephine received her very kindly and
asked her to stay to dinner, without saying anything
about it to her husband. At table Bonaparte was
visibly annoyed; he hardly spoke to her, and after
dinner he turned his back upon her. Josephine did
her best to atone for his impoliteness, saying that he
was much preoccupied and anxious about some
despatches that had not arrived.

The Duchess of Abrantès narrates a talk she had
with the First Consul a few days after Madame Hulot's visit to Malmaison. "Do you know Madame
Moreau?" "I used to see her in society when we
were young." "Isn't she very clever in a great
many ways?" "Yes; I know that she dances very
well. Steilbelt, who is my dancing-master as well as
hers, says that next to Madame Delarue-Beaumarchais,
Mademoiselle Hulot was the best pupil he had; she
paints miniatures; she knows a good many languages,
and then she is very pretty." "Oh! I can judge that
as well as any one, and I don't think so. She has a

face like a nut-cracker, a bad expression, and a very unattractive appearance." Then Josephine broke in, " You don't like her, and are unfair to her." Bonaparte answered, " It is true, I don't like her; and for a very simple reason, — she hates me. She and her mother are the evil geniuses of Moreau. Whom do you think Josephine had to dinner the other day? Madame Hulot — Madame Hulot at Malmaison !" " But," resumed Madame Bonaparte, " she came to make peace." " To make peace — Madame Hulot! My poor Josephine, you are very credulous, very simple !"

It must be acknowledged that, with all his genius, Napoleon lacked the equability and self-possession which are necessary in a drawing-room. He could not hide his antipathies, and he was subject to freaks, to outbreaks of roughness and impatience which were the despair of the people of the old régime like Talley-rand. Josephine, on the other hand, knew how to control herself, and could smile when her heart was heavy. Being courteous from principle as well as by nature, she never offended any one, and as a well-bred woman she received with charming grace even those of whom she had good cause to complain. Having lived successively in Royalist, Republican, and Consular drawing-rooms, she was very familiar with Parisian society, and by her tact and affability knew how to reconcile the most hostile elements. Had it been left to her, she would have smoothed all the dissensions that arose between her husband and Moreau.

But Bonaparte listened only to his wrath. He had, it must be said, horror of any rivalry; he would gladly have loaded Moreau with benefits, with honors, with money, but on one condition, — that no one should presume to compare the hero of Hohenlinden with the hero of Marengo. There seemed as great a difference between him and Moreau as between Louis XIV. and Condé; and if he had been in the place of Louis XIV., he would not have liked to hear much said about the battle of Rocroy. Being younger than his principal lieutenants, and having attained a wonderful position with astonishing rapidity, he fancied that the slightest familiarity would mar his reputation, and he tried to draw a rigid line between himself and his generals. He demanded as much, in matters of etiquette, for his wife, and compelled her, notwithstanding the marked modesty which always distinguished her, to assume the manners and tone of a queen. This greatly annoyed Madame . Moreau, who said it was scarcely worth while to have overthrown the old dynasty, if now they had to endure another.

To these feminine grievances were added the serious regret of a certain number of generals and officers who continued to be austere Republicans, the volunteers of the early years of the Republic, who had suffered in the cause of liberty and national independence, for which they had sacrificed themselves with a devotion void of all personal ambition. General de Ségur has drawn the portrait of these "Spartans of the Rhine," as they were then called, — sturdy ancients, who preserved great simplicity in dress and manner, and manifested a haughty and disdainful surprise at the sight of the reviving luxury and of the ambitious passions which took the place of the simple, disinterested devotion of the early Republican enthusiasm.

When Moreau returned to France without any command, he fell under the influence of unoccupied and discontented companions. There had long been a latent rivalry between the officers of the Army of Italy and those of the Army of the Rhine. The last-named gave expression to their ill-humor with all a soldier's frankness. One of them, General Domon, who had a very caustic tongue, happened to be one evening at a restaurant. He asked what they had ready. "Chicken *à la* Marengo," answered the waiter. "What do I care for chicken *à la* Marengo?" shouted Domon. "What I want is beef *à la* Hohenlinden."

We who live in a period of comparative tranquillity cannot easily form an idea of the French officers at the beginning of the century. Caring for nothing but duels and battles, they were completely out of their element in time of peace. The more rigid their discipline in the ranks, the freer and more unbridled their talk when their service was over. The officers' coffee-houses were like the old clubs, and they themselves talked like the old tribunes. It was not easy to control these men, thirsting for adventure, eager for action, for emotion, and peril. Civilian dress did not become them, and they seemed awkward when holding a little switch instead of a sabre. Averse to seeking in study and intellectual work an outlet for their activity, they crowded the coffee-houses, theatres, the galleries and restaurants of the Palais Royal, scorning everything which was not military, saying that the Consul would amount to nothing without the army, and yet opposing the growth of his power, when all the rest of the country was bowing before it respectfully. They looked on Moreau and Bernadotte as the last of the Romans.

The future King of Sweden and Norway, who at his coronation insisted on being anointed on his forehead, his temples, his chest, and his wrist by the Archbishop of Upsala, while he held a golden horn full of consecrated oil, was never tired of laughing at the Concordat and at Bonaparte's Catholicism. The future Charles XIV., who on the same occasion rode out in triumph on horseback, wearing a Spanish coat of silver cloth embroidered with diamonds, and a plumed hat like that of Henry IV., now affected in his dress and bearing a thoroughly Republican simplicity. Who could have foreseen that the time would come when he should walk beneath a canopy, while four chamberlains of the highest nobility should carry the train of his royal mantle?

Bernadotte had married Mademoiselle Désirée Clary, a young woman whom Napoleon had been anxious to marry at the beginning of his career. She was the sister of Madame Joseph Bonaparte. In 1803 he spent his time in quarrelling with the First Consul, and then in seeking to make peace. He had given up the command of the Army of the West, and was in Paris in disgrace. But the First Consul stood godfather for his son, who was named Oscar, under the influence of Ossian, at that time a much-admired poet. Méneval says: " Bernadotte, who was so obsequious before Napoleon, was forever conspiring against him; and then he resorted to everything to win forgiveness. Joseph Bonaparte and his wife displayed as much energy in securing his pardon as Bernadotte did in his alternations of offence and submission."

As for Moreau, he systematically rejected the First Consul's advances. He made a great show of never appearing except in plain clothes, even at a meeting of officers; an excess of apparent modesty, which we may well regard as an excess of pride. Rulers may always mistrust those generals who do not wish to wear their uniform.

One day Moreau refused an invitation to a formal dinner at the Tuileries, saying he preferred to dine with only a few friends. On another occasion he refused to accompany the First Consul to a review. When he was invited with the other generals to hear the *Te Deum* for the Concordat at Notre Dame, and to the banquet at the Tuileries, he did not go to the *Te Deum*, and that evening he ridiculed it in the presence of the Minister of War, with some other generals who were dining with him. Once again, there was a great supper at the palace, and Moreau was absent. When somebody expressed surprise,

Bonaparte said that since his invitations had been twice declined, he did not care to have that happen again; and Moreau was never again invited. His coolness soon became open hostility. He made, in winter, his mansion in the rue d'Anjou, and in summer his country-place, Grosbois, a centre of opposition. There the First Consul was treated as a usurper with more luck than ability, as a traitor to the Republic, and his plan of invading England was called a wild dream. When Bonaparte received the report of this talk from the police, he was furiously angry. "Moreau," we read, in his "Memorial of Saint Helena," "was ruled entirely by his wife, which is always a misfortune, said the Emperor, because a man is, in that case, neither himself nor his wife; in fact, he is nothing at all. Moreau was sometimes friendly, sometimes hostile to the First Consul, sometimes obsequious, sometimes bitter. The First Consul, who would gladly have made a friend of him, found himself obliged to have nothing to do with him. Moreau, he said, will end by breaking his head against the columns of the palace. He was driven to that by the absurd inconsistencies and pretensions of his wife and his mother-in-law, who even went so far as to wish to take precedence of the wife of the First Consul. Once, said Napoleon, the Minister of Foreign Affairs had to use force to prevent this at a grand banquet."

Moreau's position in 1803 bore some likeness to that of General Changarnier before the *coup d'état* of

December 2. He was surrounded by both Republicans and Royalists, and all the malcontents flocked to him. The Bourbons, who were as credulous as exiles always are, thought they had found in him a restorer of royalty, while, in fact, Moreau, who imagined that he had a party in the Senate and in the army, was working only for himself, and in spite of all the illusions of the Royalists, he looked upon the part of a Monk as something below him. The officers who were devoted to him had no share in the ideas and interests of the émigrés. General de Ségur, who was a grandson of a Marshal of France, the Minister of War under Louis XVI., who had felt a momentary admiration for Moreau, left him, because he found him unjust to the point of insolence for the men and things of the old régime. "It was Moreau's rudeness," he said, "which first opened my eyes to the mistake I had made. One morning I had been to the rue d'Anjou Saint Honoré, and Grenier or Lecourbe and he began to talk in my presence about the French army at the time of Louis XV. I listened to his remarks as if they were oracles, although in fact they were not at all remarkable, — for his way of speaking and his manners were noticeably common, — when forgetting or not knowing my relationship, he spoke of all the generals of the old régime, without exception, in the vilest and most insulting language. This brought all my blood to my face, and wounded by this attack on my grandfather, a brave man, maimed in his country's service, for whom I was then in mourning, I left at once. My anger was not less keen because I was unable to make any reply to this insolent brutality."

The Royalists were not so particular; they imagined that Moreau was their man, and nothing could remove this idea from their heads. But vague rumors began to get into circulation. The First Consul's friends said that his life was seriously threatened, and at Saint Cloud and the Tuileries precautions were taken which were turned to ridicule by Moreau's friends. In certain sets it was the fashion to say that the alleged plots were an innovation of the police; but the Chouans knew better. As to the general public, it awaited events. In the night of February 14, 1804, a Council of Ministers was held at the Tuileries. "I have been the kindest of men," said Bonaparte, "but I shall be the most terrible when it is necessary, and I shall crush Moreau, as I should the next man, for entering into plots odious in their aim, and disgraceful for the affiliations which they imply." The next morning a picked force was sent to the rue d'Anjou Saint Honoré, to arrest Moreau at his home. The gendarmes, failing to find him there, started to seek him at his country-place, and met him on the bridge of Charenton returning to Paris. He was arrested and conveyed to the Temple, where the famous general of the Republican army must have remembered another captive, King Louis XVI.

VIII.

MOREAU was arrested, and every one was asking the cause of this unexpected event. The provinces were comparatively indifferent, but at Paris there was much excitement in the drawing-rooms, the cafés, and in the reunions of the officers who had belonged to the Army of the Rhine. Every one was wondering what was the explanation of the mystery. The First Consul said to Madame de Rémusat: "I have just ordered Moreau's arrest. Ah! you are surprised; that will make some talk, don't you think? People will say that I am jealous of Moreau, and that this is a bit of revenge, and a thousand platitudes of that sort. I jealous of Moreau! Why, he owes the greater part of his glory to me; I let him have a fine army, and kept nothing but recruits in Italy; I asked nothing better than to live on good terms with him. I certainly was not afraid of Moreau; for I am not afraid of any one, and least of all, of Moreau. Twenty times at least I have saved him from compromising himself; I told him that they would make trouble between us, and he knew it as well as I did. But he is weak and proud, the women controlled him, and the political parties made him their tool." After speaking thus, Bonaparte went up to Josephine, took her by the chin, lifting her head, and said: "Not every man has a good wife as I have. You are crying, Josephine; why? are you afraid?" "No," she answered, "but I don't like to think of what will be said." "But what can you do? I am not moved by hate or any desire of revenge; I have thought a long time before having Moreau arrested. I might have kept my eyes shut and have given him a chance to run away, but then it would have been said that I did not dare to bring him to trial. I have the means of convicting him; he is guilty; I am the government; all this will go off very simply."

The First Consul's friends maintained that if Moreau was arrested, it was because he was guilty, and they defended Bonaparte against every charge of jealousy or injustice. But the opposition asserted that the conspiracy was an idle story, an invention of the police, and that it should not be called Moreau's conspiracy, but the conspiracy against Moreau. The prisoner's wife put on an air of majestic grief which added to the impression already produced by her husband's arrest and incarceration. It was scarcely three months since the affair of the infernal machine; and since men's memories are short in Paris, a number of people held that an attempt to assassinate the First Consul was an impossibility. It was everywhere said that it was abominable to suppose that the hero of

Hohenlinden could be a criminal. It was, to be sure, whispered that Pichegru and Georges Cadoudal were in Paris, hiding in some mysterious, impenetrable corner; but then it was added that this was a mere fancy of the police, that the alleged conspirators were not in Paris, and they defied the government to find them.

Yet there was great anxiety among those about Bonaparte, and ever since the autumn the men who had charge of his safety were in continual expectation of a catastrophe. There were sudden alarms first at Saint Cloud, and afterwards at the Tuileries. Ségur, who had charge of the guard of the First Consul, gave the watchwords and countersigns, and took the most minute precautions in concert with his band of picked men. Every day a new attempt was feared; at one time it was a projected ambush near Malmaison from which an attack was to be made on the First Consul's carriage; at another, it was a mine dug beneath the road through which he would have to pass, and where he would be stopped by a block of vehicles; once, at Saint Cloud, the guards found a man leaning against a statue very near the door of Napoleon's study, which opened on the terrace of the orange-house; and once, too, an officer, who was more anxious than usual, said to Ségur: "Didn't you see from the window where I always stand a stout, short man, with thick eyebrows, a fierce expression, whose head seemed sunk in his shoulders?" That tallied with the description of the invisible and terrible Chouan, Georges Cadoudal.

Early in February, 1804, at the Tuileries, Ségur, who was on duty, had fallen asleep on his camp-bed one night at about one o'clock, when he felt some one shaking him very hard. He sprang up, and saw that it was Caulaincourt, who said, "Get up! You must change the watchword at once, and do everything as if we were in the presence of the enemy. You understand me; there's not a moment to lose." Ségur immediately organized the rounds and the patrols in the palace, the garden, and all about, in such a way that every sentinel was obliged to challenge at least three times a minute. This system continued many weeks, until the crisis had passed.

Moreau was arrested February 15, and Pichegru on the 28th of the same month, but Georges Cadoudal, the head of the conspiracy, still eluded capture. The First Consul was very angry, and insisted that the police must lay hands on this man, who had long been laughing at them, for his arrest was absolutely necessary for the preliminary trial. To this end the most vigorous measures were taken. Paris was kept under close inspection. Entrance was permitted, but no one was allowed to leave. Any one trying to break this order was liable to be shot down like a dog. The garrison was put on a war footing; the Seine was covered with barges full of gendarmes; all the gates were kept closed; night and day Paris was surrounded by posts, bivouacs, and sentinels; orders were

given to fire on any one appearing outside of the
walls. Jury trial was suspended; the concealment
of the conspirators was declared high treason, and it
was ordered that the concealment of any information
about them should be punished by six years' impris-
onment. It was like a return to the days of the
Terror. The First Consul pursued the conspirators
as a hunter pursues his prey, for it was with him a
matter of honor as well as a means of protecting his
life. If Cadoudal eluded arrest, the plot could not
be proved, and the government would be left in a
detested and ridiculous position. At last, on the 9th
of March, the terrible Chouan was hunted down. At
about seven in the evening, when he was escaping in
a cab, he was pursued and caught in the Carrefour
de Bucy. He blew out the brains of one of the men
who were running to stop the cab-horse, but the crowd
surrounded him; resistance would have been useless;
he was captured.

Then the public began to believe in the reality of
the conspiracy. It was not a Republican plot, but,
like the incident of the infernal machine, a Royalist
plot, in which it must be acknowledged that the
Bourbon princes had taken part. The ringleader was
Georges Cadoudal, who was born January 1, 1771,
at Kerléano, near Auray; he was the son of a laboring
man, and had been the leader of the Breton Chouans.
After he had been compelled to accept the peace nego-
tiated by General Brune, January 2, 1800, he had
betaken himself to Paris, where he had had a secret

interview with the First Consul. Bonaparte, who knew men well, and had at a glance discovered the Breton leader's sturdy character, made every effort to win him over to his side. In a conversation that lasted nearly two hours he did his best to persuade him to choose between a position as general in command of a division of the Army of Italy and an annual pension of one hundred thousand francs, on the sole condition that he should abstain from politics; but Cadoudal was inflexible.

Bourrienne has given an account of this mysterious interview which took place at the Tuileries. Rapp introduced the famous Chouan into a drawing-room overlooking the garden. The doors were left open, and Bourrienne and Rapp, who were in the adjoining anteroom, saw the First Consul and Georges Cadoudal walking up and down the whole length of the room for a long time in animated conversation. At times their words and gestures became excited. " You don't look at things in the right way," said Bonaparte, " and you make a great mistake in not coming to any agreement. But if you insist on going back to your own country, you shall leave Paris as freely as you entered it." When the talk was over, and nothing had come of it, the First Consul said to Rapp, " Tell me why you left the doors open and stayed there with Bourrienne." " If you had closed the door," answered Rapp, " I should have opened it again." Bonaparte, who took a very low view of human nature, but had a high feeling about matters of honor, said, " For

shame, Rapp; you would have done nothing of the
sort! Cadoudal," he went on, "takes a faulty view
of things, but the exaggeration of his principles is
due to very noble feelings, which must give him a
great deal of influence. We must put a stop to it,
however."

After this interview, the Breton chief felt insecure
in Paris and went to England, where he was warmly
greeted by the English government, and he received
from Louis XVIII., through the Count of Artois, the
position of lieutenant-general, the grand ribbon of
Saint Louis, and a congratulatory letter on his conduct. The treaty of Amiens put a stop to the plotting, but it began anew at the outbreak of hostilities.
There was no limit to English perfidy; their minister
at Munich set in motion a far-reaching conspiracy.
He communicated to his agents in France a way to
win over the guards of arsenals and powder-magazines,
so as to be able to burn them or blow them up whenever necessary. Lord Hawkesbury, in the face of all
Europe, loudly proclaimed this doctrine, that " every
wise government owes it to itself to take every possible advantage from any dissatisfaction that may exist
in a country with which it is at war, and consequently
it should lend aid and encouragement to the plans of
the malcontents." Georges Cadoudal organized his
conspiracy with the aid of English money. He re-
solved to go secretly to Paris, where Pichegru should
join him, and there to enter into communication with
Moreau, on whom he thought he could count, and to

set on foot a criminal attack on the First Consul. With him out of the way, Moreau and Pichegru would take control of the army, and Louis XVIII. would be called to the throne. Since he intended to take a band of conspirators with which to attack Bonaparte surrounded by his escort, he said to himself, in palliation of the murder, that it would not be an assassination, but a fair fight: singular casuistry, which shows how blinding are political passions!

Near Dieppe, towards Biville, there is a cliff more than two hundred and fifty feet high, and there it was, less than a hundred paces from a signal-tower occupied by a lookout, which, however, left it at night, that Cadoudal mysteriously returned to France, August 22, 1803. A rope as thick as a merchant-vessel's cable was let down the cliff; it was made fast to a series of stakes set deep in the earth every six feet. It was in nightly use by smugglers, — the last to ascend coiling the rope and fastening it to a post in order to hide it from the patrol below; and by this perilous climb Cadoudal, and a few weeks later, Rivière, Polignac, General Pichegru, and many other conspirators were able to enter the country. Hiding by day and advancing by night they succeeded in reaching Paris in disguise, and there for a long time they eluded the police. Pichegru, who had landed at the cliff of Biville January 16, 1804, was in Paris four days later. He had an interview with Moreau one dark night on the boulevard de la Madeleine. The two generals had not met since the time when they had fought together so gloriously on the banks of the Rhine. They were joined by Cadoudal, to Moreau's great surprise and evident annoyance, for he was anxious to work for himself rather than for the Chouans. " This is a bad beginning," the Breton leader said to himself; and a few days later, when he saw that the intriguers had misled him with regard to Moreau's real intentions, he said, " Usurper for usurper; I prefer the one who now governs to this Moreau who has no head and no heart." Pichegru did not deceive himself about his old comrade; he said, with some bitterness, " He, too, is ambitious and wants to govern France; but, poor fellow, he couldn't govern it twenty-four hours." Meanwhile, the Count of Artois, who was misled by false reports, exclaimed with joy, " Since our two generals agree, I shall soon be back in France." The conqueror of Holland was given up by a treacherous friend. " Pichegru," said Napoleon, " was a victim of the most infamous treachery. It was a disgrace to humanity; his intimate friend sold him; this man, whom I will not mention by name, so odious and disgusting was his action, an old officer, since then in business at Lyons, came with an offer to give him up for a hundred thousand crowns."

All this is like a novel, or a melodrama, with this curious setting and series of adventures, with the mysterious, invisible men who defy the police; with the Biville cliffs at which English boats secretly touch in the darkness; the hiding in the woods, and in the very heart of Paris; the bold Breton who plays fearlessly with danger and death; the hero of Hohenlinden arrested like a common criminal; the conqueror of Holland banished and tracked like a wild beast! All these strange, unexpected incidents were very impressive, and threw a gloom over our giddy Paris. There spread vague rumors of the speedy arrival on French territory of a prince of the house of Bourbon. Was it the Count of Artois, the Duke of Berry, the Duke of Angoulême, the Duke of Enghien? Were the Vendeans going to renew the fight? Did the English mean to land troops, arms, and supplies on the coast? Was the First Consul to be assassinated? And was he to be killed with a dagger, or by a new infernal machine? And what would happen then? Would the Republic or a monarchy be established? All the questions were answered by each party according to its wishes.

Meanwhile Bonaparte was uneasy, nervous, agitated; and he watched at the same time Paris, the provinces, and foreign countries, observing the Vendeans, England, and the Rhine, ready to ward the blow, from whatever quarter it might come. He was in a state of extreme tension; and he employed all his resources as a tactician, all his activity as general, as if he were on the field of battle. He commanded the agents of the secret police as if they were soldiers, stimulating the activity of the picked force who all had the most ardent devotion to his person. The instinct of self-preservation put him in the state of legitimate defence. It is easy to understand the wrath that filled him, believing what he had so often been told, that he was the regenerator, the saviour of France, the Messiah of the nineteenth century, when he thought that a miserable band of assassins might perhaps destroy him and his vast work. Naturally he was indignant with the perfidy of England in hiring murderers and putting weapons in their hands; and with the ungrateful émigrés, of whom he asked nothing more than they should return to their estates and their country, while they expressed their gratitude by these abominable plots. It is easy to understand what must have filled the soul of a man so violent and impetuous, who was accustomed to triumph over every obstacle.

Nor is it difficult to picture Josephine's distress when she saw her husband and herself so beset with perils. But with her experience of danger, she kept up a good heart. In the Reign of Terror, on the evening of the infernal machine, she had seen death near her without a tremor. With all her anxiety, she did not lose her head; she continued to be amiable and kindly, appeasing and advising her irascible husband. She especially urged that a distinction should be made between the innocent and the guilty, and that no steps should be taken under the impulse of blind fury. She maintained that the whole Royalist party was not to be held responsible for the excesses of a handful of fanatics. Unfortunately for Napoleon, he refused to listen to Josephine; in his exasperation he lost all self-control; he yearned to do something terrible, to strike some strong blow. He represented vengeance; his wife, kindness. At the Tuileries there was a struggle between anger and pity. The Consular Court put on a gloomy aspect, and every one wondered whether Bonaparte was to be victim or executioner. What is more inauspicious than the prologue of the eventful drama, called the death of the Duke of Enghien?

IX.

THE ARREST OF THE DUKE OF ENGHIEN.

NOTHING so disturbs and upsets rulers as plots against their lives. The same man who, on the battlefield, looks at death without a quiver, loses his self-control when he thinks that he is encompassed by assassins. The thought that the freak of a fanatic, of a madman, may overthrow the vast structure of power and pride, this bitter and cruel thought recalling to the great man — sunk in infatuation with himself — the nothingness of human life and the irony of fate, becomes an incessant torture. A paltry kitchen knife may strike down the most formidable sword, the most majestic sceptre. The merest fool may make of triumphant Cæsar a corpse. The men who are most fearless before the enemy cannot accustom themselves to this idea. They see murderers everywhere; inoffensive persons appear to them as terrible as spectres. A profound sadness and melancholy accompany this anxiety. A man of powerful imagination thus haunted by gloomy visions loses all the cool wisdom of a statesman; anger, revenge, the instinct of self-preservation drive him to extreme steps.

Bonaparte's irritation grew continually. The arrest of the Bourbon aides-de-camp, who were allied with Georges Cadoudal and Cadoudal's own confessions only added to it. He waited with feverish impatience for news from Colonel Savary, who, with men in disguise, had for some weeks been watching the cliff at Biville, not far from Dieppe, where it was expected that a prince would land as the conspirators had done. There were jutting rocks beneath the cliff so that a landing could be made only at high tide and with a smooth sea. Savary, who was always on the watch, saw no one land there; Captain Wright's brig, on board of which the prince was supposed to be, appeared one evening and tacked about, but no one came ashore from it.

Thereupon Bonaparte turned his attention to the banks of the Rhine. He knew that the Duke of Enghien, son of the Duke of Bourbon, and a Princess of Orleans was then at Ettenheim, in the Grand Duchy of Baden. This Prince, who was born in 1772, was renowned for his bravery; in Condé's army he was regarded as a hero. After the battle of Bersheim he had given proof of a noble humanity, by saving the life of the French prisoners whom the émigrés wished to shoot in retaliation. In 1801 in consequence of the treaty of Lunéville, he had to lay down his arms and inhabit Ettenheim, a former residence of the Cardinal of Rohan, on the right bank of the Rhine, four leagues from Strassburg. There he lived as a plain private citizen, in the society of a young and charming woman who warmly loved him, the Princess of Rohan. He cultivated flowers, hunted, and with youthful carelessness scorned the wise advice of those who blamed him for living so near the French frontier. It was even thought that he carried his boldness so far as to go occasionally to Strassburg, when, if rumor was true, he would go quietly to the theatre. But his father had written to him from London: " You are very near, take care, and take every precaution to get word in time and to get off in safety, in case it should enter the Consul's head to abduct you. Don't think that there is any courage in foolhardiness in this respect." This letter was dated June 6, 1803.

When Bonaparte learned of the non-arrival of any Bourbon prince by the cliff at Biville, he imagined that it was through Alsace that one of the princes, probably the Duke of Enghien, would enter France. He sent to Ettenheim an under officer of the gendarmes in disguise, to secure secret information. At that time there was with the Duke of Enghien an émigré, General, the Marquis of Thumery, and the way in which the Germans pronounced this name (Thoumeriez) led the under officer to think that the hero of Jemmapes (Dumouriez) was with the prince, and he made haste to send a report to this effect, adding that the Duke of Enghien had often entered France, according to some, going only as far as Strassburg, but according to others, as far as Paris. This report arrived March 10, 1804. "What!"

shouted the First Consul, when he saw M. Réal come in, "You didn't tell me that the Duke of Enghien is only four leagues from the frontier! Am I a dog to be knocked on the head in the street? Are my murderers sacred? Why didn't you tell me they were gathering at Ettenheim? This is a direct attack. It is time for me to fight fire with fire. The culprit's head shall pay for it."

That same morning a servant of Cadoudal, named Léridant, who was arrested with his master, had testified that a young man, well dressed, and an object of general respect, had often visited the conspirators in Paris. Bonaparte immediately decided that this young man must have been the Duke of Enghien. Often the vulgarest details, the pettiest circumstances, settle the destiny of the world. If the Germans of Ettenheim had pronounced the name of the Marquis of Thumery a little less incorrectly, if a servant had not mentioned a person who was wrongly supposed to be the last of the Condés, perhaps Napoleon's diadem would not have borne this bloody stain. The whole affair bears the mark of fatality. The First Consul, had he been cool and in possession of full information, would not have committed the deed of which he was guilty under the influence of passion, misled by inaccurate reports.

A council was held March 10, at the Tuileries, when were present the three Consuls, the ministers, and Fouché. In spite of the opposition of Cambacérès, it was decided that the Duke of Enghien and the alleged General Dumouriez should be abducted from Ettenheim by French troops, and that Colonel de Caulaincourt should take to the Grand Duke of Baden a letter explaining this violation of German territory.   Caulaincourt, who was related to the Condés, had no knowledge of the contents of the letter; but yet he was uneasy.   After the council, March 10, he received the order to depart immediately, as did Colonel Ordener, who was to command the fatal expedition.

Five days later, March 15, Colonel Ordener, with thirty men of the Twenty-sixth Dragoons and twenty-five gendarmes, crossed the Rhine at Rheinau, nearly opposite Ettenheim, leaving three squadrons of dragoons in reserve on the left bank.   The little party under Ordener's command advanced rapidly in the darkness, and passed through three slumbering villages without being seen.   It was about dawn when they reached Ettenheim.   They surrounded the house in which was the Duke of Enghien with two aides-de-camp, eleven servants, nearly two and a half million francs in a money-box, and loaded firearms.   One of the two aides, General de Grunstein, hastened to the prince's chamber when he heard the boots of the gendarmes on the pavement and the clatter of their weapons.   He shouted out, " You are surrounded! " Then the Duke of Enghien sprang out of bed, seized a double-barrelled gun, threw open a window, and took aim at Major Charlot, the commander of the gendarmes.   There were twenty windows opening on the street, and from these the prince's servants might have fired on their assailants, while the prince, perhaps, might have got away on the other side of the house, and have fled towards the mountain. But just as he was taking aim, was about to fire the shot which would have been the signal for the fight to begin, M. de Grunstein put his hand on the prince's gun and prevented him firing. "Gentlemen," said Major Charlot, "we are here in force; don't resist, it would do no good." Then the gendarmes entered the house, and the prince let himself be disarmed. They looked everywhere for General Dumouriez, but they found only the Marquis of Thumery, whose name had given rise to this fatal error. Major Charlot examined M. de Grunstein; and the Duke broke in, "If it had not been for him, I should have killed you; you owe your life to him." When they were seizing his papers, he said, "Don't be surprised, you are going to see the correspondence of a Bourbon, of a prince of the blood of Henry IV." Remembering that there were a good many letters of the Princess of Rohan in the package they had seized, he added, "I hope you will exercise all possible discretion about things that don't concern the government."

A few minutes later, the gendarmes led away the unfortunate prince with his two aides-de-camp and some of his servants. The Duke passed through Ettenheim on foot; at the town gate he was met by Colonel Ordener, who had him carried in a peasant's cart to the river, which he crossed in a boat, thence he was driven in a carriage to Strassburg, and locked up in the citadel. On the way, the prisoner said to Major Charlot: "This expedition must have been prepared very secretly, and I am surprised that I didn't get wind of it, for I am popular at Ettenheim. You would not have found me this evening, for yesterday the Princess of Rohan besought me to leave; but I postponed my departure under the impression that you would not have time to get here to-night. I am sure that she will come and want to follow me; she is very much attached to me; treat her well."

The unfortunate duke was right; Madame de Rohan wished to share his lot. She reached the citadel in tears, begging for permission to see the prince, to go to Paris where doubtless she would have tried to move Bonaparte. Her efforts were vain; the poor young woman was never again to see the man she loved; she could not even take leave of him, even see him a single moment. Not only was she expelled from the citadel, but she was arrested and forbidden to go to Paris. "Am I to be prisoner for the rest of my life?" the duke asked sadly; "I esteem Bonaparte and look upon him as a great man; but he is not a Bourbon, he has no right to rule France; he ought to restore the crown to my family." He remained in the citadel of Strassburg from the 15th of March till the morning of the 18th, when he was awakened and told that he was to depart alone, without his aides-de-camp and his servants. After dressing hastily he said to them, "My friends, I am sorry that I can do nothing more for you." Then he got into the post-chaise which was to carry him directly to Vincennes, the termination of this fatal journey.

What was going on meanwhile in Bonaparte's mind? He was gloomy and agitated, and he preserved an ominous silence. No one dared speak to him. It was a Sunday, — Palm Sunday, — and mass was said at the Tuileries as usual. After mass, Josephine told Madame de Rémusat that she was going to spend the week at Malmaison. "I am very glad of it," she added, "for Paris frightens me now." A few hours later, the carriages of the Consular Court started from the Tuileries for Malmaison; in one was Bonaparte, in the other, Josephine with Madame de Rémusat. On the way thither the following dialogue took place between the two women. "I am going to tell you a great secret. This morning Bonaparte told me that he had sent M. de Caulaincourt to the frontier to seize the Duke of Enghien. He is to be brought here." "Heavens! and what are they going to do with him?" "Apparently he is to be tried. I have done my best to get him to promise that the prince shall not be put to death, but I am much afraid that his mind is made up." "What! you think he will have him put to death?" "I am afraid so."

The two women were in great consternation when they reached Malmaison, where they were obliged to conceal their emotions. The next day, Monday, March 19, in the morning, Madame Bonaparte had a cypress set out in a part of the garden which had just been arranged. "Ah! Madame," said to her Madame de Rémusat, "that tree is very appropriate to the day."

Tuesday, March 20, the Duke of Enghien reached Paris with his guard at eleven in the morning. He was kept in his carriage at the gates for part of the day, and at four in the afternoon he was driven by the outer boulevards to the Castle of Vincennes.

Meanwhile Bonaparte at Malmaison assumed a calmness which he did not feel. After dinner he played with his nephew, the young Napoleon, Louis's son. Observing Madame de Rémusat's pallor, he said to her, "Why didn't you rouge? You are too pale." She replied that she had forgotten it. "What! a woman forgetting to rouge! You would never do that, Josephine. Two things are always becoming to women, — rouge and tears."

Then he began a game of chess with Madame de Rémusat, and while playing he repeated to himself these lines from Voltaire: —

> Of the gods we worship, know then the difference :
> Thine have commanded thee murder and vengeance ;
> And mine, when thy hand has but just now slain me,
> Orders me to pity thee and to forgive thee.

He repeated also Corneille's great scene : —

> Let us be friends, Cinna; it is I who ask thee.

But it was not clemency that was to prevail.

X.

THE DEATH OF THE DUKE OF ENGHIEN.

MARCH 20, before the end of the day, the Duke of Enghien, who had no anticipations of what awaited him, reached the Castle of Vincennes, where he was to die. The castle was then dilapidated and unused. The governor, one Harrel, had received orders to prepare accommodations for a prisoner; and he had also been requested to dig a grave in the courtyard. He answered that this was not easy, since the courtyard was paved. He was told to choose another place, and he accordingly had it dug in the moat which encircled the building. The Prince was hungry, and they sent out into the village for food. He sat down to the table, and, while eating, questioned Harrel about Vincennes and all that had happened there since the Revolution. He said he had been brought up near the castle, and added, "What do they want of me? What are they going to do with me?" But his words and his face expressed no anxiety; and after dinner, being tired from his journey, he went to bed in perfect calmness.

Meanwhile the preparations for the tragedy were

going on. The First Consul had the orders made
out, and signed them himself. Then at about five in
the evening, he had Colonel Savary, the commander
of the picked band of gendarmes, summoned to his
room, where he gave him a sealed letter, with orders
to carry it without a moment's delay to General
Murat, the governor of Paris. When he reached
Murat's house, Savary met Talleyrand, the Minister
of Foreign Affairs, coming out. The colonel was in
complete ignorance of what was going to happen;
and he was expecting to return to Malmaison, when
he received orders to take the command, in addition
to his gendarmes, of a brigade of infantry which was
to be that same evening at the Saint Antoine gate;
and this force he was to lead to Vincennes. Savary
led the gendarmes through the castle gate, and drew
them up in the courtyard, cutting off all communication with the outside. He then posted the brigade
of infantry on the esplanade, on the side of the park.
Meanwhile the military commission that was to try
the Duke of Enghien was assembling. It was composed as follows: General Hulin, commander of the
foot grenadiers of the Consular Guard, president; five
colonels of the Paris garrison, judges; and a major
of the picked gendarmes, secretary. The meeting
was held in one of the large rooms of the inhabited
portion of the castle; that is to say, the building
over the entrance, towards the park.

At midnight the unfortunate Prince was examined;
at two o'clock in the morning he appeared before the

military commission. The spectators were one of
Murat's aides, some officers and gendarmes. The
accused had no defender. He answered the questions put to him with calmness and dignity. He con-
fessed that he had served against France, and that he
was ready to serve again in the same way; but he
denied all affiliation with Pichegru, who, he said, if
report was true, employed abominable methods. He
concluded by expressing, first by word of mouth, then
by writing, his desire to see the First Consul. "My
name, my rank," he added, "my way of thinking, and
the horrors of my position convince me that Bonaparte will not refuse my request."

But the victim was mistaken. The orders brought
by Savary were peremptory; they provided that, in
case of condemnation, — and condemnation was certain, — the sentence should follow at once. Everything must be done that very night. The judges, after
unanimously convicting the Prince, were willing to
send his letter to the First Consul, but that was useless.

While they were deliberating about his sentence,
the Duke of Enghien had gone back to his room, and
there he had lain down on his bed and fallen asleep.
When the matter was settled, they came to awaken
him and led him away. He was so free from any
anticipation of what was about to happen, that as he
went down the stairs to the ditch he asked where
they were going to take him, but he received no
answer. Harrel went in front with a lantern. When

he felt the cold air rising from below, the unhappy young man pressed Harrel's arm and asked, "Are they going to put me in a dungeon?" It was not a dungeon that was opening for him; it was the grave. When they got out into the ditch, he was stationed before the squad who were to shoot him. Then when the whole truth dawned before him, he wrote a letter to be sent with a ring and a lock of his hair to Madame de Rohan, and prepared for death like a true heir of the great Condé. When some one proposed that his eyes should be bandaged, he declined with dignity, and, addressing the soldiers who were to shoot him, he said, very gently: "You are Frenchmen. You will, I am sure, do me the great favor not to miss me." Then he fell, his body riddled with balls.

The day was beginning to dawn when Savary started for Malmaison, where he was to report to Bonaparte what had just taken place. On the way he met Réal, a Councillor of State, who was going, too late, to Vincennes. An order had been sent to him to examine the prisoner with regard to his alleged complicity with Cadoudal and Pichegru, but he was asleep when the order reached his house; and he was worn out by some work which had taken several days and nights. He had given orders to his servants that he was on no account to be disturbed. Thus he had no knowledge of the letter until it was too late to save the victim.

At Malmaison, Savary at once entered Bonaparte's

study. " The First Consul," he says in his Memoirs, " seemed to hear me with great surprise. He could not understand why he had been tried before Réal's arrival, for he had sent orders to him to go to Vincennes to examine the prisoner. He looked at me with his lynx eyes, and said: 'There is something here I don't understand. That the Commission should have given its verdict on the confession of the Duke of Enghien does not surprise me, but this confession was only made at a trial which should not have taken place until after M. Réal had examined him on a matter which it was of importance for us to have cleared up." Then he said again, 'There is something here beyond me. A crime has been committed which leads to nothing ! ' "

Savary then went into the drawing-room, where he awaited Madame Bonaparte. His face was very pale and bore marks of agitation. As soon as Josephine appeared, she said, " Well, it's over ? " " Yes, madame," he answered ; " he died this morning, and, I must say, with great courage. After his death permission was given the gendarmes to take his clothes, his watch, what money he had on his person ; but no one would touch him. People may say what they please ; it is impossible to see such men die as calmly as one can see others ; and as for me, I find it hard to recover myself."

Then came Eugene de Beauharnais. " My mother was in tears," he says in his Memoirs, " and was bitterly reproaching the First Consul, who listened in silence and soon withdrew to his study. In a few moments Caulaincourt entered, just back from Strassburg. He was surprised to find my mother in distress, and she hastened to state the cause. When he heard the whole story, he beat his brow and pulled out his hair, saying, 'Why was I mixed up in this unhappy business?'"

When Madame de Rémusat saw Caulaincourt, she started back. "And you, too," he said, "you are going to hate me, and yet I am only unfortunate, but very unfortunate. In reward for my devotion the First Consul is going to disgrace me. I have been shamefully deceived, and I am a ruined man!"

The dinner-hour came; besides those regularly in attendance, there were present Louis Bonaparte and his wife, Eugene de Beauharnais, Colonel de Caulaincourt, and General Hulin. "The sight of this man impressed me most unpleasantly," said Madame de Rémusat, who was one of the company. "The First Consul did not assume any gayety; on the contrary, throughout the dinner he remained sunk in deep thought, and we were all very silent. Just as we were about to leave the table, the Consul, as if thinking aloud, said in a harsh, dry voice, 'At any rate, they will see what we are capable of, and I hope that in the future they will leave us alone.'"

After dinner they went into the drawing-room, and one after another there appeared Joseph Bonaparte, M. Bacciochi and his wife, with M. de Fontanes, Murat, Dubois, the Prefect of Police, some Council-

lors of State, and other officials. After a long conversation on many literary and historical subjects, the
First Consul had some extracts read from the correspondence of Drake, the English minister at Munich,
who had had a hand in the recent conspiracies. When
the reading was finished, Bonaparte said: "These are
undeniable proofs. These people want to kindle dis-
order in France, and kill the Revolution as embodied
in me. I have shown of what it is capable. I have
been obliged to defend and avenge it. . . . I have
shed blood; I had to do it, simply because bleeding
figures in political medicine. I am the man of the
State, I am the French Revolution, I say once more,
and I shall uphold it."

This was a gloomy period at Malmaison this week
in March, just when the spring was beginning. This
brilliant residence, once so animated, so joyful, became
a sombre spot. Josephine, generally so affable, grew
anxious, fearing both to speak and to keep silence.
Bourrienne thus describes a visit which he made
Thursday, March 22. "On arriving, I was at once
taken to her boudoir, where she was sitting with Hortense and Madame de Rémusat. I found them all
three in great dejection. . . . 'Ah! Bourrienne,'
said Josephine when she saw me, 'what a terrible
misfortune! . . . At any rate, no one can say that
it's my fault, for I did everything that I could to turn
him from this project. He had not said anything to
me about it; but you know how I read him, and he
admitted everything. He was indifferent to all my

prayers. I hung about his neck, I clasped his knees, — "Mind your own affairs!" he shouted in anger, "this is not a woman's business."'"

Josephine added, in great emotion, "What must people think in Paris? I am sure that every one must be cursing him; for here, even his flatterers seem downcast when they are out of his presence. Ever since yesterday we have been very depressed. And he! You know what he is when he is not satisfied with himself and yet tries to seem so; no one dares to speak to him, and we are all in deep gloom. . . . How Savary distressed me yesterday when he came to me to see about something the Duke of Enghien entrusted him with before his death. Here is his portrait and the lock of his hair which he wanted me to send to some one who was very dear to him. Savary almost had tears in his eyes when he told me about the duke's last moments, and when he tried to recover himself he said, 'It's no use, madame, one can't see a man like that die and not be moved.'"

While Josephine was grieving, Talleyrand, the Minister of Foreign Affairs, was giving an entertainment to which the whole Diplomatic Body was invited. Count Miot de Melito speaks of it in his Memoirs as follows: "Amid all these scenes of terror and alarm, M. de Talleyrand found a way to distinguish himself by a piece of marked flattery; he gave a ball three days after the death of the Duke of Enghien. Two months before, Madame de Talleyrand had refused an invitation to a ball to be given by M. de Cobentzel, the Austrian ambassador, on the 21st of January, the anniversary of the execution of Louis XVI. How can one dance on that day? she said, and the Minister put it off to another day. What needs to be said of these scruples and of the indecency of an entertainment given, one might almost say, when the guns were firing which had just killed a relative of the same Louis XVI?"

At the end of the week the First Consul left Malmaison and returned to the Tuileries. On Palm Sunday, March 25, mass was celebrated as usual in the chapel of the palace. General de Ségur, who was present, thus describes the scene: "Bonaparte made his way through the silent crowd that opened to let him pass. There was no change in his face. During the prayer, when the host was elevated, I watched him with renewed attention. Then, before God, in presence of his victim whom I seemed to see in his gore finding refuge at this Supreme tribunal, still bearing the traces of his swift punishment, I thought in my agonized heart that some remorse or at least some regret would show itself on the features of a man who had done so cruel a deed; but, whatever may have been his feelings, nothing about him changed; he remained calm, and through the tears that filled my eyes, I saw his face like that of a stern, impassible judge."

The mass over, the First Consul, as usual, betook himself to the large rooms of the palace where there awaited him every Sunday a throng of courtiers and suitors. "I had just seen him in the presence of God," adds General de Ségur, "I wanted to see him in the presence of men, hence I kept close to him in the audience that followed. His manner was alternately one of forced calm, and of gloom, but he was more readily approached than was usual. He walked slowly up and down the great rooms, more slowly than was his wont, and he himself seemed to notice this. He stopped at almost every step, letting the crowd gather about him and saying a few words to everybody. He made continual reference, directly or indirectly, to the night between the 20th and 21st of March. He was evidently sounding public opinion, waiting, even suggesting answers which he hoped would be satisfactory, but he only got one; it was intended for flattery, but it was so clumsy that he interrupted it and turned his back; it unintentionally charged him with meeting an attempt at murder with murder itself."

The arrest of the victim on the soil of Baden inspired the Russian government to make vigorous remonstrances against this violation of the territory of the German Empire. The First Consul replied in the *Moniteur* with an article recalling the assassination of Paul I. At St. Petersburg a funeral service was held for the peace of the soul of the young Condé. On the cenotaph was this inscription: "To the Duke of Enghien, *quem devoravit bellua corsica.*"

"The two foes," Chateaubriand said, "had an apparent reconciliation; but the wound which poli·

tics made, and insult enlarged, remained in the heart
of each. Napoleon thought himself avenged only
when he slept at Moscow; Alexander was satisfied
only when he entered Paris."

An uneasy conscience tormented every one of the
men who took part in this terrible affair. Napoleon
and every one of his assistants tried to justify the
action; and their efforts attest their anxiety. His
share in it racked the martyr of St. Helena with cruel
memories on his lonely rock; he kept returning to it
continually, and his explanations were contradictory.
His companion, the Count of Las Cases, wrote thus
in the "Memorial of St. Helena": "The Emperor
often spoke of this subject, and when he did, as on
many other occasions, I could see the private citizen
struggling with the public man, and the natural sentiments of his heart contending with his pride and the
dignity of his position. In the freedom of intimacy,
he did not show indifference to the fate of the unhappy
prince. One day, after he had spoken to me of his
youth and sad fate, he concluded thus: 'And I have
learned since that he favored me; I have been told
that he never spoke of me without expressing admiration, and yet that is the way justice is distributed in
this world!'"

That was the way Napoleon spoke of it in the freedom of private talk, but in the presence of strangers
his language was very different: "The Duke of Enghien and all his allies had no other aim than to kill
me; I was threatened from all sides and at every

moment. There were infernal machines, conspiracies, ambushes of all sorts. I grew tired of them. I grasped the opportunity to fill even London with terror and I succeeded in it. From that day the plotting ceased. And who can find any fault with what I did? What! every day from a distance of a hundred and fifty leagues these men could aim their death-blows at me; no power, no tribunal could protect me, and I was to be denied the natural privilege of meeting force with force? ... Blood cries for blood; it is the natural, inevitable, infallible reaction; unhappy he who provokes it! ... One must be foolish or mad to imagine that a family could have the strange privilege of attacking me every day, while I should not have the right of retaliation. They certainly could not reasonably suppose themselves superior to the law for the purpose of attacking others, and then reclaim their protection for self-defence; the conditions ought to be equal. Personally I had never done anything to any one of them; a great nation had placed me at its head; almost the whole of Europe had assented to this choice; my blood after all was not mud, it was time to make it equal to their own."

That is the way Napoleon talked before strangers, but to his intimates he let fall this confession: "Certainly, if I had known in time certain particulars concerning the opinions and character of the prince, and especially if I had seen the letter that he wrote to me, which was not delivered — Heaven knows why — until

after his death, certainly I should have pardoned him."
After recounting this conversation, Las Cases goes on:
" And we saw clearly that these words of the Emperor
expressed his real feeling and character, and for us
alone, for he would have felt humiliated if any one
had imagined for a moment that he was trying to lay
the blame on any one else or condescending to defend
himself. His fear of this or his sensitiveness was
such that, when he was speaking to strangers or dic-
tating for the public, he would limit himself to the
assertion that if he had had knowledge of the prince's
letter, he should have perhaps pardoned him in view
of the great political advantages of such a course.
And in writing down his last thoughts, which he
knew would be regarded with reverence by his contemporaries and by posterity, he said on this subject,
which he knew was one of great importance to his
reputation, that if it were to be done over, he should
act in the same way. Such was the man, such the
quality of his mind, the nature of his character."

Before the altar at the mass of the Tuileries, before
eternity at Saint Helena, Napoleon tried to harden
himself against remorse. He wrote in his will: "I
had the Duke of Enghien arrested and tried, because
it was necessary for the security, the interest, and the
honor of the French people, when the Count of Artois,
by his own confession, was keeping sixty assassins in
Paris. In similar circumstances I should do the same
thing." Yet those who forgive the great Emperor
so many victories cannot forgive this drop of blood.

The great singer of Napoleon, Victor Hugo, who called Napoleon the sun of which he was the Memnon, could not forget the moat of Vincennes in the magnificent poem in which he sings the dialogue of praise and denunciation. Lamartine, severer even than Chateaubriand, in his " Ode to Bonaparte," has also written this : " His tomb has been built beneath the vaults erected at the Invalides by Louis XIV., where the statues of twelve victories, each carved from a single granite block, and forming part of the massive pillars that support the temple, seem to form the guard of centuries round the porphyry urn that contains his ashes. But in the shadow, seated on his grave, there is an invisible statue, which darkens and dims all the others ; it is the statue of a young man, torn by midnight ruffians from the arms of the woman he loved, from the inviolable asylum in which he thought himself secure, assassinated by the light of a lantern at the foot of the palace of his fathers. A cold curiosity carries the visitor to the battlefields of Marengo, Austerlitz, Wagram, Leipsic, Waterloo ; he wanders over them with dry eyes ; but one is shown, at a corner of the wall near the foundations of Vincennes, at the bottom of a ditch, a spot covered with nettles and weeds ; he says, ' There it is ! ' he utters a cry, and carries away with him undying pity for the victim and an implacable resentment against the assassin. This resentment is vengeance for the past and a lesson for the future. Let the ambitious, whether soldiers, tribunes, or kings, re-

member that if they have hirelings to do their will,
and flatterers to excuse them while they reign, there
yet comes afterwards a human conscience to judge
them, and pity to hate them. The murderer has but
one hour; the victim has eternity."

The crimes of the Legitimists do not justify the
imitation of their misdeeds, or render the Duke of
Enghien responsible for acts in which he had no part.
Humanity is a sad thing! What great man is absolutely pure? What party is unsullied? There are
stains on Royalists, Republicans, Imperialists; no sun
free of spots. We are told that the augurs could not
look at one another without laughing; may we not
say that the different parties in France cannot look
at one another without shuddering? Why was it
that Napoleon, after seizing the Duke of Enghien, to
show his power, did not set him free, satisfying himself with saying, "I might have put you to death!
I forgive you"? What a better way of laying the
foundation of the Empire with this act of clemency!
It would have been a stroke of genius to disclose the
plots of the Bourbons, their complicity in detestable
conspiracies, and then to set free the heir of the
Condés in memory of the hero of Rocroy! What
true-hearted Royalist would not have admired the
great man? That would have been to act like a hero,
a way of disarming hate, of preventing coalitions, of
wringing from Europe a cry of gratitude and surprise,
of doing something noble, grand, sublime. As a matter of fact, there is nothing more politic or wiser than

virtue. I am sure that often when he recalled the death of the Duke of Enghien, Napoleon must have repented in the bottom of his heart that he had not followed the recommendations of clemency that were urged upon him by Josephine, his best friend.

XI.

THERE is no city in the world where memories are shorter than in Paris. The impression made by the death of the Duke of Enghien was brief as it was deep. As M. Paul de Rémusat has said in the preface of his grandmother's Memoirs, "Even in the Royalists, who were absolutely hostile to the government, this event called forth more grief than indignation, so confused were men's ideas upon questions of political justice and statecraft." Yet on the day after the event the First Consul had been struck by the altered faces of those he met. But far from being alarmed, he was anxious to show himself in public as usual, and he went with his wife to the opera, although some people advised him to wait a little. Madame de Rémusat tells us that she accompanied Madame Bonaparte, whose carriage followed close behind that of the First Consul. Usually he did not wait for his wife, but went straight up the staircase to his box; but this time he waited in the little room behind, giving Josephine time to join him. " She was trembling," Madame de Rémusat goes on to say, "and he

337

was very pale. He looked at us all, and seemed to be trying to read from our faces what we thought his reception would be. At last he went forward as if he were charging a battery. He was greeted as usual, whether it was that the sight of him produced its usual effect — for the multitude does not change its habits in a moment — or that the police had taken precautionary measures. I had been much afraid that he would not be cheered, and when I perceived that he was, I gave a sigh of relief."

March 27, a week after the death of the Duke of Enghien, the Senate, in response to a communication concerning the criminal correspondence of the English emissaries in Germany, said to Bonaparte, "You have delivered us from the chaos of the past, you make us grateful for the benefits of the present; guarantee to us the future. Great man, complete your work; make it as immortal as your glory." The First Consul's reply to this official overture was measured; he said that he would reflect upon it; but every one knew that the Empire was imminent. As Miot de Mélito has said, the people of Paris had no recollections of the Bourbons or any love for them; they were entirely lost from sight. And, unfortunately, the Parisians had been too long accustomed to bloody scenes to find anything in the events at Vincennes more extraordinary than in many others which they had witnessed. "The spring was beginning, and fashion had brought back the walks to Longchamps with more than their old-time brilliancy.

After criticising the show of faces and fashions, people began to discuss the great political change which was about to take place."

The First Consul and his wife left the Tuileries for Saint Cloud, where there was to be a general rehearsal of the great spectacular drama entitled The Empire. The tribunes were transformed into courtiers; the red caps gave place to red heels. Nothing was thought of but etiquette, high-sounding titles, and court uniforms. The time of revolutionary songs had gone. How those rough Brutuses must have laughed at themselves! And the Royalists, who were rivalling the flatteries of the regicides, must have been surprised by their own recantations. From the moment when the palace doors were reopened they felt themselves drawn thither by an irresistible force; for in the nature of great lords there is, as some one has truly said, a catlike quality which keeps them attached to the same house, whoever may dwell in it. As to the poor Duke of Enghien, after a few weeks no one ever mentioned him; he was buried in the same oblivion as the victims of the Terror. The Parisians hate gloomy memories. Moreover, the bloody deed at Vincennes did not prevent the Pope from coming, before the end of the year, to crown the new Emperor. Was not this ceremony to be one of the greatest religious formalities that had ever taken place in the history of the Catholic Church? Could one be more rigid than the Vicar of Christ?

It is easy to imagine how this vision of a future

court excited longings, jealousy, ambition, flattery, and intrigue. Every one hastened to the hunt for place and money. The Republican familiarity, the pretended austerity of the modern Spartans, had wholly disappeared. It was curious to observe how promptly the newly rich people turned themselves into aristocrats; it was they who were the hardest to please in luxury, in their fare, in their liveries. They were the more eager to shine, that their shining was a thing of new growth. They who ought to have been astonished at this good fortune, instead of trying to astonish others, only thought of dazzling others, and were simple enough to think that the whole world admired their splendor. The men were vain of their laced coats, and the women rejoiced in ordering their ball-dresses, their trains, and their jewels.

Amid all this monarchial excitement, which was the fashion and sole interest of the day, there was one person noticed, who was conspicuous for his opposition; for, having a few months earlier been interested solely in dynastic plans, he had suddenly become Republican again, contrary to his interests. This man had been the leading supporter of the *coup d'état* of Brumaire, and was the own brother of the future Emperor, — Lucien Bonaparte. To get to the bottom of this new transformation, we must again ask: Where is the woman? The woman was a very pretty, very attractive widow, twenty-six years old, Alexandrine de Bleschamps, whose husband, M. Jouberthon, after having been a stock-broker in Paris, had died in Saint

Domingo, whither he had followed the French expedition. Lucien had fallen in love with this woman, and, in spite of the formal commands of the First Consul, had married her. May 24, 1803, a son had been born to them, who later was to marry the Princess Zenaïde Julie, daughter of King Joseph. Napoleon looked upon Lucien's marriage as most inappropriate and inadmissible, and he was very anxious to annul it. What he wanted was to marry Lucien to Queen Marie Louise, the third daughter of Charles IV., King of Spain, and the widow of the King of Etruria, Louis I., the first king whom he had set on a throne. Lucien was inflexible, and obstinately refused his brother's most brilliant offers ; he preferred a woman's love to a crown.

According to Count Miot de Mélito, Joseph Bonaparte was then entrusted with the following commission. He was to try to persuade Lucien to write to the First Consul a letter promising not to allow his wife to bear his name, not to present her to his family, and to wait until time and circumstances should permit with regard to this marriage a legal publicity, which, moreover, was to depend on his brother's consent. For his part he would consent to see Lucien again as if nothing had happened and would let him live with this woman. The negotiation fell through.

Napoleon was anxious to make one last effort, and he had an interview with his brother which he thought would be decisive. This took place at Saint Cloud, late one evening. About midnight the First

Consul came into the drawing-room, and said, " It's all over! I have just quarrelled with Lucien, and ordered him out of my sight." When Josephine tried to interfere in behalf of her brother-in-law, from whom she had suffered a great deal, he said, " You are very kind to plead for him," and he kissed her tenderly. Then he was heard to say, " It's hard to find in one's own family opposition to such great interests. I shall have to isolate myself from every one and to depend on myself alone. Well, I shall suffice for myself, and Josephine will console me for everything."

What added to Napoleon's distress was this, that Madame Letitia Bonaparte, his mother, sided with Lucien, and went with him to Italy, where he withdrew in the spring of 1804 to escape the importunities and reproaches of his all-powerful brother. As it was, Napoleon recommended Madame Letitia and Lucien to the friendly offices of Pius VII., saying that his brother had gone to Rome out of love for the arts, and his mother on account of her health.

Joseph Bonaparte, although he did not break with Napoleon as Lucien had done, showed that he was not contented. " He was dissatisfied," Thiers has said, " and no one would guess the reason if history were not to take pains to record it. He was sore because the First Consul was anxious to appoint him President of the Senate, and he had refused that high position with an air of offended dignity when M. Cambacérès had offered it to him at the suggestion of the First Consul. Bonaparte, who detested idleness, had sent him word in that case to seek for greatness where he himself had found it; that is to say, with the army. Joseph, appointed colonel of the 4th of the Line, left for Boulogne at the moment when the great question of the re-establishment of the monarchy came up for discussion."

As for Jerome Bonaparte, the youngest of Napoleon's brothers, he was in rebellion against his brother, like Lucien, and for a similar reason. In 1803, after the renewal of the war, after the treaty of Amiens, Jerome, at that time a naval officer, had been chased by English ships, and had landed in the United States. At Baltimore he had fallen in love with the daughter of one of the richest and most respectable citizens of that place, Miss Elizabeth Paterson. He had communicated to M. Pichou, Consul-General of France at Washington, his intention to marry this young woman, who was very charming, and the marriage had taken place. Jerome, who was born November 15, 1784, was not then quite twenty years old, and the law of September 20, 1792, declared null and void every marriage contracted by a person less than twenty years old, without the consent of both parents. It was only February 22, 1805, that, by command of the Emperor, Madame Letitia Bonaparte placed in the hands of M. Raguideau, notary, a protest against her son's marriage. In 1804, Jerome, whose resistance to his brother's commands was destined to be of but brief duration, had sworn that he would not for an empire repudiate a woman whom he esteemed as well as loved. Napoleon, who was dreaming of crowns for his brothers, was annoyed at this opposition, and excluded Jerome, as well as Lucien, from the right of succession to the Empire.

Thus the situation of the Bonaparte family did not favor the establishment of the principle of hereditary succession. Napoleon was married to a woman who could have no children. His eldest brother, Joseph, had no sons; and his other brothers, Lucien and Jerome, had just contracted marriages which were, in his eyes, misalliances which could not be pardoned.

There was then left only his brother Louis to perpetuate the imperial race. By his marriage with Hortense de Beauharnais he had one son, Napoleon Charles, born in Paris, October 10, 1802, who was destined to die at the Hague, May 5, 1807. Napoleon was very fond of this child, who scandalmongers pretended was his own, and he desired to make him the heir to the Empire, excluding Joseph and Louis, but Louis offered an insurmountable opposition to this plan. " Why," he asked his brother, " why must I resign to my son a part of your succession? Why do I deserve to be disinherited? What will be my condition, when this child, having become yours, shall find himself in a position superior to mine, independent of me, holding the place next to you, and eying me with uneasiness, or possibly even with contempt? No, I shall never consent to it; and rather than consent to bow my head before my son, I shall leave France and take Napoleon with me, and we shall see if, in the face of the world, you will dare to take a child from his father!"

The Monarchy was not yet restored; the crown, with its succession a matter of premature dispute, was not yet placed on the First Consul's head; and already we see in the embryonic court the same passions, jealousies, and dissension that we find in the court of an old kingdom, or of an old established empire. But Napoleon, whose mighty figure eclipsed and dominated everything, soon caused all the cupidity and rivalries of his courtiers to be forgotten. Joseph, Lucien, Louis, and Jerome, who all were dependent on their brother's favor, were soon lost in the background. Lucien, in his voluntary exile in Rome, indulged in a few lamentations, but his voice found no echo. He wrote: "Why has not Bonaparte, that great general, remained steadfast to philosophic and humanitarian ideas? I can positively affirm that they were the first belief of his youth and of a soul liberal by nature. . . . A horde of improvised flatterers preferred the childish and servile dignity of an absolute ruler to the wise and austere representation of a popular chief magistrate. My admiration for Washington's character does not prevent my thinking that he would have found it difficult to withstand the current which my brother has not wished, or has not been able, to resist. If all the fellow-soldiers of the American hero, and the officials who had an equal share in founding the Ameri-

can Republic, had agreed to substitute a crown for
the Presidential toga, what would the modern Cin-
cinnatus have done?" And again he wrote as follows: "Yes, Napoleon, you were without doubt
guilty of absorbing our public liberties in the splendor of your military glory, but it must in fairness be
acknowledged that they were already destroyed by
those who should have been their guardians and
defenders; and never, it must be said, was any great
political body so openly abject as was the majority of
the Senate, which could not hear without a blush,
and without applying it to itself, that line of Racine
in which he says that the ready servility of the
Roman Senate wearied Tiberius."

The great bodies of the State began to rival one
another in monarchical enthusiasm. A tribune on
the 28th of April proposed an hereditary empire. On
the 3d of May the whole Tribunate, with the exception of Carnot, adopted the proposal. All the members of the legislative body who happened to be in
Paris agreed to it most eagerly. The next day the
Senate tried to disprove the statement that the Tribunate had taken the first steps, and boasted that they
had themselves made the beginning six weeks earlier.
As to the Council of State, it had accepted it by
twenty votes out of twenty-seven. At its meeting on
May 18, the Senate adopted a Senatus-consultum as
follows: " The following proposition will be presented
to the French people: ' The French people desires the
hereditary succession of the Imperial dignity in the

direct, natural, legitimate, and adoptive line of Napoleon Bonaparte, and in the direct, natural, legitimate line of Joseph Bonaparte and Louis Bonaparte.'" As soon as the vote was taken, every senator rushed to his carriage to drive to Saint Cloud, hastening thither to see the new sovereign and to be seen of him, with their faces full of devotion, joy, and admiration. Ten years later these men were to assume a very different attitude when they had learned the difference between the setting and the rising sun, as well as the fact that in France more than anywhere else a sovereign's first duty is to be fortunate. Now, however, everything was radiant with joy; it was in the spring, the weather was faultless, and Napoleon was surer than ever that he controlled fate. The more it had given, the more he wished to ask, and his demands were to know no bounds, for he regarded it as his servant who could refuse him nothing. At the moment when the Senate came to salute him with his new title of Emperor, he was standing in uniform in the magnificent Gallery of Apollo decorated with mythological frescos by Mignard, and brilliant with all the pomp of the great century. Josephine, joyful and uneasy at the same time, was by her husband's side, modestly sharing his triumph.

Cambacérès, as the spokesman of the Senate, uttered a formal speech, which began thus: " Sire, the affection and gratitude of the French people have for four years confided to your Majesty the reins of government, and the different bodies of the State entrusted

to you the choice of a successor. The imposing title
which is given to you to-day is nothing more than
a tribute which the nation pays to its own dignity
and to the need it feels of offering to you every day
the testimony of a respect and devotion which every
day sees increasing." And he thus concluded his
speech: "Happy the nation which after so many
troubles finds a man capable of pacifying the storm
of passions, of conciliating every interest, of harmo-
nizing all the voices! If it is one of the principles
of our Constitution that the part of the decree which
establishes an hereditary government should be submitted to the people, the Senate has thought that it
should request your Imperial Majesty to consent that
the necessary measures should be taken at once; and
for the glory as well as for the happiness of the
French Republic, it proclaims at this very moment,
Napoleon Emperor of the French." At once enthusiastic applause broke out in the Gallery of Apollo,
as well as in other parts of the palace, even in the
courtyards and gardens.

The multitude, in its credulity and optimism, imagined that the Empire was a talisman, a panacea,
curing all woes and bringing every benefit. This
cry of "Long live the Emperor!" which was to be
heard on so many battle-fields, now filled the air for
the first time. Napoleon, who had attained his object,
hides his pride and exultation beneath an impassible
calmness. One would say that he was born to the
throne, so readily does he adapt himself to the part

of a monarch, such obedience, respect, and devotion does he find about him. As soon as silence prevailed he spoke thus in reply to Cambacérès: "Everything which can contribute to my country's happiness is intimately connected with my happiness. I accept the title which you consider important to the nation's glory; I submit to asking the sanction of the people to the law of hereditary succession; I hope that France will never repent the honors it bestows on my family. In any event, my spirit would no longer be with my posterity whenever it should cease to deserve the love and confidence of the grand nation."

Then it was the turn of the new Empress to receive the homage of the Senate. Cambacérès addressed her in these terms: "Madame, the Senate has still an agreeable duty to perform, that of offering to your Imperial Majesty the homage of its respect and the expression of the gratitude of the French people. Yes, Madame, France makes known the good you are never tired of doing. It says that, always accessible to the unfortunate, you never exercise your influence over the head of the State, save to console their misery, and that to the pleasure of obliging them your Majesty adds that amiable delicacy which makes gratitude sweeter and the benefit more precious. This happy disposition is a sure token that the name of the Empress Josephine will be the signal of consolation and hope, and, as the virtues of Napoleon will always serve as an example to his successors to teach them the art of governing nations, so the undying memory of your kindness will teach their august companions that the art of drying tears is the surest way of ruling over men's hearts. The Senate congratulates itself on being the first to greet your Imperial Majesty, and he who has the honor to be its spokesman presumes to hope that you will deign to count him in the number of your most faithful servants."

Josephine, the modest and gracious creole, was then exalted to the rank of a sovereign, and the prophecy of the black fortune-teller was verified. France was about to sanction by an almost unanimous vote — five and a half millions to two thousand — the Napoleonic dynasty. The few objectors who might have wished to put themselves in the way of this triumphal chariot, stepped aside. Amid the chorus of noisy applause which burst out everywhere, no discordant note was heard. In all quarters there was nothing but flattery, congratulations, the flourish of trumpets, in towns, in the country, under gilded ceilings, under the roofs of huts, in public places, in the camps; and yet, though she had reached this height, Josephine was rather anxious than happy. She did not care to rise to such a height, and the sight of the abyss from this lofty elevation made her giddy. She felt that as her fortune grew her happiness diminished, and that a crown would lie heavy on her brow. It was enough for her to be a loving woman. She had no need to be an Imperial Highness. The sceptre was an idle toy; a fan sufficed her.

While Napoleon's sisters were rejoicing at the thought that they were to be princesses, and their brother an Emperor, Josephine, tormented by this lofty rank, could not accustom herself to the idea that she was succeeding the unfortunate Marie Antoinette on the throne of France, and her unexpected sovereignty seemed to her an anomaly, almost a usurpation. In her eyes the throne was surrounded with snares; and her instinct was right. Something said to her: Nothing of all this will last, nothing except sorrow.

Strange lesson for human pride, clear proof of the nothingness of glory; ignorance was clearer-sighted than genius; the eyes of the dove saw further than the eyes of the eagle! Napoleon despised men who took counsel of women, and yet he would have done well, and would probably have escaped his ruin, had he listened to Josephine. What did she advise him? Moderation, clemency, fidelity to the Republic to which he owed his unexampled good fortune. If she had had more influence over him, he would not have put to death the Duke of Enghien, an incident which, though forgotten in France, was to be, as Thiers has pointed out, the main cause of a third general war and the inspiration of the successive coalitions which finally crushed the hero of so many battles. He would not have renounced the glorious title of First Consul for another, more majestic, but less lasting; he would not have made his brothers kings of a day; he would have remained the first citizen of a great

Republic.   He would have controlled his genius, his ambition, and his pride.   But instead of letting himself be controlled by his wife's gentler charm, the giant, fascinated, intoxicated by his own glory, made of his existence a vast romance which could end only in a catastrophe as great as his triumph.   Such was the mockery of Fate!   The humble creole judged events more wisely than the great Emperor, and said to herself, that if the wife of the First Consul had been less happy than the wife of the Citizen Bonaparte, the Empress of the French, the Queen of Italy, would be more wretched than the wife of the First Consul.

INDEX.

www.ingramcontent.com/pod-product-compliance
Lightning Source LLC
Chambersburg PA
CBHW021214090426
42740CB00006B/219